I, Too, Am Tar Baby

a memoir

John Warner Smith
Former Poet Laureate of Louisiana

Legacy Book Press LLC
Camanche, Iowa

For my grandchildren:

John Elisha
Joseph Warner
James Clayton
Autumn Rose
Jeremiah Monroe
Kerry Charles
Layla Naomi
Roman Dean
Nolan Patrick
Devyn Pierre
Isaac Omari

Who looks outside dreams. Who looks inside awakes.

—Carl G. Jung

TABLE OF CONTENTS

PRELUDE

My mother gave me the first name of my father. My middle name was given to me by her mother, my Grandmother Rose. Grandmother's only natural brother, James Warner Chaisson, was killed in a knife stabbing in July 1951 at the age of thirty. For reasons never told to me, no one called him by his first name. He was called J. Warner. At the time of his death, Grandmother was pregnant with her ninth child. Before her brother died, she had planned to name her next child Warner if it were a boy. Born a month later, the baby was a girl, whom she named Margaret. I was born the following year on December 22nd. To my relatives and the people of Morgan City, Louisiana, who knew me as a child, I am J. Warner, not John.

I own the pocketknife that slit the jugular vein of my grandmother's brother outside a nightclub that sweltering summer night in Lafayette, Louisiana. The knife was given to me on February 5, 1996, by Mike Harson, the then-District Attorney of the 15th Judicial District. For over forty years, the knife had been taped inside a legal-size manila folder and filed away on the seventh floor of the parish courthouse.

I own a clipping of a news article that appeared in the *Lafayette Daily Adviser* on July 16, 1951, the day after my great uncle's death. The first paragraph of the article reads:

"Murder charges were filed today against Curley Morrison, 20-year-old Negro, in connection with the knife slaying of J. Warner Chaisson, a 30-year-old Duson Negro, Sheriff W. S. Comeaux stated today."

W.S. Comeaux was Walter S. Comeaux, who had served as Sheriff of Lafayette Parish since 1948. In July 1989, thirty-eight years after Sheriff Comeaux arrested the man who killed my great uncle, I was interviewed by the Parish President of Lafayette for the job of Chief Administrative Officer (CAO), the top administrative position in the government. That day was the first time that the Parish President and I had met. Two weeks later, he offered me the job. His name was Walter S. Comeaux Jr., son of the former Sheriff.

I served as Walter's CAO for eight years, including a year heading up the newly created consolidated government of the City and Parish of Lafayette. For eight consecutive years, our names appeared together in news articles of the *Lafayette Daily Advertiser.* How and why our paths crossed with those two names is one of the many unexpected, surprising, seemingly bizarre occurrences that I've experienced over the course of my life. They have grounded me in the firm belief that nothing in my life happened by chance or coincidence. Everything happened with purpose. I am especially cognizant of that now, as I begin the journey of my final years.

This is a story about a black boy who grew up in poverty in the Jim Crow and Civil Rights eras, and who in 1966 became one of five black students who integrated an all-white junior high school in Lake Charles, Louisiana. It is a story about the decades that followed, when despite this young man's education, the color of his skin was a dominant factor in whether he succeeded or failed. It is a story of his personal experiences with racial intolerance and how his responses to them largely shaped who he would become. As such, it is very much a story about the problem of race in America.

Lastly, it is the story of an individual who, as a student of human experience, embarked on a long journey to know the essence of who he was and what purpose he was created to fulfill.

Accounts of where I came from and went, where and how I was educated, and what I achieved are small rocks skipping across a vast, deep river of the inexplicable, unexpected events and inward reflections and intuitions that for decades were molding me while being hidden from a conscious awareness of who I was becoming, experiences which to this day are hidden from the world that looks at me. Ultimately, these are the experiences that made and defined who I am.

I was not a candidate for long life and dream fulfillment. Born to a poor, sixteen-year-old black girl and living in a low-income housing project, I was raised by a grandfather who never learned to read and write and who had served time in prison for manslaughter. I was fed and nurtured by a grandmother whose father had stopped speaking to her for seventeen years because she gave up an opportunity to teach school to marry a poor, illiterate farmer, raise babies, and work as a maid for white families. Together, my grandparents bore twelve children, nine of whom were born after my grandfather returned home from prison.

I cannot say why I did not die or become disabled or imprisoned long ago when circumstances portended that I would or should have. My life has not been my own. I can claim no triumph or achievement that I earned. All has been given. I owe all to love, especially the love that I failed to give back. I have been carried on a soft, gentle wind, for which I am forever grateful and indebted. I am blessed to have had the love of a strong mother and stepfather, to have married a strong, beautiful, virtuous woman, and to have children with the heart and spirit of angels. I am fortunate to have discovered my God-given gifts and to have been given the opportunity to use them. There was no mold to pattern, no preconceived plan in my journey toward selfhood, only the constant prod, fall, failure, and step forward, only hands that held and lifted me, shoulders that carried me, and the long, darkened nights that let me see the light of day.

Since my earliest awareness or consciousness of being an individual and having a mind, I was aware of my individuality, of something in me that set me apart from the world around me, even when I didn't know what that was and didn't know or understand the world that I considered foreign. I was a deeply introspective child and young adult, probably to a fault, who didn't quite "fit in" with members of my family or with friends, but who adjusted and adapted, sometimes awkwardly. Whether they were long walks alone in the woods while feeling resentment toward my mother, or questioning why my natural father had abandoned me or why I was too shy to date a girl in high school, or whether they were days when I sat in a business meeting and was the only black man in the room, I always sensed that I was unique.

Introspective moments were the reality that I trusted most. There I found repose and peace. They carried me through many valleys and across many lonely, barren, desert sands when, by all outward appearance, I had failed or was not going to succeed by standards set by the outer world. I don't think my parents knew the confused, private side of me that I was struggling to know in my early and young adult years. In some respects, I felt like a stranger to my wife and children, not by their doing, but because of my comfort with solitude and aloofness. I was a natural introvert who learned the necessity and value of extroversion in my professional life. Later in life, as a poet,

I rediscovered the introversion that had caused so much dissonance in my youth, and I lovingly embraced it.

Long before I became a writer, I often prayed that I would find my highest purpose in life. Something inside me clung to the thought that what I was doing and achieving wasn't who I was; it was who I had been. I was in my early forties when poetry discovered me, and I was fifty-seven-years-old when, after obtaining three degrees, I went back to college to formally study creative writing and get a Master of Fine Arts degree. What drove me in that direction was a strong sense of the reality of the "self" or wholeness of an individual, and the idea that I was incomplete. I felt that there was more to me than what I had become and accomplished.

The influences and distractions of contemporary society make finding wholeness a nearly impossible task. Outside of prayer, meditation, and religious teachings and beliefs, there are few mediums through which we can travel to connect with our hidden, innermost yearnings and possibilities. We are easily pulled into the brokenness of life and the numinous infatuation and obsession with the physical world that our senses experience. So much human energy and effort is spent on the race to achieve and attain or to simply cope with the difficulties and challenges of everyday existence. Time moves swiftly and our lives are busy and noisy. We depend on technology to get us through every hour of the day, so much so that we literally can't function without a cell phone or a computer. It is no wonder that the silent voice that speaks to us from within and provides the guideposts to self-actualization goes unheard or ignored. Seldom are we quiet enough to hear it. And there are those inner, psychological demons of neuroses and obsessions that somehow come to possess us, the silent, dark spirits of mental unhealthiness that we don't understand or are not consciously unaware of that we mask in our strivings to function and appear normal.

As a freshman in college majoring in psychology, I was an avid reader of the works of Carl G. Jung, the Swiss psychiatrist who advanced the theory of a collective unconscious, a discovery that Jung made in his treatment of patients with mental illnesses. In reading Jung, I began to question reality as I saw it and question what I didn't know about why and how I responded to the world around me. Through his writings, I discovered that to be truly conscious of who we are requires us to know the content of the unconscious, a part of our psyche that is beyond our awareness of what we generally perceive as reality. It is there that the self lies.

Unconscious experiences, both personal and collective, are buried in the mind. Our inability to know their content and tap into them does not diminish their influence over our daily lives. In fact, though unaware, how we behave and respond to ordinary, everyday circumstances is due in large part to the forces of our unconscious mind. The problem we face in knowing and understanding that deepest, innermost part of us is that the unconscious speaks in a different language and through mediums that we are not generally accustomed to thinking about, through dreams, reflections, and "inherited" universal symbols that are not easily noticed and understood. The very definitions of those terms are abstractions that drown in the concreteness and practicality that command our daily attention. It is no wonder that we don't know and understand what moves beyond and beneath what our physical senses define as reality.

I don't claim to have that understanding. I only speak about the little that I was blessed or fortunate to learn about the complexities of human experience, lessons that none of us is taught as a child, student, and young adult. We are nurtured by loving parents and taught to study, learn, pray, and persevere, but no one teaches us how to hear so-called silent inner voices that point directions for the journey we will travel. Life simply pulls us into the abyss to figure things out as we grow, live, and learn. I was no exception, but for reasons beyond understanding, except perhaps for the purpose of this memoir, I was given a light to carry into the darkness.

Seeing and knowing does not necessarily mean that one has the answer to life's problems or the ability to cope with them. In my experience, there was no substitute for religious faith. It was no coincidence that the stage of my life when I fully embraced the power of religious faith and tried to live by the teachings of it was when I began to discover my higher purpose. No dream, reflection, intuition, or knowledge of anything sustained me as much as my belief in God and life after death.

Like the Apostle Paul, I had my moment on the road to Damascus, but I was not chosen to preach the Gospel of Christ, only to be a follower of it. Admittedly, I often failed miserably in being that individual, and even now I struggle to live up to Christian ideals, but that is what and who I am. In some ways, the thought that I am real and that the world outside me is real is myth. I can only prove its existence with what I call my mind, which I know very little about. I have learned that knowledge can explain mountains but faith can move them. Even though I have eyes that see, I am blind to absolute truth and to the ultimate reality of a world that seems impossible for any single being to create. Still, unlike Jung, I would rather believe than see and know. To some, that might all sound self-righteous, esoteric, or philosophical, but for me it is simply truth.

But faith does not come easily. Although I would rather cling to belief than be needful of evidence for things not seen, believing in the face of disappointment, hardship, sickness, and death has been a constant trial for me, and I wonder sometimes whether those things happen merely as a test of my faith. The ability to have oneness of mind and heart, to have faith and to exercise it every day in all that I think, feel, and sense, is part of the brokenness of me and the journey toward wholeness that I still travel.

I have experienced many setbacks and failures in life. This book recounts many of them. The successes, if measured by traditional standards, came unexpectedly but not without sacrifice and preparation. My work as a professional striving to achieve the American dream and provide for my family was gratifying, despite its long-term cost to my health and physical well-being. But what I deem my greatest achievement in life, discovering that whatever gift I might have as a poet comes with a great obligation to give that gift to the world, is a realization that came long after I had been a public administrator, a banker, and a public education policy advocate.

I know now that becoming a writer and teacher was not accidental or incidental. I was always a black boy and a black man facing obstacles that seemed insurmountable. The color of my skin was a constant determinant. I have a much better understanding of how I overcame those obstacles than why. Education clearly made a difference between living in poverty and growing beyond it, but all the knowledge and experience that gave me the capacity and tools to achieve outward success could not equip me for the journey to seek the wholeness of me.

Although I did not travel the conventional path to finding my best use, I did not simply stumble upon the realization of it. I was always moving toward it but would never have realized that I was going there had I not listened to an inner drumbeat, the haunting whisper that led me to where the window of heaven opened. Only the constant look and listen inward to see the hidden path and hear the silent voice led me to the ultimate discovery that I am a poet.

I inherited a penchant for storytelling from a grandfather who didn't know how to read and write and who was a surrogate father of my early childhood. He might have inherited the oral tradition of telling stories from his father or grandfather. My narrative is written in that vein and probably does not conform to the generally accepted pattern and structure of a memoir. In memory, I had to leap past prose to rush on to truth and catch up with the swift passage of time and rapid movement of place and circumstance that would ultimately reveal the singular purpose that my journey encompassed. l did not wish to show insignificant details or to give fictionalized dialogue to entertain readers. Frankly, much of the detail is forgotten. Only that which is significant is remembered. The outer events are recounted only insofar as they reveal the pattern of wholeness embodied in my journey toward the realization of who I am, a journey that continues in my later years.

This is not a "how to" book on self-discovery. It is merely an account of one person's experiences of that journey. It is my talking book, a story that I would not have set out to tell if I felt that it could not teach some lesson and offer some hope to people everywhere, regardless of race, gender, religion, or national origin. But as an African American, my hope is that my story will offer lessons to black boys and young black men about the power that lies within them to rise above the barriers of race and above the meanness and hardness of a sensate world to find their highest purpose through the redemptive, liberating power of self-knowledge.

The first seven chapters of this book attempt to show that journey through stories and anecdotal incidents. At the point in which I discovered that I am a poet or that poetry had discovered me, I attempt to describe how my collections of poetry were born and what meaning my poetry strives to give to life. It is my hope that much of that meaning is embedded in the poems themselves, which are woven through every chapter of the manuscript and are as much my talking book as the narrative itself.

Three months after my seventieth birthday, my life took a surprising, unexpected turn. My account of it is literally, I think, the final chapter of the journey in search of the purposes I was created to serve. But that is only what I think. As I enter the final stage of life, what I mostly know about who I am is that there is so much more that I don't know, a lesson taught by the many years lived before I became a writer. I am broken and incomplete, but I know that the wholeness of me is evolving. I have at least been put on a path to seek it.

REFLECTIONS ON FORGETFULNESS

On May 14, 2005, I left my car, a small but sporty 2003 BMW, with my father while I went to the Callaloo Creative Writing Workshop in College Station, Texas. My plans were to drive two hours from Baton Rouge and fly out of Lake Charles Regional Airport. Daddy would drop me off, keep the car, and pick me up two weeks later. I knew he was in some stage of dementia, but at that time he was more stable than not. He spoke coherently, answered phone calls, and heeded good advice.

I felt a little anxious about leaving my car with him, but Daddy knew cars; he cared about them. He always drove below the speed limit, obeyed traffic signals, and was meticulous about maintenance, which he usually did himself. As a child, I watched him take engines apart and put them back together. Still, sitting at the gate waiting to board the plane, I worried that he might move the car to cut his lawn and forget to lock the door, or he might mistakenly push a button and the windows would roll down. So, I called a friend and a cousin and asked them to drive by Daddy's house from time to time and check on the car while I was away.

Though I hadn't lived in Lake Charles for nearly thirty years, I had driven the streets long enough to know them quite well. But while driving my father to the airport that Saturday morning, he insisted on navigating me to our destination—pointing at nearly every turn. He had done this before on our visits to his doctors. Sometimes I took a different turn just to show him that his way wasn't the only way and that mine would get us there just as quickly. But that day, I followed his direction. The pointing was mostly habit, but I sensed his need to reassure me and himself that he was still in control of the ground below him even though the world was slowly passing him by.

One afternoon at the Callaloo workshop, I strolled across the courtyard and saw someone doing a Tarot Card reading for Percival Everett, the award-winning novelist and visual artist who was instructing the fiction writing workshop participants. When I got close to the table, the reader sensed the presence of another spirit and asked me to back away. She said that the spirit force wasn't of Percival, whose bright future was being foretold. She had seen or felt the dark, foreboding clouds that would soon hover over me.

Upon returning from Callaloo, Daddy picked me up in his truck and drove me to his home to get my car. I was relieved to find that he had cut the lawn but hadn't moved my "Beemer." That afternoon, as I sifted through his mail, my father spoke the only true confession he ever entrusted to me. "Something has fallen out of my head," he said, brushing his forehead with his right hand. "I don't remember some things I used to know." No words that Daddy had ever spoken to me rang as clearly and sank as deeply into my heart. His confession struck me as quiet desperation, a revelation that he was beginning to feel unsure of his familiar and predictable corner of the world. I was just beginning to know the real tragedy of my father's dementia, the fast approaching moment when Daddy would not know that he was forgetting or that he had a mind that once remembered.

Many incidents would follow in which my father showed visible signs, both frightful and humorous, that his brain was changing. As time passed, he grew uneasy and distrustful of visitors. He didn't want company. He became keenly sensitive to time, obsessed actually, and never wanted to be late for the crossing guard work he did mornings and afternoons after retiring from Union Pacific Railroad. So he wore two watches, one on each wrist. On my visits to see him, he'd point nervously to his watches, stuttering and searching for words, as he talked about going to work or to visit his sister in rural Iberia Parish. He often mentioned trips he had to take to Texas and California for reasons he could never explain.

That was uncharacteristic of Daddy. He had always been a homebody. Except for trips my mother insisted on taking or the truck driving he did for the railroad between east Texas and southwest Louisiana, Daddy seldom traveled anywhere. But when his brain began to deteriorate, he started going places, in his mind at least. In reality, he only left his house to go to work or the bingo hall or to run errands for himself. One afternoon, when he politely told me to leave, insisting on the urgency of a trip to Houston, I hid my car around the corner and watched him circle his truck a few blocks and then return to the house.

Daddy had begun to show signs of memory loss and disorientation long before my mother's death in 2003. When she grew ill, he became her caregiver. When she died, he suddenly found himself having to manage a household. He continued to do crossing guard work, drive his vehicles, play weekly bingo, and manage his checkbook, but his memory loss made daily living increasingly difficult and stressful. His judgment grew poorer with time, as did his hygiene. On my visits, I'd discover that he had forgotten to turn off heaters and lock doors. He cashed pre-approved bank credit checks that he received in the mail not knowing that he was borrowing money. He found it necessary to carry large sums of money in his pockets and was often seen waving the wad in public. He had several brand new weed whackers piled under his carport. Everyone, including me, became an intruder to his privacy.

Daddy's neurologist was slow to diagnose the dementia as Alzheimer's due to the presence of a tumor on Daddy's pituitary gland. He underwent the usual diagnostic tests such as MRIs and ophthalmology exams but refused to do a spinal tap. Eventually, he was prescribed Aricept, a medication that slows the loss of memory. Daddy refused to take the pills.

Three months after my return from the Callaloo workshop, Hurricane Katrina hit southeast Louisiana. In the days and weeks after Katrina, one was easily lost for words to describe New Orleans, a city so loved for its vitality and spirit and for the richness and diversity of its expresion—an American city so modern yet old with tradition. Langston Hughes said he saw the muddy bosom of the Mississippi River turn golden in the New Orleans sunset. No one could speak of the waters of Katrina in the revering way that Hughes described his river.

One of the paradoxes of this very tragic event is that, in spite of the vastness and absoluteness of its physical and human destruction, those of us who did not live the flood first hand, were forced to experience it in abstraction. We experienced it from a distance, mostly in past tense, through what we read in newspapers and in the rapid click of our computers and televisions. Those accounts, including the progress of the state's recovery, eventually faded with world headline news.

So it is with the raw statistics of this tragedy. It is impossible to talk about Katrina without mentioning the speed of the wind, the volume and height of the water, the number of people dead and displaced, and the homes, schools, churches, and hospitals destroyed and severely damaged. It is impossible to fully appreciate the storm's impact without noting the number of businesses destroyed, the jobs lost, and, of course, the human, physical, and financial costs of the destruction.

At the time of the disasters, I was serving on the cabinet of Louisiana Governor Kathleen Blanco as Secretary of the Department of Labor, in charge of training for the state's workforce, unemployment insurance, and workers' compensation. I learned of the levees breaching while sitting in the vigil and communication fire of the emergency operations center at State Police headquarters. At first, I didn't fully appreciate what it all meant. . .billions of gallons of Lake Pontchartrain pouring into the city…80% of the city underwater…8…9…10 feet of mucky water filling buildings and dwellings in the poorest neighborhoods of the city…neighboring St. Bernard Parish obliterated. And then the stories flashed about tens of thousands trapped in the city, unconfirmed reports of thousands drowning in the streets.

I, like the rest of America, saw the horrific images reeling across the screen, stories of the exodus and rescue efforts, the military command and control, bodies floating, rape and looting in the streets, mothers crying for their babies. We saw the nightmares at the Superdome and the Convention Center unfolding in real-time in the sweltering daylight and nighttime of a Louisiana September. I had seen and lived big hurricanes, including Betsy and Andrew, but Katrina was different, a storm of storms. A part of me felt that this wasn't really happening, but as quickly as I saw the bad dream unfold, I was drawn into the reality of it, pulled by the weight and gravity of the catastrophe and the urgent need to respond.

Several weeks after the hurricane, I flew to New Orleans in a helicopter with several National Guardsmen and state cabinet members. We visited Jackson Barracks, the National Guard headquarters, and saw the watermarks on the walls that nine feet of water had inundated. We went to the Lower Ninth Ward and stood on top of the levee that breached at the Industrial Canal. The infamous 200-foot ING 4727 steel hull cargo barge that floated through a break in the floodwall still sat inside the neighborhood. Looking inland at the Lower Ninth Ward, a neighborhood inhabited by many of the city's black, poorest residents, I saw every building lying flat on the ground, massive rubbles of sticks and concrete—a deep, vast ocean of destruction as far as I could see.

A month after Katrina, Hurricane Rita struck southwest Louisiana and east Texas. My father lived in the direct path of Hurricane Rita and refused to comply with a mandatory evacuation order. After repeated pleas to Daddy, at one point screaming to him through the telephone that if he didn't get out he would die, he agreed to go. We made arrangements for him to be picked up by an uncle and brought to Fort Polk Army Base, several hundred miles north. When my Uncle Earl went to get him, Daddy refused to leave the house. Roads were closing and telephone communication was starting to break down. When I eventually connected with Daddy, he lied and said that Uncle Earl never arrived. At that point, it was too late for him to get out; the storm was approaching.

Rita hit the Louisiana coast as a Category 3 hurricane. Late that night, the state emergency operations center reported that every building southwest of Interstate 10 to the Gulf Coast had been severely damaged. Daddy was far enough from the coast and inland waterways to not be flooded, but with peak winds gusting 130 miles per hour, I was afraid that his roof had been blown away. Through 911, I contacted the Sheriff's Department in Lake Charles to report that my father might be in danger, and I began making plans to drive there the next day. I packed food, water, hand tools, and a first aid kit. The Superintendent of State Police arranged for me to get a pass to enter the city. They offered a personal escort but I refused it.

Accompanied by Girard Melancon, a co-worker, I left Baton Rouge shortly after dawn. It was a breezy Sunday morning. Gray clouds thickened as we got closer to the city. When we approached the I-10 exit ramp, armed National Guardsmen stopped us, checked the access pass, and warned us to enter at our own risk. Suddenly, we were driving through the ruins of a long, devastating war. The entire city lay tangled in debris. Roofs had been blown away. Fallen trees and power lines covered the streets. There were no people or sounds. Nothing moved. No birds flew overhead. The stillness was surreal and eerie.

Carefully navigating streets to get to Daddy's neighborhood, I approached his house, relieved to see his roof intact. Then I noticed that one of the three mature pine trees that stood in his backyard wasn't there. I braced myself for the worst as I rushed to the backyard, finding the tree lying on the neighbor's carport. Daddy appeared behind the glass screen of the back door. I was never more relieved to see that unwelcoming half-smile that my visits always prompted. "Boy, we had some rain last night," he said. To him, a bad thunderstorm had passed. I honestly think he slept through the entire horrifying night oblivious to the massive destruction around him.

For weeks after the storm, Lake Charles was nearly uninhabited, with no water, electricity, and health services, and no place to buy food, gas, or living supplies. Farther south, in Cameron Parish, where wind gusts reached 180 mph, the fisheries and towns were totally demolished and the coast was sucked into the Gulf of Mexico. In the aftermath, daytime temperatures rose above 90 degrees. Daddy, who had survived the storm with no injuries and only minor damage to his property, still refused to leave, preferring to live half-beast and half-child. I drove from Baton Rouge several times a week to bring him ice, water, and food supplies, but he barely touched them. He insisted that I not throw anything away, including the spoiled food in his freezer.

His mental condition declined sharply, but he refused to see a doctor. He was a tall man, rather well-built, and the poor nutrition took a visible toll on his appearance.

Eventually, the city was restored, schools reopened, and my father went back to crossing middle school children on the corner of Highway 14 and Oak Park Boulevard. Daddy's supervisor was aware of his mental condition and didn't allow him to work the corner alone.

My days were consumed with a continuous string of meetings and briefings on the state's recovery efforts. Our agency was responsible for leading the state's efforts to pay unemployment benefits to the more than 250,000 workers who were displaced by the storms and to help businesses find workers. Seasons changed, as did Daddy's grip on gravity and the ground beneath him. The cool winds of November fanned the blue roof tarps.

December brought yet another tragedy. The week before Christmas, my car was hit in a high-speed broadside collision that sent me spinning across the road into a steep ditch. I crawled through the front passenger door with minor injuries, but the car that I feared leaving with Daddy those two weeks in May was totaled and hauled to a wrecker yard.

That same week, Jonathan, our oldest daughter Karen's husband, drove to the woods of Hattiesburg, Mississippi and took his life.

I went to see Daddy to tell him about Jonathan's death. Daddy hadn't seen Karen, Jonathan, and their four young sons in several years. He reacted with sadness and disbelief. "He shot himself, Jay? Lord, Lord, Lord," he said shaking his head. The emotion that Daddy showed was a sign that he still remembered his grandchildren and great-grandchildren.

On the morning of December 19th, we drove to Hattiesburg for Jonathan's funeral, seeing remnants of Hurricane Katrina in the hilly forests we passed along the way.

With Christmas Day fast approaching, I asked Daddy about his plans for the day, hoping to persuade him to go to Baton Rouge. He declined my offer, of course, and said he was planning to spend the holiday with his sister, which I interpreted to mean *I want to be alone.*

Just when we thought nothing more could go wrong in 2005, the last week of the year brought yet another shocking, tense moment. I was driving home shortly after dark on Christmas Eve. Stores had closed and traffic was calm. My cell phone rang. Seeing an unknown number, I hesitated to answer, but on second glance I saw the 337 area code. *Could be a family member from Lake Charles or Lafayette*, I thought, so I took the call.

"Is this Mr. John Smith?"

"Yes, this is John."

"Mr. Smith, I'm Officer Peterson with the Lafayette Police Department. Mr. Smith, I have a Mr. Sylvester Antoine in custody, whom I believe is your father. Is that correct?"

"Yes, sir, that's correct. Is there a problem?"

"Mr. Smith, I responded to a call about your father about a half hour ago. He was seen stranded on Point des Mouton Road in Lafayette. From what I can see, he had a flat tire and drove his truck down to the rim of the wheel. The axel appears broken."

"Is he okay?"

"Mr. Antoine appears to be very confused and disoriented and doesn't really know where he is. He was being a little quarrelsome, but I managed to settle him down. If it's okay with you, I can transport him to the emergency room at Our Lady of Lourdes Hospital. I have a number you can call to have his truck towed."

Daddy had finally gone to visit his sister in Iberia Parish, 100 miles from home. He took the wrong turn on his return trip, got lost, blew out a tire, and kept driving to find his way. Seeing that Daddy's wallet contained his photo identification card as a deputized crossing guard, the police officer contacted the Sheriff's Department in Lake Charles. A 911 emergency operator took the officer's call. She remembered my father's name, *Sylvester Antoine*, not a common name and unusual enough to be remembered. She remembered that his son had called 911 three months before on the night of Hurricane Rita to report that his father had refused to evacuate and might be in danger. She had entered the father's name and the son's name and cell phone number into her call log. And so it happened, that a chance connection between a 911 operator in Lake Charles, a police officer in Lafayette, and me in Baton Rouge had prevented my father from spending Christmas Day of 2005 as a missing person.

That night, I drove to Lafayette with my son Patrick to pick Daddy up and bring him to Baton Rouge. He insisted that we take him home, seventy-five miles to the west. I told him that it was late and we needed to get home to prepare for Christmas Day. Only when I threatened to drive away and leave him at the hospital did he agree to get in the car. It would be the last Christmas that Daddy would spend with us before he was confined to a nursing home.

I wish the story ended happily there, but it didn't. In the months that followed, my father grew increasingly forgetful and paranoid. He began to hoard things—money, used Styrofoam plates, half-empty plastic soda bottles, and little cups of syrup and butter he'd get with his McDonald's pancakes. He stacked the cups neatly side by side and on top of each other until he built the Great Wall of China on the kitchen counter. It stunk, of course, and ants crawled everywhere. I discovered the wall one morning when I went to visit him and had decided to check on the house while he was doing crossing guard work. When he walked in earlier than I expected, all hell broke loose. My father was always a man of meek and calm demeanor. Until that day, I had never heard him curse. The only time I ever feared that he would strike me was when he saw me tearing down that wall. I backed off and let him have his way.

In late March 2006, not long after the "Great Wall" incident, Narva and I went to Lake Charles to clean Daddy's house while he was at work. Daddy had refused to get rid of Mama's things. Her clothing, jewelry, and personal papers were still there. I don't know why I started looking in his dresser drawers. I pulled one of his drawers and saw a pistol, old packs of Viagra, and envelopes full of dollar bills. I spread the bills across the bed. As I counted, I called Narva and asked her to quickly go to the front of the house and let me know if Daddy arrived. I counted hurriedly . . .$5,000 . . . $10,000 . . . $15,000 . . . $17,000. I was shocked. We immediately went to the bank to deposit the money.

Concerned that Daddy might think he was robbed, or worse, that I had robbed him, I returned to the house to tell him what happened. I wondered how he would react. I thought about the gun and was sure it was loaded. The thought crossed my mind that in anger he would overreact, get the gun, and shoot me, but instinct told me otherwise. Nearly everyone, including friends and relatives, had become strangers to Daddy, but he still called me by my nickname, and I believed he knew me as someone he loved and trusted. He returned home before we got there and was standing in the driveway as we drove up.

"Hi Daddy, we were here earlier and cleaned up a bit. The place was a mess. I found the money you had in your drawer. That's too much money to keep in the house, Daddy. I put it in the bank."

He spoke in a soft shout that showed more surprise than anger. "You did what? What? Why did you do that?"

"I put the money in the bank, Daddy. It wasn't safe in the house. Suppose the house catches on fire or you get robbed. See, here's the deposit receipt. Look, it's all there, every penny of it, and it's safe. It's in the bank." I didn't tell him that his name wasn't on the newly opened account, but he discovered that the next day when he tried to withdraw the money. He questioned me about his money for several months every time we spoke. "Where is my *l'argent*?" he would ask. Daddy had grown up in a Creole environment and knew a little French, but he rarely spoke it. I thought it odd that, despite his memory loss, he remembered that particular Creole French word. Eventually, he forgot the money incident entirely.

I feared for my father's life and safety. Living 150 miles away was more than distance.

Daddy had stopped answering the phone and wouldn't return calls. I knew that I was racing against time. Sooner or later he was going to seriously injure himself or someone else.

I obtained a Power of Attorney and took control of his affairs—rerouting his mail, managing his bank accounts online, and paying his bills. I filed an application with the State Office of Elderly Affairs to have my father examined to possibly be involuntary committed to the care of the state.

And then, one scorching morning in mid-August 2006, I answered another unknown number on the cell phone. It was my father's supervisor at the Sheriff's Department. Daddy had been arrested at a Kroger's grocery store for shoplifting a bag of cookies. He had simply wandered down the aisles and out the door, forgetting to go to the checkout register. Coincidentally, I was in town that day shopping for an assisted living facility for Daddy's placement.

On the day of his arrest, I signed a state protective order to have my father involuntarily committed for psychiatric examination. All that he worked for was lost when we put him in the back seat of a Sheriff's car and took him to a locked down unit on the tenth floor of Lake Charles Memorial Hospital. As the deputy sped down the road, Daddy spotted his truck parked on the lot of the store where he had been arrested. He opened the door of the car and tried to jump out. His entire life was reduced to one locked door and the minutes to separate him from his job and all his possessions, not to mention the loss of his pride and dignity as an honest, hardworking man. I broke down in tears when I heard his loud growl as two hospital assistants gripped him in a bear hug, one in front and another behind him, to empty his pockets—finding his keys, a small pocketknife, and $1,600 in bills folded neatly inside a rubber band.

I can recall no personal decision more painful than committing my father. At that point, the journey became a pilgrimage, his and mine together. I had taken my father's life into my hands. I had become the father and he had become the son.

Over the course of my father's illness, I moved him four times for various reasons—better care, surgery, or security. At his first nursing home, Daddy refused to eat, requiring a feeding tube to be inserted into his abdomen. Four months later, at a party celebrating his birthday, he opened his mouth to eat a piece of cake. As months passed, he ate so much that he was put on a diet. At another nursing home, Daddy caught pneumonia and again stopped eating. Again, a feeding tube was inserted. When the hospital prepped him for the procedure, they cleared his esophagus and removed a small, unopened pack of seasoning that had apparently been put on Daddy's plate several weeks before. Thinking it was food, he swallowed it, leading to an infection and high fever. Had I not authorized the tube surgery, he would have suffocated in his sleep and his death would have been attributed to pneumonia.

Alzheimer's patients are prone to wander, putting themselves and others at risk. They require close supervision and must be placed in secured, lock-down facilities to restrain movement. When I first began to search for a nursing home to place Daddy, I visited one facility that literally puts Alzheimer's residents behind a steel caged wall. My father did more than wander. He never gave up on going back to his house and was always trying to unlock a door—always "going somewhere." In May 2007, he fell while walking the slippery hallways of a nursing home in the middle of the night, suffering a hip injury that required surgery and permanently confined him to a wheelchair until his death in 2013.

As I reflect on my father's journey—the progression of the disease, his stubbornness and paranoia, his frightening and sometimes humorous attempts to fake reality and sanity—I am certain that angels had been camped around him. Thinking back on the turns and steep climbs, the chance occurrences and coincidences, all that could have gone terribly wrong or tragic but didn't, I can't help but be amazed and thankful that Daddy lived through it.

I don't know why the worst didn't happen, why Daddy didn't burn himself down by leaving the gas heaters on or driving off the road and into a canal in the middle of the night. I can't explain why he picked up a fork and opened his mouth after refusing to eat for four months. I can't explain why the 911 operator who took my call on the night of September 24th was working on Christmas Eve when Daddy got lost, or why, when I closed my eyes and spun the steering wheel, my car was hit broadside and not head-on. I don't know why I happened to be in Lake Charles searching for an assisted living facility for my father on the morning that he was arrested, enabling me to commit him to psychiatric treatment on an emergency basis.

I can't explain why those things happened or didn't happen, but I know that the answers to those questions are what made our journey together unforgettable. Perhaps that was our destination, the unknown. My life has unfolded that way, with many incidents and occurrences that happened for my good but beyond my understanding of them. Something outside of me was always present in the dark, unseeing days and nights, carrying me on a soft, gentle wind, and pointing the direction I should go, as Daddy had done when I drove and he rode beside me.

EARLY YEARS

My earliest memory of reading and writing was when I started kindergarten. In 1957, Reverend and Mrs. Phillips of Mount Pilgrim Baptist Church started a preschool program for the Negro children of Morgan City. They taught us the alphabet and numbers and read books to us, although I don't recall the children having books of their own. At Mount Pilgrim, I had my first public recitation of a poem at the Christmas program:

> *Jingle, jingle, bright and clear,*
> *I love my ears with which I hear.*

To be taught to pronounce and understand the meaning of words that I had not heard at home and would not have known at that age were it not for the love and guidance of a black minister and his wife was unquestionably the most important and impactful learning experience of my life. One of my most cherished pieces of art is an enlarged photograph of my kindergarten class of thirty-one children seated at our desks, dressed in our Sunday best, and posing in front of a camera. Two students stood at the blackboard, one of them pointing at the alphabet, as Reverend and Mrs. Phillips stood beside them. The girl on the front row with the "wooden stare" was my Aunt Antoinette, my grandparents' tenth child, who was seven months younger than me.

Picture Day at Mount Pilgrim, 1957

> Blackbirds perch on every stalk
> of the bean garden,
> their eyes open wide
> for this still morning shot.
>
> Little one in the front row,
> I see your wooden stare,
>   hanky balled tightly,

your sister's Sunday-worn socks,
feet barely touching down
with loose-buckled shoes,
worn and cracked
like your grandma's hands,
a story in every line,
like this morning
when she warmed the iron,
one by one gathered
and pressed the cancan pleats
that drape your pebbled knees.
I see the ribbon she unraveled
to bow-tie the braids she curled
thinking...

Any minute, child, the taxi will blow.
Ms. Gillespi's sheets need wash
and I ain't even soaked my feet yet.

Colored girl,
    someday you'll know why
    miles away in Little Rock,
    at this hour,
    time stopped
    and warriors marched
    only to a drummer's beat
    with a steady bird's-eye aim
    on freedom.

Look up!

When I started first grade in 1958, my grandmother bought me a writing tablet, but for some odd reason, I'd fill line after line and page after page of the notebook with the letter "X," written neatly and slowly as if I were creating something that was more than a string of one alphabet. Maybe in not knowing what to write, my blank mind, staring at a blank page, was in search of something that the letter X symbolized or represented. I must have known other alphabets at the time, but for some reason that I wasn't consciously aware of, I'd sit alone for hours and days writing X's, making sure that each X neatly touched each other and sat perfectly on the line. It was consuming, probably obsessive, and I remember hearing words said by others that maybe something wasn't right or normal about me.

It was around that time that I had my first encounter with "the other," something that I felt the presence of but didn't see. I felt it inwardly and only when I'd close my eyes while sitting or lying down in the presence of other people. In those moments, I felt my mind being encircled by layers and depths of something unseen and intangible, something other than me, and I'd feel that I alone had been visited. I call it "the other," because it clearly was something connected to me yet outside of me, but not the person whom I referred to as *I*. I was so consciously aware of the force that I would purposely lie down while in the company of other people and close my eyes to summon it. Whether the visitations had any relation or connection to the X marks is unknown, but I vividly recall them both happening around the same time. There would be many such occurrences in my life, when something unknown and outside of me was present and made its presence felt, not in a ghostly sense but clearly letting me know that I was not alone.

Around the age of ten, I took a taxi ride with one of my mother's younger sisters to the icehouse on the Morgan City riverfront, where my Grandfather Andrew worked. My aunt, who was only a couple of years older than me, was going to pick up Grandfather's paycheck to go grocery shopping. I thought nothing of a teenage black girl walking into Cannata's, the town's only supermarket, to cash her daddy's paycheck, but in a town as small as Morgan City, it was not uncommon for a white store owner to know the black families who shopped there. I remember the tall, concrete seawall lining the downtown street, the icy-cold room, and my grandfather standing in his calf-high, black rubber boots with the paycheck and a pencil in his hand. He must have sat down on a block of ice when I looked down at the "X" that he signed for his name.

Until then, it hadn't occurred to me that the man who was raising me as a father was illiterate and couldn't write his name. I knew that neighbors called him "Mr. Frenchy" but I didn't know that he was of French Creole descent and barely spoke English. I also didn't know that he had spent time in prison in his late twenties for killing a man. I knew nothing about my grandfather's life except where he lived and worked, and when his workday ended, he came home and made me, his first grandchild, the center of his life. I'd sit at his feet and slip his slimy boots past his smelly wet socks, and he'd let me eat from the plate of food that Grandmother had kept warm for him atop the hot water heater.

Dixie Homes was a federal housing project built in 1953 for Morgan City's poor black families. My grandparents moved there when I was two years old. I was too young to remember their former home but it was a small three-room house with an outdoor toilet. At 1416 Dixie Homes, we lived in a four-bedroom, one-bath duplex. Sumpter Williams, a new school for Negro children with all twelve grades, had been built a block away. The road leading to the project was Railroad Avenue, named as such because of the railroad tracks that ran parallel to it. The town's cemetery was directly across the street from the school. Our backyard butted up against a motel that fronted a highway. One night the motel caught fire. Seeing the flames jetting in the backyard trees, my grandmother, in a state of fear and rage, screamed. My grandfather slapped her. Years later, as I reflected on his past life, I understood that his hitting her was not an act of violence or abuse but of love.

Torched

> Grandmother wind whirled,
> screaming prayer to the stars.
> Granddad circled half-moon
> to a crucifix in her eyes,
> uttered something damning,
> then raised his palm
> and slapped water out of her.
>
> He had been at the sea wall all day,
> shoving ice for boats that stirred
> the Atchafalaya's deep roux silt.
> His feet sloshed inside wet wool socks,
> rubber boots up to his knees.
> His beans and salt meat still warmed
> on the hot water heater.
>
> Like a patient soprano,

fire shattered the glassy night,
leaping from the rooftop
to teary willows swaying
to an old-fashioned freedom song.
Memories flashed of time he had spent
in the iron-bending Angola sun,
the deaf drum of a wooden bench
against his skull, how it felt
to butcher a man
as easy as cards turned flush,
feeling his hands blister and swell
in a sweat-dripping dream
and not levitate and free-fall
with her scent clinging to him.

What's one torched sky
to a life branded by color
and days that can't be counted,
loving the only way
a once caged heart can?

My grandmother worked as a maid for white families. By the time I was born, she had given birth to nine children, eight girls and one boy. Three more children, two girls and a boy, were born after me. Mary, my mother, was the oldest. She and the second and third oldest daughters had left home by the time I started kindergarten. One of my most vivid recollections of my grandmother was hearing her come down the hall in the middle of the night gritting her teeth and cursing while praying to Jesus, knowing that not all the older girls were in bed and not knowing where they were, or even worst, that boyfriends had not left the house.

Memphis Soul Hour

Nights my grandpa gambled,
Grandma lay awake
with her rosary beads
draped to the bedpost.
Dragging heavy, crusted
feet, she'd rise to open

her door, squeaking,
and let all the bone heat
of hell fly. Chewing clumps
of corn starch, she'd rattle
her teeth like a tin can.
On the living room couch
two daughters slump
with their lovers
while Memphis Soul crackles
softly in the blue-lit dark.
Sultry and sweaty, they slither
like snakes between
whispers and a sex wish.
Then, a tongue-spewing
holy water and fire,
a soliloquy of cuss and prayer
seething like boiling grits.
Sheetrock walls shimmy,
porch screen hinges pop,
and a breeze cools the house.

I got to know a lot of children while living at Dixie Homes, most of them since kindergarten. My two best friends were Spencer Colbert and Calvin Welch. Caboon, as Calvin was called, was a silly, fun-loving kid whose mischief brought out the worst in me. Years later, Calvin went to Viet Nam and sustained injuries that left him paralyzed and barely able to speak. His face and body were badly deformed. The last time I saw him was shortly before his death, a visit that Victor, my mother's second brother who was two years younger than me, had arranged on one of my visits to Morgan City when I was in college.

If there was any benefit to growing up in a low-income housing project, it was being sheltered, not by buildings but by love. Like all the families in Dixie Homes, we were poor, but I didn't know it. All the families knew all the children and treated them like their own. When I got hungry and there was no food in the refrigerator or on the stove, I went to one of the neighbors and asked for a slice of bread. Their children did the same. All the neighborhood children were especially fond of my grandmother's biscuits, and there were times when they literally fought over the last one on the plate. If any neighbor was short of an egg or two or needed a little butter or a cup of flour or milk, they sent one of the children next door or a few houses away to borrow it.

Atchafalaya

Here, poor black men fish
or shove ice for the shrimp boats.
Women bear children, then work
where they're not seen, cleaning houses
and cooking in cafes across town,
bringing the ironing home
with a bundle of hand-me-downs
and leftovers for their own babies.

On workday evenings, they gather
in the quadrangle of small yards made
by the buckling, cross-shaped sidewalk
that connects their red brick duplexes,
government-built in the Eisenhower years.
In the air, the scent of beans, biscuits,
and pork fat, Motown and Memphis
blues blaring through the sheetrock walls.

Girls skip hop-scotch and rope
and spread handfuls of stars
to gather them before the rubber ball
bounces twice. Boys throw stick pegs
and crouch down in dust and twigs,
lagging and flicking glass taws.

Old soles, worn, heavy with troubles,
thin with hope, press against
the hand-drawn lines of Jim Crow.

At least once a week, Grandmother cooked a pot of cush-cush, a mixture of cornmeal, salt, oil, and water, cooked in a black, cast-iron skillet and served with milk and sugar. It was my favorite meal. On occasion, she would send one of us to the neighborhood store to buy stage planks for a treat. My earliest recollection of counting was seeing Grandmother slice one stage plank into four pieces and two into eight.

The only time that it occurred to me that we were poor was during Christmas, when white people gave us gifts. Every Christmas, we'd walk several miles to a building *across the track* and stand in line to get toys that white Sheriff Deputies handed out. Although no one said it, I assumed that the deputies knew that our family couldn't afford to buy us lots of toys. Still, like every child there, I was excited to get what they handed out. One year, I got my first set of six-shooters with a holster and a box of caps.

That aside, I don't recall ever interacting with white people in my early years. The most I saw of them was at the neighborhood grocery store, which they owned. In general, I didn't think about them, but I knew that they were privileged to have rights that were not afforded to colored people. The society in which I grew up was entirely segregated. Dixie Homes was all colored. I attended a colored school, a colored church, drank from the colored water fountain at the city's park, and sat in the colored balcony at the local theatre. My grandparents didn't own a car, and I knew that my grandmother took a taxi every morning to go clean, cook, and iron for white people. Occasionally I went on taxi rides with one of my aunts which enabled me to see places where white people lived, worked, and shopped.

Some days, Grandmother would send me to a meat market located close to downtown. I distinctly remember buying liver or kidneys. I had a practice of running all the way to see how quickly I could get there. On one trip, I took a turn without realizing it and got off course. By the time I looked up, I was several feet from a large body of water. It was then that I realized that the Atchafalaya River existed. I had never seen a river before and I surely didn't know how to swim. Standing so close to such a large body of water frightened me. It was the first time that I became aware of grace, as if a hand had raised my head to look up just in time. I knew that if I had not looked up, I would have run into the river, panicked, and drowned. I was keenly aware that some unknown, unseen force had held me back and kept me alive.

My mother became pregnant for me when she was fifteen years old and dropped out of school. She turned sixteen four months before I was born. By the time of my birth, she and my father had gotten married, but they never lived a day together. The marriage was strictly a legal arrangement. The day I was born, Mama took me to her parents' home. Shortly after my birth, my father joined the Army. They divorced soon after he completed his two years of military service.

I later learned that the relationship between my grandmother and mother grew very strained after my birth. They argued frequently. My mother, seeing no future for herself in Morgan City as a poor teenage girl with little education, and who was somewhat of an outcast for having a child at such a young age, felt the need to try to make a life of her own. When she turned eighteen, she left home and moved to New Iberia, Louisiana, to live with relatives. I saw very little of her in the years that immediately followed.

Upon returning home from the military, my father became the first colored mailman in town. On occasion, I'd see him from a distance, but we didn't have a relationship. My most memorable childhood experience of being with him happened the summer before I started the third grade. He stopped by to deliver a new bicycle that he had bought me and took me for a short ride in his car. When my mother, who happened to be visiting me that day, learned what had happened, she was extremely upset and had him pick the bicycle up. My father had long ago stopped paying child support and Mama didn't want me to have any part of him. I would not see my father again until I was thirty-six years old.

I would only see my father's parents, John E. and Margie Smith, on Sundays. They lived not far from the Catholic church that I attended, and I'd walk over to visit after Sunday mass. I have fond memories of playing with Darrel and Rodney, my father's youngest brothers, who were close to my age. My fondest memories are that of my Uncle Claude, who was paralyzed from the neck down but was able to move his right hand. Claude was a gifted child and had gone to college on a full scholarship. He was in his early twenties when I started my visits and had been in that condition for several years after being thrown from a car in an accident that occurred while on Spring Break from Southern University in Baton Rouge. My grandmother had cared for him since taking him home from the hospital. Although I had difficulty understanding Claude's speech, I looked forward to my visits with him. His body was ravaged but his mind was completely whole, and his spirit was always full of life. I would often think of him long after my visit.

In the fall of 1958, my mother remarried. She had been living in Mossville, a community near Westlake, Louisiana, and was working for one of my grandmother's first cousins, who owned a restaurant and bar with a small adjourning hotel. Twenty-five-year-old Sylvester Antoine, the man who would become my stepfather, was a native of Loreauville, Louisiana, and had served in the Army during the Korean War. He had moved to Lake Charles to find work and met my mother at the restaurant and bar where she worked. One afternoon, I got summoned out of my first-grade class to go to the principal's office. My mother, whom I hadn't seen in quite a while, introduced me to her future husband. The tall, slimly built man immediately won my heart by giving me a t-shirt emblazed with a red 1957 Chevy and the words "Conoco, Hottest Brand Going."

Just before the start of second grade, I went to Lake Charles to live with my mother and her new husband in a small duplex apartment where a railroad track ran almost to our front door. First Ward Elementary was directly across the street. What I remember most about the apartment was the smell of bananas, chocolate and vanilla cookies, and my mother's cooking.

Mama cooked at a local restaurant and my father worked for a milk company. At the end of the school day, I would stay with neighbors who lived in the adjourning duplex until my parents got home. That's about as much as I knew about my mother and stepfather in those days. They were complete strangers to me and in my own way, I rejected them. I had a terrible time adjusting to a life without my grandparents, aunts, and uncles. I wouldn't eat and hardly talked at home or at school. My mother wanted so badly to make her new family work. I recall being aware of how my aloofness affected her and I purposely kept up the charade to upset her.

In October of that year, I went to my first state fair. I was afraid of the rides but Daddy let me play games until I won a stuffed animal. The next morning, I put the toy monkey that I had won in the oven to bake it. And it wasn't an accident. Mama yelled at me and whipped me, then she fainted. That proved to be her breaking point. Before the start of the spring term of second grade, she moved me back to my grandparents. The only shining moment I had in those months was being taught by Mrs. Pye Brown, my second-grade teacher. She showed a genuine interest in my academic progress, and I felt it. I started off rather slowly with "needing improvement" in every subject area, but by the time I left, I was performing satisfactorily or better in every area. She remained very interested in my academic progress in the years that followed.

I returned to Morgan City to live with my grandparents for the spring term of second grade and remained through the third grade. Toward the end of that school year, I cut my left knee while sliding at home plate in a pick-up baseball game in a lot at Dixie Homes. In a state of trauma, I hid inside the living room closet instead of telling someone that I had been injured. I had no idea that the cut was so bad until my Aunt Betty saw the large pool of blood on the living room floor and called an ambulance. The cut required eighteen stitches. My left leg was inches from being severed in half.

After a month of recuperation but still unable to walk, I had another unexpected visit by "the other," the second time in which I did not consciously summon its presence. My Aunt Rita, who was fifteen years old, came into the room to clean up while I was lying in bed. Suddenly, I saw her levitating above the ground and moving toward the top of the curtains. I became so frightened that when she left the room I crawled out of the bedroom window and started limping toward the nearby school. Luckily, one of the neighbors saw me and got me safely back home. Many years later, Aunt Rita told me that when she was a child she suffered from rheumatic fever and would see angels flying around on the ceiling. She'd talk to them, and when she'd tell her younger sisters that the angels had appeared, it frightened them.

Except for the children I grew up with or were related to, I have little recollection of my years at Sumpter Williams. I do recall that I was an excellent speller. In the fall of my third-grade year, I was one of two students selected to represent my class in a district-wide spelling contest to be held in Baldwin, Louisiana. My cousin Gale Granger, who lived next door, was the other third-grade student. For the occasion, my grandmother bought me a new pair of Buster Brown shoes and she starched and ironed a white shirt and pair of blue pants for me to wear. I vividly recall sitting on the school bus during the ten-mile trip to Baldwin because it was the first time that I had been on a bus. After arriving at the school, I was told that it would be several hours before my spelling bee started, so I drifted off to the playground, where I discovered a set of monkey bars. I was alone at first, but when a little girl showed up and joined me, I completely lost track of time. My teacher had no idea where I was, and by the time she found me, the contest had ended. I knew that I would win, and I felt very badly that I had missed the opportunity to win my first prize. The experience haunted me for many years and taught me a valuable lesson about responsibility and being conscious of time.

By mid-summer of that year, I was beginning to feel the walls of my grandparents' home close in on me. I was no longer the darling little grandbaby and had begun to feel neglected in a home with nine other children, including three who were younger and several who were teenagers. I wrote my mother a letter and told her that I was ready to move back to Lake Charles. Knowing that her mail was delivered late in the day, I stayed close to home in anticipation of her phone call, knowing intuitively that she would. She did and within a month I was back in Lake Charles. To help make my transition easier, my grandparents allowed Victor to go with me. Although he was an uncle, Vic was like a little brother. He and I were inseparable.

By then, my parents had bought a home on Gelpi Drive, a mile from Chennault Air Force Base. The base was shutting down, and the neighborhood where my parents lived had homes once occupied by Air Force personnel. Several officers, including one of our next-door neighbors, were still working to close out the base before assuming responsibilities of their new orders at a base in Oklahoma. I mentioned the officer next door because he was the first Negro military officer that I had met, and before moving, he gave me his prized collection of several dozen handcrafted airplanes.

There couldn't have been more than a half-dozen non-military families living on Gelpi Drive when my parents moved there. They were all Negro, and most of them, like the Walls and Williams families, had all or mostly boys. In the neighborhood down the street, which somehow got the nickname "Car Shop," more boys lived— the Jones, Guillory, Simon, and Bellard boys. Chennault Air Force Base, although largely vacated and unguarded, had not shut down completely, and it soon became our playground. In the absence of a public recreation center, we played in the base swimming pool and gymnasium, and we had miles and miles of open space runways to ride our bikes, with pet dogs and stray dogs that they had befriended running alongside us. Our second playground was a large vacant lot on Legion Street, directly across from Gelpi Drive. Legion Street field became our baseball and football field, where every boy in the neighborhoods gathered for outdoor sports. It remained so until our late teens and early twenties.

In the fall of 1961, I started fourth grade at St. John Elementary School, a school built for Negro children, located ten miles away in a then unincorporated area of the city called Prien Lake. The long bus ride was fun to say the least. It never occurred to me that the school was that far or that there were white schools much closer that we could have attended, but we were fortunate to have young, talented Negro teachers who were genuinely interested in our education.

My absolute worst day of that year was the Monday morning when I refused to get on the school bus when it stopped in front of the house. It was bad enough that Mama had Victor and me start the school year wearing short pants, two of only a few boys who wore them, but when the fall weather drew near she bought my first pair of blue jeans . . . two sizes larger, thinking that I would be wearing them for a while and would grow into them. She made me wear them to a church rodeo the day before, which wasn't so bad because all the men riding horses and bulls appeared to be wearing big pants. But when she told me to put them on for school that Monday morning, I couldn't bear the thought of wearing jeans with six-inch cuffs. Without mentioning the jeans, I told her that I wasn't going to school. She asked what had gotten into me but I kept to my story: I didn't want to go to school.

By the time the bus pulled up, she had had enough of my stubbornness and pulled out the belt. I ran toward the side door of the house, but before she could get another lick on me, the spring of the screen door broke and hit her, giving me just the time I needed to run across a neighbor's backyard. I stayed gone until I saw her drive away to go to work. What I hadn't thought about was the bus stopping in front of the house and every child on it seeing Mama swinging the belt, the door spring snapping, and me running. I could hear the loud laughter as I streaked across the back yard. When Mama got home from work, she gave me the whipping that I had escaped. When I got to school the next day, Mrs. Conway, my fourth-grade teacher, gave me another one in front of my classmates, most of whom had been on the bus and got a second laugh watching me jitterbug around Mrs. Conway's paddle. From that day forward, I had perfect attendance in school, and getting a good education was the priority of my life.

That was the year I met Charles Roland Floyd and David Walls. I mention them because Charles was severely mentally challenged and David was exceptionally gifted. We started out in fourth grade together. There were no special accommodations for students with disabilities and gifted children in those days. We all sat in the same classroom. Eventually, Charles was pushed back to the second-grade class where Victor was. Teachers tried homeschooling him, but he later dropped out.

Charles and I lived a few houses apart and became close friends. He wasn't the first child with a disability that I had met, but the first one that I befriended. There was something about his outgoingness that attracted me. In addition to his learning problem and slurred, foreign-like speech, he was never quite on the beat. He was very pigeon-toed and couldn't run far without being tripped by his own feet, but his name always got called when we picked teams for a sandlot football game. He never got a hand-off, or a pass thrown to him, but you could always count on Charles to play hard and give his best.

During my early college days, Charles had a job making wooden pallets. It was cool…Charles employed, making money, wearing new shoes, and putting a few coins toward the cigarettes and wine we'd buy at Jones Liquor Store. One morning, he was shot and killed by a neighbor who saw him breaking into his car to steal a CB radio. The shooter was a black police officer. I can't picture Charles today. I have no photo of him and can't see his face, remembering only his light skin, long curly hair, spastic moves and broken speech, but I loved him.

In addition to having an exceptional intellect, David had unusual penmanship. He was the only student who wrote with a fountain pen and ink well, and his letters and words looked like visual art, which I greatly admired. I first discovered his gifted intellect when Mrs. Conway, our fourth-grade teacher, was teaching the class about the Bay of Pigs crisis that had the entire school doing regular fire drills in preparation for what might be a Cuban nuclear attack on the United States. When she asked the class what an I.C.B.M. was, David said "Intercontinental Ballistic Missile." I had no idea what that was, but the fact that David was the only student in class who knew told me that there was something special about him. In time, I learned that he was much more; he was a genius.

On occasion, I went to David's home to play with him and his brothers. On one visit, he invited me to his bedroom, where I discovered that he was an avid reader of *Time* and *National Geographic*. It greatly encouraged me to begin reading magazines and books outside of schoolwork. David and I developed somewhat of a competition for getting the best grades in every class. I managed to surpass him during our entire sixth grade, but it was short-lived. In every grade, we ranked at the top of the class, but his achievement test scores were always a grade or two above mine. There was never a doubt in my mind that he was smarter, but the competition pushed me to be my best and excel.

The second summer of my return to Lake Charles turned out to me to be one of my most fun-loving. My mother had taught me how to write cursive, and I composed my first letter in cursive to my grandmother on June 2, 1962, in which I wished her a belated Happy Mother's Day. Among other things, I mentioned that Victor and I had both passed to the next grade and that I had won a spelling certificate, although I misspelled the word "passed" and "certificate." I also told her about my experience crabbing and how my stepfather had fished a bicycle out of the coulee bordering our backyard. It wasn't a plain bicycle. It was a brand-new silver-colored Schwinn, fully equipped with chrome rims, front spring suspension, and a chrome headlight. I named *her* Silver Bell, and she would be the joy of my life for many years, not to mention the envy of every boy in the neighborhood.

All the boys of the neighborhoods bonded, but my two best friends at St. John Elementary were Garston Guillory and Martin Guillory. We were in the same class and remained so until the start of ninth grade. I'm not sure what made us click. We loved sports, particularly baseball, although they were much more talented than I was. We had met in fourth grade but really started bonding as fifth-grade students. By then, Victor had moved back to Morgan City and I was once again an only child. Martin and Garston became my brothers. That year, Erb Fontenot, who would later become my sixth-grade teacher, started a Boy Scout Troop at St. John. Our troop was No.148, which we soon gave the slogan, "The Best in the State." Every boy in the school who was age-eligible joined, and we became the largest troop in the district.

Mr. Fontenot wrote comments on my final sixth-grade report card that I often returned to in times when I felt like I could not and would not succeed: *You have done excellent work this year. The summer offers a great opportunity to further educate yourself. Use the library. Continue to read. A good education is precious.* The last time I spoke to Mr. Fontenot was in late 1980. He had become a dean at Florida State University and I was living in Natchitoches, Louisiana. I called to thank him for his instruction, guidance, and love. He died several years later of a brain tumor.

In early November of my sixth-grade year, several classmates and I were recruited by Mrs. Sonnier, the fifth-grade teacher, to be in the cast of a Thanksgiving play. One afternoon, Mrs. Sonnier heard that President John F. Kennedy had been shot and killed. She immediately broke down in tears. I had learned of President Kennedy the year before when the school had evacuation drills during the Bay of Pigs crisis and I had heard my parents talk about him as a man who cared about equal rights for Negroes. Kennedy's assassination proved to be an initiation, the moment when I began to pay attention to the non-violent protest movement led by Reverend Martin Luther King Jr., although it would be several years before I understood what Dr. King and other leaders were protesting about. I did not fully understand it until I came face to face with racism.

I completed my seventh-grade studies at St. John under the homeroom instruction of Mrs. Delores Beaco, whom I had great respect for. My only recollection of Mr. Bennett, our math teacher, was the awkward lecture he gave the boys about masturbation and how dumb David made him look when he found a math textbook error that Mr. Bennett insisted was the correct answer. David went to the blackboard and proved him wrong. That was also the year that I discovered poetry, although I didn't know what poetry was. One evening, my father took me to a debutante competition in which Debra Jones, a classmate, was a contestant. She recited a poem that to this day she doesn't remember, but the words made an indelible impression on me. It was a long recitation, but I particularly remember these words:

Freedom, I'm tired.
I'm tired of being born in the shadows,
smothered by my hopes and dreams.

Freedom, I'm tired.

I don't know why I remember those words or why they have lingered in my subconscious for over sixty years, but they are thematic of much of the poetry I have written.

In the summer of my seventh-grade year, one of our neighbors, Mr. Rankins, started a Sheriff's League baseball team, the Monarchs. By then, Garston had moved down the street and we played catch incessantly. He was a pitcher with a strong curveball. I ended up playing center field after losing the first base position to Edgar Bryant, a lefty. Martin played second base. I would never drop a catch and could throw a ball from deep centerfield to a foot within the back catcher's glove, but I couldn't hit a lick. I might have gotten one hit the entire summer. My father, a big fan of baseball, had a truck and took us to most games. Nothing was more exciting than putting on that sparkling green and white uniform, sitting on the back of the truck with my teammates as we rode to the other side of town, and standing under the glaring lights. We won the league championship among black teams our first year.

The following year, I enrolled in Carver Elementary, located in a colored neighborhood called Fisherville. It was my first experience being bullied, mostly by boys who had a history of reform school and who were regularly truant. I soon won them over by pushing my exam papers to the side of the desk to let them see my answers. Two of them, Vincent August and Albert Malveaux, eventually became my bodyguards, not allowing any of the other bad boys to bully me. Carver was also where I learned that I had somewhat of a natural talent in public speaking. I would be called on from time to time to introduce a guest or give the occasion for certain programs.

I had four teachers at Carver, including Mrs. Placide, my homeroom teacher. One day, Mr. Henry Williams, who taught English, gave an assignment to write an essay titled, "The End Justifies the Means." I have no recollection of what I wrote but I recall one of his written comments, that I should not use words unless I fully understood their meaning. He particularly noted my misuse of the word "aspect." After class, he pulled me aside and said that I had a gift for writing and that I should think of becoming a writer. Of course, I had no idea what he was talking about. I didn't know that Negro people were writers.

I had never read anything written by a Negro man or woman, and I surely didn't know how to become one.

I can add little more meaning to my early years beyond what is evident in the experiences that I have recounted. From the beginning, I was set on a journey to be introspective enough to distinguish the *I* from the *Not I*, and to embrace an awareness of a world beyond what I saw and sensed outwardly. My mother moving me out of the housing project to live with her and my stepfather, as trying as that would later prove to be in building a mother-son relationship after years of separation from her, was a turning point. I will never know whether the conditions or quality of my present life would be better or worse had she not moved me to Lake Charles, but I do know how positively and profoundly the experiences of living with her and my stepfather, and the love that I received from them, shaped me into being who I am today.

As an only child, the friendships and caring teachers of my middle school years gave me an extended family. I was carried on a soft, gentle wind that was just beginning to lift me out of poverty. I knew that the path would be through education and that I had the ability and desire to achieve it. I was nurtured, protected, taught, and mentored by people who sheltered me, intending only to help make the best of my circumstances and to help me realize my fullest potential. I had not yet felt the sting of racial prejudice or had any direct experience with white America. In ways that I had yet to appreciate, all the love that was given to me in those years was preparing me for the bitter hatred that I would soon begin to encounter.

THE FIRE THIS TIME

On July 2, 1964, President Lyndon Johnson signed the Civil Rights Act of 1964, which banned discrimination based on race, color, religion, sex, or national origin. On the day of the signing, I was at a Boy Scout camp carving a pinewood derby car and working on scout merit badges. Two years later, at the age of 13, I started ninth grade as one of five black students who integrated all-white Rosteet Junior High School in Lake Charles.

I don't recall who initiated the discussion, my parents or me, but I do remember that they allowed me to make the final decision. I had the choice between Washington High School, an all-black school, and Rosteet. I hadn't given any thought to *white* schools before then or white people in general for that matter. The only ones I knew by name were Mr. Johnny, who owned a neighborhood grocery store, and Ms. Irene, his cashier. I knew that white people controlled most things, including the government, and I had been paying attention to the work of Dr. King and others who were marching, going to jail, and dying for racial equality. When "freedom of choice" was presented to me, I naturally assumed that a white school would be better. Geography was also a factor. Rosteet was within walking distance of home, a measurement that I grossly miscalculated, especially on mornings when it rained. Oddly, no one suggested that I simply cross over to the white neighborhood down the street and hop on a school bus.

We were two boys and three girls. I had the distinction of being the darkest of the five. Nicholas, the other Negro boy, was a mulatto who had hair and eyes like Elvis Presley and sang like Smokey Robinson. White girls loved him. The black girls, Debra, Blanche, and Glenda, made a click among themselves. I hung out with them on occasion, but I mostly kept to myself, standing around at times with other misfits like the nerdy, pale-skinned boys who walked in short steps and carried textbooks pressed against their chests the way girls did.

Soon after school started, I joined the football team. We were champions that year, and I gained the distinction of being the first black player to be in the varsity team photograph that hung on the walls of the school lobby. I later joined the basketball team.

That year was the first time in my life that I felt hated and only because my skin was brown. Students laughed and snickered at me. Some called me nigger in my face and spat on the back of my head in lunch lines. With a blob of warm saliva dripping down my head and neck, I'd turn to see a chorus line of faces that all looked alike, all sneering, grinning, and white. I took the harassment and humiliation in stride, never striking back verbally or physically. I felt completely alone. My only friend was me. Somehow, I walked through the school doors every day with my head up, willing to face the hell that awaited me, and feeling confident that I could succeed.

I remember only a few names of the white students, Ricky Johnson, because he was the smartest student in class and who very much reminded me of David Walls, and Hugh Morton, because he was the one student who wasn't subtle about his dislike for me and my blackness. He never got physical, but his name-calling and "nigger jokes" were quite annoying. Of course, he only spoke meanly when he was around his pals. I'd wonder sometimes if he would behave that way if his friends were not around.

One afternoon in the fall of that year, I went to a nearby pond to get a sample of water for the study of paramecium in my Biology class, and "the other" surfaced out of the water.

Rebirth

> When I was fourteen,
> I went searching for paramecium
> and it's predator, didinium.
> Alone inside the water hyacinth,
> dipping my Mason jar
> into the pond, I heard
> Careful, don't fall in,
> as a hand behind me
> cupped my crotch.
> Like a mosquito hawk,
> I darted deep into the air
> until I could feel
> the drum in my heart
> and look back to see him—

his white mane palomino,
his cocked chapeau,
the mannequin-like grin
of a classmate's father.
I never told Mama and Daddy
how I became endowed
with the cheetah's speed,
the stealth and cunning
of a big catch that got away,
how life inside black water
had been fed and eaten, and
something inside me had died.

Years later, I discovered that the man who had come close to molesting me, the father of a child whom I had once gone to school with, was a gay person who later died of AIDS. For reasons that I can't explain today, except that I was a quiet, thinking child who kept his feelings to himself, I never told my parents about any of those experiences. I kept my feelings to myself but I was determined to prove that I could read, write, compute, and play ball as well as any white boy in the school.

My last essay in Freshman English was a writing assignment on the topic of our most memorable experience of the school year. I expressed my pain and regret for having attended Rosteet, "mixed feelings" I called them. The paper prompted a summon to the principal's office for a meeting with my teachers, none of whom had a clue that the quiet, well-mannered, and seemingly well-adjusted Negro boy was hurting and hating back. Among the teachers present was Ms. Troutman, a short, Tasmanian devil-looking woman who taught civics. Although she seldom smiled, she seemed to take much pride in her collection of film documentaries on un-American activities. In one of the films, J. Edgar Hoover, then Director of the Federal Bureau of Investigation, chronicled the public and private life of Dr. Martin Luther King Jr., noting that Dr. King was a "dangerous communist sympathizer." As the only Negro student in the class, I watched attentively, knowing that that was a lie, even when Ms. Troutman said it was the absolute truth. Not present in the meeting was Mr. Kravchuk, the Russian algebra teacher with a strong accent, who had privately and with a great deal of tact extended the courtesy of correcting my pronunciation of the word "ask," a politeness that made a life-long impression.

41

My father had suffered a severe back injury that year, and part of my morning routine before leaving for school was to cook breakfast for him. Years later, when Daddy had no memory of me as his son, I sat beside his wheelchair after rolling him onto the patio of a nursing home. While reading Natasha Trethewey's poem, "Southern History," I reflected on my experience at Rosteet and the struggles that he must have had growing up in the South.

Gazing

One King Holiday, I wheeled you
to the nursing home patio.
Drifting in and out of your blank stare,
I read Trethewey's "Southern History,"
recalling the year at Rosteet Junior High
when Ms. Troutman, the Civics teacher,
said Hoover was right to call King
a Communist. That was a lie,
I knew, but enough to make
Hugh Morton and his pals hate more.

That year, the one before King's death,
a bad spine kept you home
for weeks. On those mornings,
I rose early to cook two eggs for you
over easy. Keeping the flame low
and blue beneath the old black skillet,
I dragged the spatula slowly
to gather the frothing butter,
careful not to break the yolk
nor harden the thin white.
Across town, Mama's polished
corn-slit shoes and air-dried nylon dress
had already stained with grease
from Mr. Woody's hot oven broiler.

Daddy, gazing into your eyes,
the longleaf swaying
as the sun's yolk peeked
through gray clouds behind you,
I wondered if I'd ever really known

the burden you bore:
a black man living in the South.

The final essay assignment of my ninth-grade year was written during class. With little time to think, I felt words swelling in my hand, words I had spoken to myself many times before, spoken silently in tears with the feeling that I was alone and no one cared. It was my chance to strike back, the first time that I felt the courage and need to fight. I had endured their hell and shown them that a Negro boy can learn and be well-behaved, but I needed to make them know my pain. Maybe it was my audacity and surprising display of courage that caused the teachers to summon me and hear me say to their faces what they had already read and known, or certainly should have known, about the racially intolerant white children they taught, who came from the good white families they prayed and sang with on Sunday mornings. I restated the words exactly as I had written them. My best recollection of the teachers' response was that they were dumbfounded. Several apologized, but nothing they said changed my feelings and impressions of white students and that school year.

I finished the year with academic honors, making my parents and me somewhat of a sideshow on honors night, a proud night for my parents and one that I vividly remember, mostly for the stiff, piercing stares and kindly spoken words that made me feel more Negro than smart. The hatred and prejudice that I experienced at Rosteet had such a profound impact on me that even now, over sixty years later, I wonder how different my life would have been, for better or worse, if I had gone to Washington High School. To some degree, the experience molded my tolerance and patience with racial prejudice and my ability to cope with it, but it also cemented deep intolerance for racism, a quiet militancy, and a desire to fight injustice and inequality.

From Rosteet I went to Lake Charles High, which had also enrolled its first black students the year before. There we had strength in numbers. A black Catholic high school had closed and many black seniors and juniors decided to attend Lake Charles High instead of enrolling in the private, all-white boys and all-white girls Catholic schools a few blocks down the street. By my junior year, the Catholic school transfer students had graduated, leaving a much smaller number of black students. Many of them later transferred to one of the black high schools or dropped out. My graduating class consisted of twenty-two black students in a class of three hundred fifty.

In a population of over 1,000 students, I had two worlds: a black student community that included a few neighborhood buddies and new acquaintances, and a white student community within which I could freely move to suit my likes and interests. All in all, the social adjustment to a larger predominantly white school was relatively easy.

Racial tensions were high during the late 1960's. Social unrest and militancy permeated the air all across America. In April 1968, my junior year, Reverend Martin Luther King Jr. was gunned down in Memphis. The morning after King's death was especially tense. Before the first bell rang, I huddled with a group of black students who chose to sit on the steps of the stairway of the main lobby instead of sitting outdoors, so that white students had to walk around us as they went to the second floor. At least one of us was hoping to hear a complaint that could trigger a fight. White students silently walked around us.

Two months later, U. S. Senator Robert Kennedy was killed for campaigning for the Democratic nomination to the presidency. That summer, I watched television with amazement and pride as world-class sprinters Tommie Smith and John Carlos stood on the award podium at the Mexico City Olympics wearing black socks and no shoes with their black-gloved fists hoisted in the air. The era was marked by riots, protest marches, sit-ins, Black Panther militancy, and anti-Vietnam War demonstrations.

Although tension was also high on the school campus, there were no demonstrations. By choice, black and white students socialized and ate in segregated spaces. We had our stately columns and old majestic oaks beneath the "Wildcat" sky, and white students had theirs. As would be expected, there were fights, but they were always one-on-one.

My only fight with a white student was at the start of tenth grade. Actually, it was more of a punch than a fight. Some mornings, while showering after physical education class, a tall, heavy-built white boy would pass by and thump me on the head. That went on for several weeks, until I had had enough. That morning, he thumped, and I spun, leaped, and landed a solid right hook on his upper lip. He fell to the floor, got up, and didn't swing back. Minutes later, he showed me a silver tooth in his mouth and said that if I had knocked it out he would have "kicked my ass." Not only did he not thump me again but word quickly spread that the quiet, shy, moon-face black boy in the third-hour Physical Education class was not to be messed with.

That was the year that I had my only black teacher in four years of junior high and high school. Mr. James Ambrose taught me Geometry. He was young and talented, and greatly impressed me with the way he handled the *bad* white boys in class, who showed very little interest in learning but went out of their way to try to ridicule him. He quickly and tactfully dealt with their noise and belligerence, sometimes putting them out of class for a visit to the principal's office.

I began my senior year as a starting right cornerback, one of only two black players on the varsity football team. Unfortunately, my playing time was cut short by an injury after the second game. While being an athlete helped my assimilation into the white student community, it also created awkward moments, like watching black students sit in protest at pep rallies while I stood with the team and my white schoolmates and teachers as the band played "Dixie." At some point in the season, I decided to join the black student body and sit on the gymnasium floor when the song was played. The injury had me sidelined, so I had nothing to lose. The coaches didn't make a fuss about it.

The most awkward but fun moment that I experienced as a black athlete was the night our team took a three-hour ride home after playing a school in Shreveport. The other black player, a sophomore, sat near the front of the bus. I took a seat in the rear, near two underclassmen whom I hadn't interacted with much but who I suspected lived a lifestyle much different from the low-income family life I lived. While bragging about senior girls that they had sex with, one of them asked if I could "hook them up" with a black girl. On the spot, I made up a story about a black girl in my neighborhood who would give it up to any boy who asked, not mentioning the fact that I was a virgin. I offered to set them up with her at 4:00 p.m. the following Sunday if they each gave me $5. We agreed to meet in front of the grocery store that was owned by the family of one of them and was located near my neighborhood. With $10 in my pocket, I went to the bowling alley that Sunday afternoon to shoot pool with my friend Garston, treating us to burgers and sodas afterward. When I returned to the neighborhood corner that evening, I was told that two very angry-looking white boys were asking about me. Needless to say, they made threatening remarks and demanded that I return the money when they saw me at practice the next day. I told them that the "deal" fell through and that I would repay them later. I never did.

I was extremely self-conscious of my close association with white students. Being black on a predominantly white high school campus, one had to be careful not to be too "whitish" in speech, appearance, and actions for fear of being labeled an "Uncle Tom" by black students. I wore penny-loafers, Levis, and cardigans, but I wouldn't have been black without my Chuck Taylor All-Stars, iridescent slacks, and colorful double-knit shirts. I walked a high beam between two cultural extremes and found a comfort zone, a sense of identity that was rooted in Afro-American culture yet conveniently white, a convenience driven entirely by my desire to simply fit in.

That year, I also fell in love, although I didn't call it that until I felt the loss of it. I don't remember how the relationship with Leotha Eaglin started. I thought she was cute and I probably showed my interest in some awkward way. I was a shy boy who didn't quite know how to be personal with a girl. All the friends I had up to that point were boys from the neighborhood. Before long, I started carrying her books and walking her to class. I was much too shy to date and in fact dreaded the thought of being on one for fear of looking and sounding stupid and showing my ignorance about girls. But I grew to like her a lot. What I remember most about our relationship was talking on the telephone so late into the night that one or both of us fell asleep holding the receiver. Sometime during our senior year, the relationship ended. I was rebelling against the overprotective, controlling discipline of my mother in those days. I can't explain why, but I'm certain that my relationship with my mother had something to do with me suddenly ignoring Leotha and stopping taking her phone calls. Eventually, she moved on. When I tried to get her back, she ignored every plea for forgiveness. The loss of her haunted me for many years.

I was my mother's only child. She always wanted more children but couldn't have them. In December 1968, she and Daddy adopted a child. They brought Tracie Monique home directly from Morgan City General Hospital after she had been in an incubator for three weeks. Tracie was the child of Thelma, one of my mother's sisters, who had gotten pregnant at the age of eighteen while living in Dixie Homes with my grandparents. She spoke to Mama about ensuring a good life for Tracie, and Mama offered to take the child on the condition that she and Daddy would legally adopt her. I had just turned sixteen and Mama was thirty-two.

I've never known my mother to do anything but cook in local restaurants, and she was one of the best, making a few white business owners quite wealthy. People knew *Mary's* cooking and followed her when she quit one restaurant and went to another one. She was an attractive, fair-skinned woman who dressed well and spoke articulately. She once told me that people often asked if she was a schoolteacher, not realizing that she didn't have a high school education.

Mama and I stayed on a collision course for many years. Much of it, I think, was due to my being raised by my grandparents and her being absent during much of my early childhood. Much was no doubt due to our closeness in age and the stage of life I was going through. We were only sixteen years apart, and I was a teenage boy struggling with puberty. She seemed more like a bossy big sister than a mother. It took both of us many years to understand that we had two entirely different and opposite personality types. She was a talkative, outgoing extrovert and I was a quiet, socially uncomfortable introvert.

The summer after my junior year, my mother started a business. Lockheed Corporation had leased much of the Chenault facility to run a military helicopter maintenance operation. Mama and Daddy leased the cafeteria to provide breakfast and lunch services for the workers. The very first job I had was working for them. I was a dishwasher and did custodial work, but during the lunch hour, I drove from hanger to hanger delivering lunches that had been called in. I was more excited about driving the open-space runways than delivering lunches.

One day, I had an incident with a Lockheed employee that nearly cost me my job. Mama covered each meal with a sheet of wax paper and then placed it on a Styrofoam plate. Apparently, my speeding and turning curves en route to one of the hangers caused some of the plates to tilt, and the meals scattered. The employee, a white man, opened the box and expressed disappointment that the gravy had spilled onto the bread and vegetables, but in doing so he called me "boy" and told me that he wasn't going to eat "this shit." He threw the plate on the ground. I picked it up and tossed it back at him. Another employee, apparently a supervisor, immediately stepped in and told me to get my "ass" away from there. I had reached a point in my life when I wasn't going to take "shit" from any white man. Although I was only sixteen and smaller than the average boy my age, I was ready to fight if he had put a hand on me. By the time I got back to the cafeteria, Mama had gotten a phone call. Needless to say, she wasn't happy and scolded me.

My stepfather was a quiet, reserved man who seldom fussed about anything. I always had the feeling that he was in my corner, even when he didn't express disagreement with my mother's disciplinary measures. He was a good dad who took an interest in all the things I got interested in. Like pals, we hung out together, doing father-son stuff like tinkering with his cars and going to Friday night football games. I always felt that he was dominated by my mother's extrovert personality. In that sense and more, he and I had much in common. Mama often complained about something he didn't do right or didn't do enough of but he quietly took it all in stride. Sometimes, I'd feel sorry for him and felt comforted knowing that I wasn't the only one who got fussed at.

I don't recall Daddy ever raising his voice, and I can think of only a few times when he whipped me. Even then, it seemed like he was just doing what Mama expected him to do. He was a Dodger and Astros fan and loved watching baseball, which I thought was a little too slow for television. We'd never miss ABC's *Fight of the Week*, and I enjoyed spending Saturday and Sunday afternoons with him watching college and professional football. Of course, Mama was a great cook and we both looked forward to her meals. But she also talked a lot on the telephone, even while cooking. On many Sundays, he and I sat watching the Cowboys while waiting for dinner, and without speaking we'd look at each other as if to say, "I wish she'd be quiet."

Daddy was a hardworking man who at that time was doing highway construction work. Years later he was hired by Southern Pacific Railroad and would retire there after more than thirty years of service. I'd often see him walk through the back door at the end of his workday, wearing a hard hat and oily overalls, and carrying the lunchbox that Mama had packed that morning. With a smile on his face, he'd called her "Honey," and they'd embrace and kiss. On payday, he reached into his shirt pocket, pulled out his paycheck, and gave it to Mama, who handled the bills and was somewhat of a financial wizard in making ends meet.

My relationship with my mother grew increasingly strained as I entered my senior year in high school. I felt that she was too protective and controlling and I wanted more freedom to do the things other boys my age did, such as hanging out after sundown without a curfew. The strain of our relationship had started as far back as the years when I began to grow into puberty. In those years, I was two people, a quiet, withdrawn child when I was in her presence and a talkative, outgoing kid when around my friends. We both saw the difference. She'd whip me often, sometimes for things that I hadn't done but that she was convinced I had or for things that weren't bad enough to justify a whipping. She was always counseling me about matters of growing up that I didn't care to listen to or had grown tired of hearing.

While working at the Lockheed cafeteria, Mama insisted that I save my earnings in preparation for my senior year. In early August, I decided that I would ignore her directive and go shopping for new clothes. It would be the first time that I had money to buy what *I* wanted to wear, not what she bought me to wear. She was extremely upset and let her displeasure be known and felt. Our relationship deteriorated to a point where I felt like I hated her. When school started, I wasn't adjusting well socially and was struggling academically. I was underachieving and knew that much of it was my way of rebelling against Mama's discipline. My grade point average fell so low that I was kicked out of the honor society and lost eligibility to compete on the track team. At the start of the second semester, Mr. Hurlburt, my homeroom instructor and English IV teacher, pulled me aside and told me that if I didn't shape up I would not have enough credits to graduate. That got my attention and I became laser focused on finishing the semester strong. Fortunately, I did.

I was always somewhat domesticated, cooking, washing the clothes, and cleaning the house when I was out of school and she and Daddy were at work. I took pride in doing it, and Mama often bragged to her friends about how good a job I had done doing chores around the house. By my senior year in high school, I didn't want to do those things anymore. I couldn't imagine any other boy my age doing those things, and I felt that it was a burden that had befallen me just because

I was the only child old enough to do it. Shortly after graduation, she and I argued over my having to wash clothes and hang them on the clothesline. I told her that I had had enough of her bossiness and was going to enlist in the Army, during escalation of the Viet Nam War, to which she replied, "Go ahead. I can use another picture of you." That remark sent me to the Army recruiting office the following day. Because I was only seventeen, I had to get a parent's signature before leaving for Houston in a few days to be inducted. I never did.

The summer after high school graduation, I suffered another personal injury, this time playing football in the rain with the neighborhood boys. I stepped on a railroad spike that cut deeply into my right big toe, severing the tendon. My parents were at work but luckily my cousin Donald, who had come to live with us to take a job cooking at a local restaurant, was home and drove me to the hospital. The sight of my blood caused him to nearly faint, and he had to be treated in the emergency room. I stayed in bed and on crutches nearly the entire summer and became addicted to all the daytime soap operas and to smoking cigarettes. When I was able to walk, I started hanging out with Donald, who like Mama, was very talkative and outgoing. Two years older than me, he was single and drove a 1966 Chevy Super Sport and a Harley Davidson motorcycle. On his days off from work, we traveled the roads of south-central Louisiana. On one occasion, "the other" reappeared.

Hands
FOR MY GRANDSONS

I.

No one might ever say what I am about to tell you.
When strong men die, you don't bring up their dark pasts.
So years ago, when I eulogized your Great-Great Paw Paw Andre,
I didn't say that he had spent eighteen months in prison
for killing a man. The year was 1939. He was 27 with a wife
and three baby girls. The oldest, your Great Granny Mary,
was three years old. It was Saturday night, a poker game
the backroom of a gambling shack in Broussard.
Suddenly, an argument, a fist fight, a wooden bench slung
at Andre's head. The blade he pulled, smaller than his hand,
quicker than his thought, sank into a man's heart
as if Andre had played magic to make the knife disappear.

Named for African slaves, bound on three sides
by the murky Mississippi River, Angola Penitentiary
had been cut out of cane and corn fields of South Louisiana
plantations. The scorching sun bent iron and melted
men's spines. Shovels and sledge-hammers of the farm
and quarry pulled flesh from men's hands. A good meal
was raw potatoes, bread, and water. A good night was one lived.

II.

As a young man, I had close encounters with death
and imprisonment: blue lights flashing, the life ahead of me
unreeling, told to step away from a car, show my hands,
a cop's finger pointed at my face, his hand on a holster.
One frigid Saturday morning just short of my turning 19,
Cousin Donald and I on a Harley, daredevils tunneling
wind drafts of the wheelers, got pulled over by a trooper
onto a lonely gravel road at the mouth of a cane field.
He said you boys but we heard "niggers." *Slam the door
on his leg*, Donald said, *and I'll reach in and grab his pistol*.
Scared but angry, I looked down at the trooper seated
behind the wheel, pen and ticket book in his hand,
driver's door open, his foot on the ground. I felt a hand
leave my body, and for more than a second I reached
for the door. Something, I don't know what, pulled me back.
So when I say that any goodness in you and me is penance,
I mean that the life we think is ours is not. Strong men cry
us into existence, and prayers of good women are answered.

That was my first direct encounter with a law enforcement officer.
I had gotten a traffic ticket in high school for an accident in which
I was at fault and that required me to endure a week of afterschool
counseling at the detention center. But nothing prepared me for
that moment when I literally came within seconds of being killed
or incarcerated for life. I know that I had reached for the trooper's
door, but I can't explain what pulled my hand back. I often think
of the lives of young black men that hung on that thread but who
for some reason were not spared life or the freedom to live it. It's
a humbling thought and a constant reminder that my life is not my
own. My mother, who was young but prayerful, was always fearful

of that moment—when the thread would break and I would make a choice that would cost me my life. That was the cause for her strict discipline and overprotection of me in those years when I was in the storm of life, unknowingly playing with fire and giving no thought to the consequences of it.

BOY OF THE NIGHT

Having sat out the first semester of college after graduating from high school, I was looking forward to getting back into school, but I wanted to leave home. I decided on the University of Houston. Mama suggested that I contact one of Daddy's cousins about staying with them and they gladly agreed. Their only child was no longer living at home and they had plenty of space. Daddy was unemployed but my parents were committed to giving me the financial support I needed. Still, I knew it would be a burden. Without telling Mama, I drove to a pay telephone one night and called my natural father to ask him for help. I had not seen or spoken with him since I was a child. Still living in Morgan City and working for the U. S. Postal Service, he had remarried and had other children, which I wasn't aware of at the time. I told him that I was planning to go to college and needed financial support to help cover the cost of tuition and books. Politely, he told me that he couldn't help. His response was terribly disappointing but I would not let it deter me.

I entered the University of Houston in January 1971. Months before I arrived, twenty-one-year-old Carl Hampton, head of the Peoples Party II, which later became a chapter of the Black Panther Party, was gunned down on Dowling Street by Houston Police after a ten-day standoff at the PPII headquarters. Although I didn't become aware of the incident until after I enrolled, Hampton's murder, the black protest aftermath, and the police investigation were still major news stories. That, coupled with anti-Nixon and anti-war demonstrations and rallies on campus, created somewhat of a revolutionary atmosphere that I found intriguing.

I was overwhelmed, not only by the size of the student population and classes but the impersonal relationship between students and professors. I literally felt like a number. As a psychology major, the first class I attended was a history class held in an auditorium filled with at least one hundred students. We were given a course syllabus and told to show up at a testing site in several weeks for an exam on a book by Cicero. At that moment, I knew that college would not be high school. One of the required readings of my sociology class was the *Autobiography of Malcolm X*. I had seen Malcolm X on television and knew that he had been killed in 1965, but I hadn't paid much attention to his words. After reading his autobiography, I was drawn to his struggles with identity and his message of black nationalism.

I don't recall the thesis of the first essay I wrote in my English composition class, but I earned a high score. In handing me my graded paper, the professor asked if I was majoring in journalism. She seemed a bit surprised when I told her that I wasn't and suggested that I think about being a journalist. It was the second time that I had been told that my writing was exceptional. Still, I gave absolutely no thought to being a writer or studying English or journalism as a major.

When not attending classes, I gravitated toward the Afro-American culture scene, hanging around the black student center, discovering the poetry of Nikki Giovanni, and attending speeches by black activists like Dick Gregory and "Black Power" advocate Stokely Carmichael, who had just returned from a long stay in Africa. Many white students left the auditorium during Carmichael's speech, apparently feeling offended by his remarks.

Even though I didn't compete in high school track, I had relatively good speed and dreamt of being a football star before my season was cut short by a fractured rib injury. At UH, my talent caught the eye of a physical education teacher, who encouraged me to join an intramural track team and asked if I had considered trying out as a walk-on for the UH football team. I welcomed the chance to run in the intramural competition but brushed aside the thought of walking on to one of the top-ranked football teams in the country.

On the day of the intramural meet, we heard that the fastest players of the UH football team would be competing as a team. I took first place in the 100-yard dash and second place in the 200-yard dash. The final race was the 440-yard relay, and I would run the third leg. Standing beside me was Robert Ford, a UH starting wide receiver and the fastest runner on the UH team. Before I took the baton, my team was in last place. Ford said something cocky like, "This'll be easy; we're way ahead." Looking at the runner approaching me, I replied, "Not for long." When I passed Ford in the curve, I turned and smiled at him. I gave our last runner the baton with a slight lead, but we got the silver. Ford and his team finished third.

My instructor later arranged for me to meet with a member of the UH coaching staff. After suiting up for several practices, I stopped going, feeling completely out of place and intimidated standing on the sidelines watching guys like Ford and fullback Robert Newhouse. Newhouse finished UH as the all-time leading rusher and played 12 years for the Dallas Cowboys. Ford went on to become All-American, the first player in the history of the NCAA to have two 99-yard touchdown receptions, and won three Superbowl championships with the Cowboys.

That spring, the Texas Legislature doubled the tuition for out-of-state students, making it unaffordable for me to remain at UH. Although short-lived, my stay in Houston was a powerful education, not to mention that bright, shining moment when I dusted the fastest player on the UH football team. If nothing else, they were the kind of experiences that I could talk about back home sitting on milk crates late at night while gulping cheap wine with Vietnam vets and street hustlers or intellectualizing with the more serious college students.

In the fall semester of 1971, I enrolled in McNeese State University, where I spent the greater part of the 1970s pursuing two undergraduate degrees with a brief stint in graduate school. Outside of school and weekend parties, the early years at McNeese were a period of introspection and questions about what I wanted to do with my life. A strange mix of individuals, including several 19th-century American writers and philosophers, a young U.S. Senator, and a 20th-century Swiss psychiatrist, would greatly influence my thinking about my individual self and the world around me.

I titled my first freshman English term paper at McNeese "Malcolm X: From Conception to Conceptions." The paper theorized that Malcolm's resistance to white supremacy and his philosophy of black nationalism were shaped long before he embraced the Muslim faith. The greater influence was the traumatic and tragic events that Malcolm and his family experienced by his 13th birthday at the hands of white terrorists, always in the middle of the night. The paper got the highest grade in class and elicited a complimentary comment by the teacher that it was the only one worth reading. I later sold the research paper to several students to earn spending change.

I don't know what drew me to psychology as a major course of study, although I'm pretty sure that my Aunt Sally, my grandparents' third oldest child, had much to do with it. She suffered from paranoid schizophrenia since childhood and lived in and out of mental institutions most of her life. During my senior year in high school, my mother took her in to live with us. Aunt Sally was thirty years old, married, and had three children, all of whom were separated from her for most of her adult life because of her illness. Under heavy medication, she behaved quite normal for a few months but eventually had to be sent back to the institution.

As a psychology student, I was greatly influenced by Carl Jung, whose theories in analytical psychology took me beyond personal experience into the world of myths, symbols, and the collective soul of contemporary society. My readings of Jung's *Man and His Symbols* and his memoir, *Memories, Dreams, Reflections*, were studies in the journey of self-realization. I was especially enamored by Jung's concepts of the collective unconscious, archetypes, and psychological types. It was then that I discovered that I was a thinking, intuitive introvert. My reading of Jung continued long after I graduated and into the middle and late years of life.

Without a job and a car, I spent much of my leisure time during my early college years hanging out with other neighborhood boys on the corner of Progressive Street and Highway 14. I was a college student during the day, but when most people were settling into bed, I became a boy of the night, wandering the streets in search of who I was and was becoming. We sat on empty milk crates on the side of Abe's Grocery Store, smoking cigarettes and reefers, and drinking cheap wine that we bought at the black-owned liquor store across the street. With few exceptions, the boys I hung with either hadn't gone to college or had dropped out, but being with them gave me a sense of belonging. Someone with a car was always at *the corner* with stereo speakers on the hood. Some nights we just rode around, and I ended up in places that my parents could never have imagined I had been.

Baptism

> One Sunday night we swayed
> in a holy wind, wearing Super Fly
> shirts and Eleganza shoes

56

we had seen at the Palace Theatre.
Life reeled in front of milk crate squats,
between reefers and the poison
we gulped out of cheap port wine
mixed with fruit juice and spit.
Hitched a ride with a Viet Nam vet
turned hustler, whose Brougham,
half-primed, half-painted, choked
like a bleeding hog, blasting funk
from a plywood, shag-covered box:
Curtis, Santana, and our favorites—
soft horns and violins, high tenors
telling of broken-hearted men
and love we dreamt of making.
Peach-fuzzed and celluloid,
we cruised over Cyclops' bridge,
crept alleyways that stunk of piss,
and stood at a slut's bedside.
Would-be-gangbangers, candles
flickering on a frosted cake, we circled
her nakedness like a prayer vigil—
Awestruck. Eyes bulging. Legs
buckling on a thin sheet of lake ice.

Sometime in early 1972, I met Narva Hebert, a girl who lived on Gelpi Drive. She was a senior in high school and the third oldest of her mother's eight children. Her mother, Edith Carter, was no longer married. Narva was raised by her great-grandmother from the age of two. Like me, she never had a relationship with her father. She met him for the first time when she was twenty years old and had attended school with siblings not knowing they were related.

I was a friend of Narva's older brothers, Lester and Mark. In time, I found myself pretending to go to their home to hang out with her brothers just to see their oldest sister. Her nickname was Teenie and it fit her perfectly. She couldn't have weighed more than 100 pounds, but she had the cutest smile I had ever seen. She was quiet and smart, and we instantly connected. I was her date at her high school prom, which I remember little of except for her pink dress, my ruffled pink shirt, and getting her home by 11:00 p.m. as her mother had instructed. Her quiet, humble nature made her easy to talk to. We were both introverts, but something about her long periods of silence baffled me. It took me a while to figure out that while I was thinking, she was sensing and feeling. By the time she started college at McNeese State in the fall of 1972, I was in love.

At the start of my junior year, I was hired as a pre-sorter at United Parcel Service. All the pre-sorters were college students and worked part-time, clocking in at 10:00 p.m. and working several hours sorting packages for trucks that drove in from parts of Louisiana and Texas. As members of the Teamsters Union, we were the highest-paid, best-dressed, part-time student workers in the city. The job enabled me to buy my first car, a 1964 Ford Galaxie. I had no sense of money management, spending my entire paycheck on clothes and music, and was always broke by the next payday.

While working at UPS, I developed a close friendship with Milton Henny, a black accounting student. He'd bring his portable 8-track player to work, and Marvin Gaye's "Let's Get It On" would get us through the night. I envied "Slim," as we called him because he was smart, insightful, serious, and funny. On weekends, we hung out at the local nightclubs. Being much taller and a good dancer, Slim was never turned down for a dance. I, of course, spent most of the night standing near the bar.

I had major disagreements with Charlie, the black supervisor, who was a UPS "company man" and showed little concern for us as students. He saw me as a rabble-rouser who purposely slowed down the unloading and stacking when he increased the speed of the conveyor belt. I refused to be treated like a human robot, and the younger, less experienced workers followed my lead. It was a classic standoff between labor and management, and I was determined to win. One night, the confrontation reached a boiling point. Charlie punched my timecard and told me that I was fired. When he escorted me to the parking lot, I grabbed a crowbar from the trunk of my car, stepped off the UPS grounds, and dared him to come near me. Thank God he didn't. The next day, I met with the union steward, who assured me that I still had a job. Charlie had failed to follow the "progressive discipline" union contract procedures for firing an employee. I clocked in at the usual time that night.

That year, I switched my minor course of study from math to English and discovered my great love for literature. I grew very interested in discoveries of the zeitgeist of the periods in which English and American literature was written and how that spirit influenced the philosophies and trends of thought that ultimately shaped the literary canon. It was a perfect match for my major study of psychology. After reading Thoreau, Hawthorn, and Emerson, I was convinced that I was a reincarnated transcendentalist who was born in the 19th century. Thoreau's *Walden* and Emerson's essays on "Nature" and the "Oversoul" drew me deeper into questions about my inner self. Who am I, really? Why am I so comfortable with intuitive feeling and thought? What is the connection between me and the natural world? Is there some connection between Jung's theories of psychoanalysis and depth psychology and the writings of Thoreau and Emerson?

More than anything, those questions caused me to become more introspective. I was living in two worlds: the one that I sensed and portrayed outwardly and the one I experienced silently, alone, and inside my own thoughts. Literature greatly broadened my view of the world. Our study of the Age of Enlightenment made no mention of slavery or the life of ex-slaves. The world I was studying was that of white men. I don't recall being taught the literature of African American writers other than Paul Lawrence Dunbar and Langston Hughes. Still, I had begun to understand the humanness of me, not simply as a "Negro" and a descendant of slaves but as a person living in a world defined and dominated entirely by the thoughts and actions of white people.

Athletics remained a great passion, and I still harbored dreams that I could be a star athlete. After taking the top awards in sprints at a McNeese intramural track meet, beating one of the track team's fastest sprinters in the 100-yard dash while wearing a pair of tennis shoes, I met with the head track coach and decided to give college track a try. At that point in the season, the training consisted of distance running, which wasn't my forte, but in time I was in top shape. By the time we started training for sprints, the job at UPS was taking a toll. I wasn't getting enough sleep, and practices interfered with the little time I had to study and do homework before clocking in at 10:00 p.m. Not being on an athletic scholarship, I had to choose between track and my part-time job. I chose the latter, finally facing the reality that being a college athlete wasn't in the cards for me. At that stage of my college experience, I wasn't sure what was.

College life at home brought joy and pain. After dating Narva for three years, she became pregnant. I panicked at the thought of being a father and drifted away, not denying that I was the father but not being there when Narva needed me most. Karen's birth on October 12, 1975, was an awakening. I now had a responsibility that I could not turn my back on. More than anything, I didn't want to be like my natural father.

Narva and I both took a break from college for a semester. I had lost focus completely and gave serious thought to not returning to school. My mother expressed her disappointment in my behavior, particularly my treatment of Narva. Her constant complaints, along with past issues between us that I had not let go, strained our relationship even more. Eventually, I left home to live with an aunt who lived not far from the McNeese campus. I stayed in school but wasn't giving my best, spending a lot of time doing what young men in the early 1970s did…partying and riding around.

There were several moments in those years when I was visited by "the other." One night, while living with Aunt Nancy, and for a reason that I can't explain, I picked up a copy of playwright Lorraine Hansberry's *A Raisin in the Sun* and read the entire book in one sitting. While reading, I played the Harold Melvin & the Blue Notes song, "To Be Free To Be Who We Are," over and over. When I finished the book, I felt the presence of Lorraine Hansberry and spoke to her. In tears, I told her that I would do what she was calling me to do and be a writer. In a moment of epiphany, I knew that I would one day publish a book.

One Saturday evening not long after that moment, I rode with a friend to buy a bag of marijuana from a cousin. On the way home, Jonathan was pulled over by a state trooper. Jonathan removed the marijuana from under the seat and told me to stuff it in my pants. Not thinking, I did. The trooper asked Jonathan to show his driver's license and registration papers and step out of the car. Minutes later, the trooper walked to my side of car, told me to roll the window down, and put his head inside the car to sniff. Luckily, we had not gone far enough to light a joint. In that moment, I saw my entire past and future life reel in front of me, and the only future I saw was prison. The trooper walked back to Jonathan, gave him a warning for crossing the yellow line in the road, and drove away.

Christmas of 1975 would be the first holiday season since I had gone to live with my mother that we were not together, hardly speaking to each other in fact. One afternoon in early November, she surprised me with a visit at Aunt Nancy's place and spoke words that pierced my heart. "Jay," she said, "you've got to give love to receive love." It was the moment when I understood the depth of my Mama's love for me and the pain that she had felt in all the years when she tried so hard to win my affection. I also knew what I had to do to heal the wounds that divided us.

That Christmas Eve, I went to a drugstore and bought her a $5 gift, a small pewter-colored rose embossed on a blue, velvety frame about the size of a child's hand. It read, "To Mom With Love." On Christmas morning I went to see her and gave her the little rose, unwrapped. I think that gift meant more to her than any I would ever give her. I moved back home shortly after that day. Years later, when my mother was very ill and had started numbering her days, she labeled objects with the names of her children and grandchildren, things that she wanted them to have when she was gone. On the back of the rose, she had placed a piece of masking tape and written the word, "Jay."

Not long after moving back to my parents' home, another incident occurred in which a soft, gentle wind prevented tragedy. I had left Narva's mother's home late one night, and as I got closer to my parents' home, the song, "Heaven Must Be Missing an Angel," by the R & B group Tavares came up on my eight-track. I liked the song and wanted to hear it, so I took a detour down a long stretch of road that I seldom traveled. As I entered a curve and applied the brake to slow down, I discovered that I had none. Being on a long road with no stop signs and signal lights, I was able to coast the car to an eventual stop.

At the start of my senior year, I thought of looking for another part-time job. Several courses that I needed to take were only offered in the morning, and the late-night work hours at UPS didn't allow enough time for study and sleep. Sears hired me as a student worker in the credit department, pulling the files of customers who needed to increase their line of credit while they were shopping in the store. It was the first job in which I regularly interacted with white employees, mostly women, and with the public. The credit department was not "back office." We worked in an open space that shoppers saw, and I was the first black male to work there. Paul, a Nigerian American who had recently graduated from McNeese, headed the cashier's office adjacent to the credit department. Neither he nor I saw a future with Sears, but I was proud to stand near him every day and watch the surprised look of white customers who stopped to do business. My mother was prouder, making sure that I had a clean, pressed shirt to wear on workdays.

With enough college credits to minor in English, I decided to take courses in education in order to qualify for state certification to teach high school English. At the start of my senior year, I was assigned to Lake Charles High School to complete my student teaching requirement and was given an English IV class of students who would not be college-bound but who had to take the course. My supervisor happened to be Mr. Hurlburt, who had counseled me about getting back on track to graduate from high school. By the end of that semester, I was absolutely certain that I would never teach English. I hated the thought of doing that for the rest of my life, especially knowing how little teachers were paid. When I eventually received the state certificate, I tossed it into a drawer and never applied for a teaching position.

Narva and I graduated together in December 1976. I distinctly recall having a feeling on the night of graduation that I hadn't accomplished anything. I didn't have a full-time job and I felt no sense of accomplishment. I felt as empty and lost as the first day that I stepped into a college classroom. Eventually, I got a part-time job working the front desk at the main branch of the public library. After a boring summer studying sociology as a graduate student, I decided to return to college in the fall of 1977 to pursue a degree in accounting. On Slim's suggestion, I had taken one accounting course as an elective and enjoyed the structured practicality of the discipline. I instinctively felt that I would enjoy the studies and do well.

On October 16, 1977, Narva and I went to the home of a Justice of the Peace and exchanged marriage vows. Karen had turned two years old four days earlier. Neither of our parents was invited. Having spent our savings on furniture for the apartment we had rented on the McNeese campus, we couldn't afford wedding rings. The morning after getting married, I went to class, and Narva dropped Karen off at the babysitter before taking the fifty-mile drive to her job as a special education teacher.

Marriage and fatherhood caused me to be more focused and committed to college, much more than I had been in pursuing my first degree. While in school, Joy, our second child, was born, giving me more reason to succeed. I enjoyed accounting and got excellent grades, hoping to land a good-paying job that would enable me to provide for my family. I joined a small study group comprised of the top accounting students and felt good that I could contribute and compete with the best.

Mr. Robert Brantley Cagle, a licensed clinical social worker and librarian who headed the government documents depository at the McNeese library, hired me to work as a graduate assistant on weekends. In doing research for other students, I discovered the work of the U. S. Small Business Administration and the programs that the SBA has established to promote the development of minority-owned businesses. Both library jobs gave me the time and quietness to read, study, and think. For two years, I was immersed in the world of books. When I had a break from work, I did accounting homework or read King, Gandhi, Jung, Toynbee, Adam Smith, Schweitzer, and the first biography on Robert F. Kennedy. It was then that I grew interested in public policy and the economic plight of black Americans.

In the spring of my final year, the tax accounting professor asked a group of us to volunteer to prepare tax returns for members of the McNeese faculty. I did the return of Mr. Cagle and his wife, both of whom had cerebral palsy and high medical expenses. Preparing their tax return was extremely challenging but I got it done and the professor approved it. I credit Mr. Cagle, not only for giving me a part-time job, but for mentoring me during a very challenging period of life. Dr. Millard Jones, an English professor under whom I had studied while pursuing my first degree, was also extremely encouraging and helpful in my realizing a sense of purpose. One day, he pulled me aside after class and told me that he saw great potential in me and felt that I needed to find some focus about what I wanted to do with my life.

Three months before graduation, the head librarian who had hired me at the public library retired. Her replacement moved me from the front desk to shelving books in the stacks. My gut feeling was that she didn't want a black male face to be the first and last face that library patrons saw, but with graduation around the corner, I accepted the reassignment without complaining. Several younger white college students also shelved books, including two young men who constantly talked and joked. I immediately sensed that they felt uncomfortable about my presence. The topics of their conversations were always simple and silly. Feeling too intellectually superior to engage in them, I mostly kept to myself. On occasion, I'd pretend to be interested to show them some friendliness. On one such occasion, one of them, out of the blue, started telling a "nigger joke." Before he could finish, I told him to stop and that I not only didn't listen to jokes of that kind, but I didn't appreciate him trying to tell them. That was the last time that either of them spoke to me.

One evening, Hussein, a Ugandan student who lived in an apartment a floor below ours and who had learned of my interest in public policy through conversations we had, gave me a book titled *To Seek A Newer World,* written by U. S. Senator Robert Kennedy. Kennedy, who by then had announced his candidacy for President of the United States, put forth a bold vision for inner-city renewal that advocated more private investment in impoverished communities and the empowerment of inner-city residents to take economic destiny into their own hands. Searching government documents, I later discovered the work of federally-funded community development corporations (CDCs) that grew of out legislation that Kennedy sponsored in 1966 with former U.S. Senator Jacob Javits of New York. I also grew more conscious of the divisiveness and economic disparities that I saw in my own community. I was keenly interested in the problems of race and poverty in America.

For many years, the thought of my relationship with God haunted me. I was raised Catholic and believed in the death and resurrection of Jesus Christ but had stopped attending church when I got old enough to make that decision on my own. I had grown bored with the routine recitations of the Catholic Church. The mass seemed canned and spiritless, and I was very suspicious of any organized religion that solicited money from poor people. Watching *The Exorcist* in early 1974 scared me to death and I began to think about going back to the Catholic Church. I visited a priest to confess my separation and discuss the process of renewing my faith. He didn't pray with me. Instead, he blew cigarette smoke in my face and told me that I needed to get reacquainted with the history of the church, giving me a book to do that. After reading about wars and conquests, I was convinced that I'd never go back. But the haunting continued. I felt God pulling but a great fear of religion was overpowering me. I'd pass St. Margaret's Catholic on the way to visit my parents, wanting to go in and pray, but was afraid to do it. I didn't know what I feared.

While attending McNeese after getting married, I met a Mormon student in class, who invited Narva and me to have dinner with her and her husband, who was also a McNeese student. They lived in a married student apartment several blocks from ours. It was the first time that I had been inside the home of a white married couple. They cooked Japanese, and we had a very pleasant evening talking about student life and course work. They talked about the belief and history of the Church of Jesus Christ of Ladder-day Saints, but it wasn't a hard pitch. Before we left, they gave us a copy of the *Book of Mormon*, which I read. I found the story of Joseph Smith and the founding of the church interesting. I had often wondered whether Jesus had visited parts of the world other than his home country, and the *Book* answered that question. Still, it was organized religion, predominantly white, and I gave no thought to getting involved in it.

Around that time, Narva started attending Refuge Temple, a small, non-denominational "holiness" church led by a young black minister named Wendell Archie. There, the Holy Ghost moved. People loudly praised God and spoke in tongues. Prophecies and healing miracles took place. Narva changed. She stopped wearing jewelry and makeup, wore only long dresses, and stopped doing the "worldly" things that were still my way of life. Eventually, I started attending weekday Bible classes and Sunday services, but I remained more of an observer than a participant. In time, I got drawn in, went to revivals, received the Holy Ghost, spoke in tongues, and left "the world." I stopped smoking and drinking alcohol. One night, I went to the dumpster and tossed my prize possession of several hundred R & B albums. I hadn't socialized much with friends since getting married, but in seeing me after my "conversion," they thought I had lost my mind. Without my knowing it, I had.

Perhaps it was my still intense study of Jungian psychology or my introvert, thinking personality that eventually led me to feel that Refuge Temple was a cult. All the signs and symptoms were there, at least from a psychological point of view, and I grew increasingly uneasy about being a part of it. I grew skeptical of prophecies and miracles that took place during church services. The members carried Bibles everywhere they went and were constantly witnessing. Jesus and the church were all they talked about. One day, several of them came into the public library, saw me working at the front desk, and practically preached a sermon in front of the patrons who were checking books out.

The dissonance of being in the church and wanting to get out of it was too much stress for a struggling college student, studying accounting and reading psychology, philosophy, literature, and history. I had grown to understand how easily dogmatism could lead to fanaticism and mass-mindedness and could lead people to destroy either themselves or those with whom they differed—all in the name of what they believed or worshipped. I felt that I was under the spell of something that had possessed me to the point that I had no control over my free will. Jung would call it being in the grip of the "God archetype." I left the church and Narva remained a member. We had been married for only two years and our living two different lives strained our relationship. After leaving, I experienced moments of paranoia, feeling that members of the church were watching every move I made and worldly thing I did. Fortunately, my college studies kept me focused and grounded. I had one goal, to graduate and get a good-paying job.

Sometime during the mid-1970s, my parents bought another home on Gelpi Drive and moved my grandparents out of Dixie Homes to live in our first home less than a block away. Still an avid hunter, Grandfather brought his hounds, which he built a house for in the backyard. He grew flowers on the front lawn and built a large garden in the backyard, growing okra, beans, cucumbers, peppers, and watermelons. I visited often and took great pleasure in listening to him tell stories of his past life. By then, his English had improved, but there were moments while listening to him when his broken English caused me to drift. He smoked a pipe, and as if he knew that I had stopped listening, he'd tap me on the forearm with the pipe to bring me back to his words. If I have any talent in storytelling, I know that it came from him. Grandmother knew how much I loved her cooking. When I stayed away too long, she'd call me to say that she had just taken homemade bread out of the oven. She was also a talented seamstress, and I'd have her patch holes and hem trousers that needed altering.

My grandfather was born in 1912 and had lived a hard life farming in his younger years. Grandmother was six years younger and had had twelve children in twenty-three years. Being poor and with limited medical care in Morgan City, their health had started to decline long before Mama moved them. Grandfather had two heart attacks while living in Lake Charles. On the night of Friday, May 25, 1979, Mama called to tell me that Grandfather had died of a massive heart attack. He had gotten out of bed to get a nitroglycerin tablet from the bathroom medicine cabinet and couldn't reach it soon enough. The following morning I drove to a mental institution in Pineville, Louisiana, to pick up Aunt Sally. I cried the entire two-hour trip.

My grandfather was the first person whom I had loved who died. He had been the father of my early childhood at a time when I most needed the love of a father. Fifty years later, I still mourn his passing. I wrote these words shortly after delivering his eulogy:

"The words I spoke for my grandfather's eulogy came to me in the sorrowful hours after he died. They came out of nowhere. As I drove my car in the pouring rain, crying out loud, feeling such a terrible loss deep down in the depths of my soul, there came a voice whispering these words in the still air. Minutes after I had heard them, I went to visit my parents, and they asked me to say a eulogy for my grandfather. I knew at that moment that his spirit had not died, that life had not ended. I had a great secret! My parents had not known that the words had already been given to me. I only had to sit and arrange them on paper. I went home that night and did it gladly. God wanted somebody to say that there was much good to be said of this man. Indeed, he was a man in every sense of the word. I know that his spirit lives. Praise to Our Heavenly Father for comforting us in our hour of sorrow. If we listen to the small, still voice within us, we can grow in much love, mercy, and wisdom. We can be prepared to fulfill those tasks in life that are far greater than us."

The 1970s, which I refer to as my college years, were a time of growth—growing into young adulthood and manhood and discovering what I thought I wanted to do with the rest of my life. I spent nearly a decade in college classrooms, preparing myself academically. If nothing else, I was persistent. In my last three years, I had spent many hours reading books that had nothing to do with my major course of study, books that had shown me a new window to the world that I now gazed at. I thought nothing of the fact that I held a college degree and was counted among the low-income, disadvantage people of my community and country. What mattered was that I was dreaming of a brighter future and believing in myself.

Still, there were doubts and questions about who I was, whether the turns and choices I made would pay off, and what the future held for us as a young family. The only value I saw in myself was the knowledge that I had gained. I questioned whether that would be enough for a young black man to succeed in a society in which race and skin color still decided what most black men could do professionally, despite what they knew and were capable of achieving. I was still just a poor black boy from Dixie Homes. No one in my immediate family had ever graduated from college. No one worked as a professional and could be considered middle-upper class. I had no model to follow, except the one I dreamt of.

LEAPS OF FAITH

In early spring 1979, nearing college graduation for the second time, I started going on job interviews. Narva and I had two small children by then, ages three and one, and in a few weeks we would learn that she was pregnant for our third. We had been living in a married students' apartment for nearly two years and were anxious to see our sacrifices pay off. I was interested in being a certified public accountant but didn't know that very few black men in Louisiana had achieved that status. I confidently sent resumes and secured interviews, only to discover that I was black, which automatically made me unqualified despite my excellent grades. I got a lot of cordialness and politeness but no job offers. On one interview in southeast Louisiana, the interviewer told me to sit at the back of the room, at least twenty feet away from his desk, where he sat asking me questions. Needless to say, it was one of the shortest interviews I had.

One morning, armed with a fresh haircut, one undergraduate degree and another one soon to be attained, I put on a navy-blue polyester suit that I bought for the occasion, stepped confidently into a cubicle at the university career center, and sat in front of a recruiter representing a publicly traded electric utilities company. My most lasting impression of that meeting is not that the recruiter considered me qualified, but that he noted my skin color as a particularly attractive attribute. "I'm going to be perfectly honest with you," he said. "We've had issues with the NAACP and we're under a court-ordered consent decree to hire black people in administrative positions. You seem to fit the profile of what we're looking for." He went on to comment on my grades and my articulation of the English language. Within two weeks the company invited me to their headquarters in Beaumont, Texas, for more interviews.

A week later, I accepted their offer of an accountant position. I would later learn that I was one of three black business graduates recruited from three universities to be "groomed" for mid-management. Each of us worked in a separate division of the company.

To a kid who was raised in a low-income housing project and whose grandparents and parents didn't finish high school, it was a dream come true to be among the handful of black professionals who entered the tallest building in downtown Beaumont every morning to work for one of the largest businesses in the South. I had arrived in corporate America, a product of affirmative action and a testament that discipline, study, and perseverance pay off.

In time I would learn, that in this and other defining, life-changing moments, past and future, I was not arriving at all. I was only passing through. Much like the state and country where I was born and lived, I was only becoming.

That summer, the country was in the grips of an oil crisis that caused gasoline shortages, higher prices, and long lines at the gas pumps. Still apartment shopping several weeks into the job, I started carpooling from Lake Charles to Beaumont with Dapo, a Ugandan who worked for a social service agency a few blocks from my office. Although ride-sharing was helpful for the 150-mile round trip drive, Dapo made it extremely tense and stressful by his habit of regularly and suddenly falling asleep at the steering wheel. One morning he decided to exit the highway about ten miles from Beaumont. He said he needed gas, but I knew he had gotten sleepy. While coasting into a long line at a service station, the car stalled and wouldn't restart. The station owner immediately confronted us about holding up the line. In his distinctly coarse Ugandan-English dialect, Dapo tried to explain that his battery died and needed a boost.

"I'll tell you what you boys can do," the owner shouted. "You can push that damn piece of shit off my property and as far down I-10 as you can get it...right now!"

Apparently not reading anger in the owner's tone, Dapo politely continued to press him for help, which only stirred more anger and belligerence. At that point, I convinced him that it was probably best to push the car away. Being safely off the lot, we tried waving down motorists leaving the station. As much as we stood out under the glaring Texas sun, two very dark-skinned men wearing neckties and neatly pressed white shirts, we were invisible. Eventually, I walked across the street to a supermarket, noticing that there were no black people present, and made a distress call to the office. I asked for Terry, a co-worker who was assigned to train me for several months.

"Man, don't you know where you are? You're in Vidor. You need to get the heck out of there," he said chuckling. "I'll be there in fifteen minutes. Meanwhile, you might want to get back in the car. I'm on my way."

I didn't know what to make of that, but in the time it took for Terry to arrive, I had put the puzzle together—the gas station attendant, unfriendly motorists, no black shoppers in the large chain supermarket—just Dapo and me. Riding to Beaumont, Terry told the story of Vidor, that it was a haven for the Ku Klux Klan. Vidor, he said, is a "Sundown Town." Black folks aren't welcome there after dark. "Rumor has it," he tried to joke, "that when a black man gets arrested by Beaumont police for being drunk or disturbing the peace, they don't put him in jail; they drive him to Vidor in the middle of the night and drop him off on the street." Although it was 9:00 a.m., I took no comfort in the early morning hour and brightly glaring sun. Beginning that day, I thought differently about that ten-mile stretch of asphalt. But as I made my way up the steps into the building, through walls of steel, glass, and plush surroundings, passing a customer service line that was always long, black, and poor, it still had not registered that Vidor was "only" ten miles away.

That incident aside, I was making a slow but gradual transition to the office environment. Work was easy. I especially enjoyed lunch breaks, which I often spent reading and browsing stacks at the library a few blocks away. Not long after the Vidor incident, our division supervisor offered to treat a group of us to lunch at one of Beaumont's finest restaurants. I gladly accepted. Terry offered to drive. Charlie, the supervisor, sat up front while I took a back seat with Sharon, another accountant. Driving through downtown Beaumont on our return from what had been a very pleasant break, Terry saw a black man being hit with a billy club by a white police officer.

"*Gollee*! Look at that nigger gettin....," Terry blurted loudly. I think he was going to say "whipped" before he muzzled his mouth with one hand and tried to crawl through the steering wheel with the other. It was too late. The word was said and the damage was done. No one uttered a sound in what became a very long ride to the office. The rest of the day seemed even quieter, a heavy trenchant silence that made you notice the pace of someone's steps against the deep carpet floors. I don't know what went through my mind in those hours. It's

71

possible that I was too shocked and numb to think or feel anything.

Terry, a red-haired, boot-wearing Texan, was several years younger than me and had been with the company two years. On at least one occasion he openly expressed his disapproval of my salary being equal to his and I clearly sensed that he was uneasy and perhaps resentful of training a black employee. But I mostly saw him hurting and trying to adjust to a painful marital separation. His wife had recently left him for another man, running up his credit cards in the process. Some mornings he sulked and cried, and I actually felt sorry for him.

The next morning I broke the ice and confronted him directly, telling him that I was offended and felt that he owed me an apology. Without looking at me, he walked away, mumbling words and shuffling papers as if something pressing had suddenly required his attention. Things were tense between us in the days that followed. We spoke only when necessary. Our work relationship was visibly strained.

Finally, the company dealt with it. Terry was abruptly but quietly transferred out of the main office to a remote substation—no notice given to his work team, no farewell cake and punch—just him walking in, grumpily gathering up his personal belongings, tossing them into a small cardboard box, and walking out.

To the company, I suppose that was enough. It would wipe the slate clean as if nothing happened. It would give me comfort. And it might have if someone in the company had apologized. No one did. I had always been able to put a name and face on bigotry—Hue Morton and his spit-throwing pals in junior high school, a few teachers and professors, and now Terry, who had come to represent more than himself. To me, he had become a symbol of the whole discriminating history and culture of that company. He had become their Jim Crow and I had become their Tar Baby. As much as I had grown to understand racial prejudice, I felt betrayed, not only by the company, but by my country and personal ambition, all of which seemed blind in the face of a strand of racism that I had not seen before. After years of preparing to walk through doors unlocked by the hard-fought battles of Civil Rights, the doors swung wide open, but with the stinging, chilling realization that I was just a "nigger" in a blue pinstripe suit. It was the rudest awakening, but a call to act, not to sit still.

Much more defining than the callous and insensitive way that an employer handled a racially disparaging comment by a co-worker, my decision to leave the company was driven largely by a discovery of who I was becoming. What the company didn't know was that I had long ago been tried by spit and fire. I had become the consummate poker face who, like them, had mastered the art of mask-making and held a hand they hadn't seen. What I didn't know or had not understood about Sundown Town, the utilities company, and my white classmates and professors, and what they didn't know or understand about me, was that once I became their Tar Baby, they were glued to me. And as Ralph Ellison notes, it was their task, not mine, to learn how to free themselves and to learn that their price of freedom was to call the Tar Baby by his name. That is the antithesis and alter-ego of being a white American and a black American.

Shortly before the Sundown Town incident, Narva had been offered a teaching position in Port Arthur, Texas. We had begun to shop for an apartment there, which would have required me to make a ten-mile commute to Beaumont on workdays. Feeling anger and resentment toward the utilities company, I started scanning want ads for other job opportunities, stumbling upon a very small advertisement by the Natchitoches Economic Development Corporation (NEDC), a non-profit organization located in Natchitoches, Louisiana, which was searching for an executive director. I knew very little about Natchitoches and knew absolutely nothing about running a non-profit organization, but I was drawn to the organization's mission and felt qualified to lead it. I later learned that NEDC was one of about twenty organizations across the country that had grown out of the legislation that Senator Robert Kennedy had championed in the late 1960s, in which locally controlled community development corporations would start, own, and control business ventures to revitalize economically depressed neighborhoods. They were funded through the then-federal Office of Economic Opportunity.

NEDC invited me to a job interview. Several weeks later, a few days before we were to sign the lease on an apartment in Port Arthur, John Winston, the chairman of the Board of Directors, called to tell me that I didn't get the job, but he asked if I would be interested in a vacant business analyst position. He was a high school principal and assured me that he could guarantee a teaching job for Narva. After discussing the opportunities with her, I resigned from the utilities company.

While working in Beaumont, I had begun a second or third reading of Carl Jung's *Memories, Dream, Reflections* and his last work, *Man and His Symbols*. I had also begun to have a series of "big" dreams that would awaken me in the middle of night, so I started keeping a daily dream log. In one dream, I told my mother that I had quit the Beaumont job to take a job in Natchitoches. In the dream, she said, "Why Natchitoches? There are already too many lawyers there." I completely dismissed the reference to lawyers, knowing that I wasn't one and had no interest in practicing law. When we moved to Natchitoches, I discovered that they had more attorneys per capita than any city in Louisiana.

The dream activity had never been more alive in me, and in those days I felt very intuitively that I was entering a phase of my life when the unconscious was speaking. I felt certain that it was a period of transcendence, and although I didn't understand the meaning of the symbols that appeared in my night sleep, I felt the need to record them. Attentiveness to the unconscious continued for several years. I would later realize the importance of those dreams and reflections in guiding me through what would soon become one of the greatest disappointments of my life.

I left the plush floors and tinted glass windows of the utilities company on a Friday and walked into the NEDC office the following Monday. The carpet was so ragged that Narva, who was now pregnant for our third child, nearly tripped. NEDC was located in what had been the Self-Help Shopping Center, in the middle of the city's poorest neighborhood. Behind it was a low-income housing project. The organization's mission was to revitalize the city's economically depressed neighborhoods by starting businesses that would provide jobs to neighborhood residents. Funding was provided by the federal Office of Economic Opportunity (OED). The organization had secured OED approval for the start-up of a business that would manufacture boat trailers. The business would be housed in the vacant 10,000 square feet of space that was once a supermarket.

What I didn't know about NEDC was that the defunct Self-Help Shopping Center was owned by Ben Johnson, one of the wealthiest black men in Louisiana and the owner of a chain of funeral homes. Ben Johnson had used his political influence to build the shopping center through a minority small business investment corporation sponsored by the U. S. Small Business Administration, a corporation which Mr. Johnson was also the majority owner of. When the shopping center failed, the investment corporation failed with it. Mr. Johnson and other local black leaders then used their influence to create and secure federal funding for NEDC, which would lease the shopping center while pursuing its development mission, thus bailing out Mr. Johnson and his investment company.

I also didn't know that NEDC had written an Overall Economic Development Plan approved by the OED that had scathing comments about the region's treatment of black people, including comments that "vestiges of slavery" still existed. Remnants of plantation life did in fact still exist, and while the bronze "Good Darky" statue no longer stood on Front Street, postcards of the relic could still be purchased in downtown shops. Needless to say, the OEDP didn't sit well with the Chamber of Commerce, local elected officials, and white men who owned the banks and other major businesses in the area. In one of my first meetings outside of the office, I accompanied the marketing director to do some damage control in a meeting with the president of a local bank and owner of one of the city's largest shopping centers. When I saw a photograph of him and former Georgia governor Lester Maddox hanging above his desk, I knew that we were in serious trouble. He expressed his grave disapproval, not only with the OEDP but with NEDC using his tax-paid dollars to compete against him as a business owner.

In addition to the public relations nightmare that I suddenly found myself in the middle of, I later discovered that members of the NEDC Board of Directors, including Mr. Winston, were actively campaigning to oust the sitting Congressman who had represented the area since 1976 and was running for reelection in 1980. Congressman Jerry Huckaby, a Democrat, retaliated by initiating an inquiry into the management of NEDC. By then, the boat trailer manufacturing company that had been established was floundering in the midst of a national recession and high prime interest rates. People had stopped buying boats.

Named after a tribe of Native Americans, Natchitoches is the oldest European settlement in the Louisiana Purchase. A small community of 16,000 residents in 1979, its largest employers were public schools, a state university, and a chicken poultry plant. Natchitoches was most famous for the Annual Christmas Festival, which, since 1927, attracted hundreds of thousands of tourists each year to see the most dazzling display of Christmas lights in America. By Christmas, Narva was less than a month away from having Patrick, our third child. On the afternoon of the Festival, we gathered up blankets and food to attend the traditional Christmas parade and camp out on the levee until nightfall to see the light show. That year, Lorne Greene, star of the television show *Bonanza*, was Grand Marshal. I enjoyed the smallness of Natchitoches and its slow pace. While living there, I discovered my love of folk art, purchasing several prints of Clementine Hunter.

One Saturday morning, two Mormons on bicycles knocked on our front door. I graciously let them in and listened to their pitch, which I had heard once before on the evening that Narva and I had dinner with a Mormon couple when we lived in the married students' apartment at McNeese. They were surprised to learn that I had read the *Book of Mormon* and met several members of the Church of Jesus Christ of Ladder-day Saints. The more they talked, the more interested I grew, eventually accepting their offer to visit the local church. I started re-reading the *Book*. Narva came along but was clearly skeptical and distant. We were the only black people present. After several church visits, I agreed to join and was ordained into the Aaronic Priesthood, the lowest order of priesthood, assigned to teenage boys and new male converts. Sometime after joining, I discovered that black men had only recently been allowed to be ordained as priests and to assume leadership roles in the church. These restrictions were apparently of divine revelation and supported by church doctrine. In 1978, the year before my ordination, Spencer W. Kimball, the church president, had declared by a supposed revelation from God that it was time for the church to remove these restrictions against black people. All of that struck me as being racist and utterly preposterous, and there was nothing that anyone in the church could say or do to convince me otherwise. I left and never looked back.

In July 1979, I dreamt a nightmare that I was a child witnessing the strangulation of children by a strange man or group of men. Later in the dream, I was an adult who was about to be suffocated by the men. Someone handed me a book about Boy Scouts and God. I awoke before being killed, finding water in my eyes. I had cried in the dream. Weeks later, I heard about a series of murders that had occurred in

Atlanta, Georgia, in which black children had disappeared or were found dead. As time passed, more bodies of dead black children were found, and the city was in the grip of a mass killer who had not been identified. That dream and what would later become known as the Atlanta Child Murders haunted me for many years.

Living next door to the townhouse we rented was Brady—a white, single, blond-haired fellow in his early twenties. A native of Mississippi, Brady had grown up poor, graduated from high school, and become a produce manager at Winn Dixie. One evening, he knocked on our door to introduce himself, holding a bag of ribeye steaks in his hand. He met Narva and the kids and we chatted briefly. After several visits, I discovered that, like me, Brady loved to play Scrabble. Having left the Church of Jesus Christ of Ladder-day Saints, I had gone back to the worldly life of drinking alcohol and smoking marijuana, and Brady always had a couple of joints. On weekends, he and I spent many late hours smoking, playing Scrabble, and talking about life.

As time went on, it became clear to me that Brady was a racist. He felt that black people were inherently inferior to him as a white man, and he gave no apology and offered no excuses for thinking and feeling that way. But unlike white guys I had met in school, he didn't show hatred, at least not toward me, and he never tried to tell a *nigger joke*. I didn't ask myself why, after knowing his racist views, I continued to befriend him. I sensed that I was somewhat of an enigma—a young, educated black man who wasn't despising him because of his racial biases. To me, he was equally enigmatic—a young, racist white guy who ate with his black neighbors, played with their children, and showed a genuine interest in their well-being.

Brady had a girlfriend in Mississippi who wanted to get married but he wasn't interested in settling down. I shared my stories about the trials and challenges of my young adulthood, of Narva getting pregnant and my not marrying her until two years later. Over time, we were just two young men getting to know each other. If I could point to one common ground that we stood on that bonded us, other than smoking weed and playing Scrabble late at night, it was mutual respect, which grew out of our talking, listening, and taking an interest in the personal side of each other's lives. I can honestly say that I genuinely enjoyed his company, and I think the feeling was mutual.

Several years after Narva and I left Natchitoches and moved to Lafayette, Brady and his girlfriend visited us. We had bought a little house in Lillian Heights, a low-income neighborhood of the city. That evening, we had plans to attend a party to celebrate a next-door neighbor's wedding anniversary. Wes and Anna were an older couple with children in their twenties. Brady and his girlfriend joined us. It was the funniest thing, seeing a racist white guy from Mississippi in a house full of black people, zydeco dancing and having fun. A year or so later, when he was promoted and moved to nearby Crowley, Louisiana, I visited him once, but in time we drifted apart and lost contact with each other.

Outside of life at home, there wasn't much to do in Natchitoches on weekends. Occasionally, I drove around town in my 1969 Dodge Dart to keep the engine fresh, but I never went out of town. The longest trip we took as a family was to Shreveport to buy Joy's first pair of walking shoes, taking Narva's 1977 Aspen. When I wasn't working or playing Scrabble with Brady, I spent time writing and reading. For no reason except to say what was on my mind, I wrote essays about poverty and race issues in America. On April 22, 1980, I wrote a letter to my mother, father, and grandmother. Twenty years later, Grandmother returned the original copy to me.

Dear Mom, Dad, & Grandmother:

> Just sitting up to enjoy a moment of quiet and peace and reflect on a bit of life's kindness. I am very grateful to you and the God who created you for all that you are and have been. You may have felt, as I think you would feel, that it is all a part of being a parent and grandparent. But you have gone far beyond that. I cannot give you in material things the measure of concern that you have shown me. I can only express my gratitude to our God and ask each day that He touch your lives in a good way.

> This old world has changed so very much since I first looked at it as a child. People that I've met along the way have come and gone on to chase dreams different from mine. Most of what I have experienced has somehow been forgotten. The things that you worked so hard to provide for me have been replaced. Some of them, though, have proved tougher than

time and I cherish them today. As you lived near me and in me, you gave. Your giving may not have always been recognized, but through all things good and bad I did learn what life had to teach me. With life, I am certain that the knowledge of that will remain.

As I live now in remembrance of the past and hope for the future, watching my own children grow, I value more and more the discipline and advice you gave, and the decency and dignity that shined through you.

I am mindful, too, that there is so much more of my life that I am required to give, that I must pass on to others, whatever there is in me that may be uplifting.

May God bless you.

I love you All.
Jay

In early May 1980, NEDC was notified by the federal government that its funding would be cut to a level that would require it to terminate several jobs. As the last person hired, my job was at the top of the list. I received a notice that I would be unemployed in four months. It was devastating news. That day, I cried all the way home, screaming to God with questions. Why, after all I had been through with the utilities company, did He allow that opportunity to happen, knowing that it would end that way? Why, after all that I had sacrificed to earn two college degrees, would He set me up to fail? I felt that God had betrayed me. It was deeply painful, especially the moment I walked inside to tell Narva what had happened. I felt that I had failed personally and had failed her and our three young children. She took the news calmly and in her usual confident, faithful way assured me that it would all work out.

Despite the disappointment and pain I felt, something in my gut told me that she was right. Over and over I silently repeated the Biblical passage, "In everything give thanks; for this is the will of God in Christ Jesus for you." I immediately began searching for a job, following up on advertisements by public accounting firms but with the same results that I had experienced nearing graduation. White accounting firms didn't hire black people in any position, especially accountants.

Joe LeBrum, the director of NEDC, suggested that I contact the Southern Cooperative Development Fund (SCDF), a Lafayette-based community development corporation that had been founded by Reverend A. J. McKnight, a Catholic priest. I had heard Father McKnight speak at a function in Lake Charles years before and was impressed by his message of self-determination and black business ownership. Joe knew one of the managers who worked there and graciously placed a call to recommend me. Edgar Jordan, who headed the technical assistance division, invited me to be interviewed and take an accounting exam. After the exam, Marvin Beaulieu, the vice president, also interviewed me. When he noted from my resume that I had a degree in psychology, he asked if I had studied Carl Jung. I knew at that moment that I would be offered a job. The afternoon that I went to the mailbox and opened an envelope containing a job offer from Father McKnight, I did a cartwheel in the street. Within two weeks, Narva secured a teaching job in Lafayette Parish. In mid-August 1980, we put our belongings into a Home Furniture truck that one of her brothers had *borrowed* to help us move. Brady helped us to pack and load up.

Lafayette was the corporate headquarters for oil companies drilling in the Gulf of Mexico. By 1980, the entire region was booming economically and there were no vacant apartments. We were fortunate to find a house to rent, a few blocks from my mother's oldest brother Andrew and his family. I started my dream job, working for the largest community development corporation in the South with a slight increase in pay.

In addition to being a cooperative bank, SCDF had several subsidiaries, including a minority small business investment company. Unlike NEDC, it had a diversified funding base comprised of investment income, federal grants, and foundation funding. As one of the largest black landowners in the South, it had five out-of-state field offices and was doing business in twenty-six southeastern States. I was a loan officer who analyzed loan applications of cooperatives and provided technical management assistance to client businesses. The company had hired some of the best and brightest black minds in America, several of whom were graduates of Ivy League schools. The leadership of the organization was also active in state, local, and national politics but with sophistication far more advanced than what

I had seen in Natchitoches.

My first assignment at SCDF was to work with the managers of Southern Consumers Cooperative to develop a comprehensive business plan for the coop's operations. Based in Lafayette, the coop owned a bakery, newspaper, finance company, and the office building where SCDF was housed. It was a fun and challenging project, requiring me to spend several weeks in Lake Charles, where the bakery was located. No business school in America could have provided me the opportunity to learn and apply business strategy so quickly.

I became a contributing writer for the *Southern Consumer Times* newspaper, collaborating with Ronald Mason, Jr, SCDF's general counsel, to write a series of articles portraying everyday practices of Nguzo Saba, the seven principles of Kwanzaa. For the paper's 1985 special edition commemorating the 100th anniversary of the birth of Lafayette, I researched and wrote an article about a criminal trial that had taken place in Lafayette Parish in 1922, at the height of the Ku Klux Klan's dominance in Louisiana. My grandfather's brother, Emile Hebert, was charged with murder in a trial that brought the National Guard to protect the courthouse, a first for the parish.

Father McKnight believed that for the employees of SCDF to effect meaningful change they had to first change themselves. To do that, they had to understand their history, know who they were, and be spiritually liberated. We were required to greet each other in Swahili and read books such as *Hunger for Justice, Plan to Planet, Souls of Black Folk,* and *Up From Slavery.* We held regular book discussion sessions or debates on the assigned books. Aside from my reading of the *Autobiography of Malcolm X, A Raisin in the Sun,* and several black poets, that was my first serious reading of African American literature. The company held an annual retreat in which employees were given the opportunity to openly express their thoughts and feelings about their experience as SCDF employees or anything personal that they wanted to talk about. What I particularly enjoyed about working there was the camaraderie with talented, young, black professionals who were politically conscious and committed to social and economic change.

In addition to working under the leadership of Father McKnight, I sat in meetings quietly observing discussions between local political activists and trailblazing Civil Rights freedom fighters like Ronnie Moore and Dave Dennis, both of whom lived in Lafayette at the time.

Moore was a member of the SCDF staff and Dennis was a practicing attorney.

SCDF was the only black-owned business that I worked for. It was an indescribably fulfilling experience walking into the office every morning and working with talented black professionals who were committed to the ideal of economic justice. I felt so much at home that one employee remarked that I walked around as if I had been there for several years. In a way I had. I had been given the opportunity to do work that I discovered since reading Senator Kennedy's policy ideas on community economic development as a college student. My commitment to economic justice and to Kennedy's bold ideas had drawn me to Natchitoches. One of his most famous quotes, "Only those who dare to fail greatly can ever achieve greatly," rang loudly. When it appeared that I had failed and that I had once again been betrayed by my sacrifices and aspirations, the window of heaven opened.

From 1979 to 1980, I held three positions at three different companies in three cities. Every step of the way, Narva was there, changing jobs just as many times, with the added responsibility of caring for our three very young children. Her support, strength, and faith held the ground steady and intact when I felt it crumbling beneath me. Out of those experiences grew an assurance that although the destination of our journey would be unknown, the path to it would get us there and be for our good. The utilities company, NEDC, and SCDF were necessary stops along the way, but there was a larger plan, bigger than my dreams, that had not begun to unfold. To go blindly into the unknown would be a great test of faith and require that I remain as attentive to the still, silent voice speaking from within as to the reality that my senses perceived.

PUBLIC SERVICE

In early 1982, I unexpectedly saw a job advertisement by the City of Lafayette Community Development Department that got my attention. I later got a phone call from Edgar Jordan, telling me about the opportunity. They were searching for an economic development coordinator to establish a non-profit organization to revitalize the city's economically depressed neighborhoods. I instantly knew that I was a perfect fit for the job. Within several weeks I was hired by Mrs. Jessie L. Taylor, the city's human services manager.

Jessie, a black woman, was a retired librarian who had been hired by the previous administration and was somewhat of a grande dame of city government. She had great influence and was well-respected in both the white and black communities. She mentored me and gave me the wings and breath to sail. A widow in her late forties, Jessie had one son and had taken a second mortgage on her home to finance the start-up of his pharmacy business. She was a chain smoker and had been diagnosed with lung cancer, which didn't stop her habit or her tireless efforts to improve the lives of Lafayette's economically disadvantaged residents.

SCDF gave me a dream job, but I soon realized that this one was made in heaven. Every skill that I had acquired and everything that I had studied academically would be put to use. More importantly, I was passionate about the mission and goals that I had to accomplish. I was given a small, open-space cubicle several feet from Jessie's office. She and Phil Lank, the department director, gave me some direction and monitored my work progress but they allowed me the latitude and flexibility to take the initiative and be creative. What I enjoyed most about the job was that the challenge was bigger than me, requiring more of me than I had experience doing, and I relished the opportunity to demonstrate my competency. I had to build from the ground up. My writing and verbal communication skills and finance background would be big assets, but I also had to employ strong organizational and people skills. I largely depended on my knowledge, instinct, and intuition.

My task was to build a membership-based community development corporation controlled by residents of the city's low-moderate-income residents, who would elect a Board of Directors to govern the organization. I would essentially function as the organization's executive director while being a City employee. The City had committed a $300,000 grant of Community Development Block Grant (CDBG) funds awarded by the U. S. Department of Urban Development (HUD) to capitalize a revolving loan fund that would be used to make loans to new and established businesses located in the target neighborhoods.

In addition to having to work internally to develop organizational systems and policies, I had to work with black community leaders and residents. I was required to make presentations to the five-member City Council to secure their support of the City's three-year contract for the use of CDBG funds. I had to establish a loan committee and lending policies for the revolving loan fund, conduct outreach activities to generate interest in the program, and eventually analyze loan applications for the loan committee's review.

Lafayette Neighborhoods Economic Development Corporation (LNEDC) was incorporated in late 1982 and obtained IRS 501 (3) tax-exempt status shortly thereafter. In early 1983, we held the first annual meeting to elect a Board of Directors. I wrote a letter for the Mayor's signature to request New Orleans Mayor Ernest Morial to be the keynote speaker. Much to my surprise and delight, he accepted the invitation. LNEDC was off and running.

The next several years were very productive and fast-paced. I implemented the City's Enterprise Zone Program, which gave tax breaks to businesses located in the target neighborhoods. I led the creation of Lafayette Centre Development Corporation, another non-profit that provided long-term fixed-asset loans to expanding businesses under the auspices of the U. S. Small Business Administration. A year later, we created Sterling Grove Housing Development as a subsidiary of LNEDC and secured funding from HUD to build an elderly housing development. Interestingly, the development was originally planned to be built on city-owned property in the Sterling Grove Historic District, where I lived, but residents of the district voiced strong objections, causing an alternate location to be selected.

To secure HUD approval of the housing development application, I traveled to Washington, D. C. with the Mayor, two members of the City Council, and Edgar Jordan, who by then was Chairman of the LNEDC Board of Directors. Our agenda was to meet with members of Louisiana's Congressional delegation and later with White House and HUD officials. While making our rounds at the U. S. Capitol, we stumbled upon William "Bill" Broadhurst, an influential attorney and oil and gas lobbyist for Louisiana. It was Mr. Broadhurst who, two years later, rented an 83-foot yacht to take an overnight trip with then-presidential candidate Gary Hart and two single women, a trip that ultimately caused Mr. Hart to withdraw from the race for the Democratic nomination.

Mr. Broadhurst invited us to join him at his townhouse for drinks later that evening. The first level of the spacious two-story townhouse had been completely gutted to accommodate receptions and dinner parties. The second floor had bedrooms, which we were not allowed to see. While we were sitting around sipping gin and tonic, Mr. Broadhurst took a phone call from Louisiana Congressman John Breaux, who was running for the U. S. Senate. Mr. Breaux had called Mr. Broadhurst to tell him that State Attorney General Billy Guste had dropped out of the race for U. S. Senate. In hearing Mr. Broadhurst's words, it was apparent that Mr. Breaux had sought his response to a statement that Mr. Breaux would soon release to the media about the Attorney General's withdrawal. To a low-ranking civil service employee whose sole task of the trip was to convey the facts and figures of the application for the housing development, it was a surreal moment, to be sitting within an earshot of a conversation between two of the most influential political figures in Louisiana about a congressman's communication strategy in the race for the U. S. Senate. Mr. Breaux, a Democrat, eventually won the U. S. Senate race against Congressman Henson Moore, the Republican contender.

Sometime in 1985, I developed a concept paper that proposed a policy to increase minority business participation in city contracting, particularly in capital improvement projects. By then, I had been promoted to a management-level position in the department. Phil and Jessie approved the concept and meetings were subsequently held with Mayor Dud Lastrapes and Chief Administrative Officer

(CAO) Glenn Weber, the city's top administrator. I reached out to key black local leaders to quietly *instigate* their engagement. In crafting a policy that eventually gained the mayor and city council's approval, I attended several meetings with the CAO and department directors.

My department was located on the second floor of City Hall, directly across from the executive offices, and I'd often see directors walking in and out. I knew that it was there that all the major decisions of city government were being conducted, and I felt a certain mystique about that part of the building. On occasion, I represented Phil in the directors' meetings when he was out on sick leave. The more I engaged with the executive staff, the more confident I grew in my management and leadership skills. The mayor had one black assistant, who I sensed was more of a political figure, and there was only one black department director, who headed the Department of Recreation and Parks. I had absolutely no interest in being a mayoral assistant or a city department head, but one day the thought wildly entered my head that I could be the chief administrative officer. I was sure that I could do the job and do it well.

A year and a half after starting the job at City Hall, Narva and I bought our second home, a house built in the late 1920s and located on Elizabeth Avenue in the Sterling Grove Historic District. We did some renovations shortly after moving in but the upkeep was constant. I did the interior painting myself and kept the refinished pine floors shining. The wiring was outdated but only needed minor periodic repairs. I also did the exterior house washing once a year, spraying the house with bleach and following up with the water hose. Because the house sat on cinder blocks, I had to climb a ladder to reach the eaves. One Saturday morning, while standing on the aluminum ladder with the running water hose in my hand, I splashed water on the electrical box. The moment I stepped off the ladder the box exploded, the force of which knocked me off my feet and shook the entire house. I immediately ran inside to check on Narva and the children and call the fire department. The explosion hadn't caused a fire but we were without electric power for several days. The electrician who did the repairs said that had I not stepped off the ladder with the running water hose still in my hand, I would have been instantly electrocuted. Once again, a soft, gentle wind had carried me.

That was the home in which we spent most of the years raising our three children, Karen, Joy, and Patrick, nurturing them through their childhood and teenage years. At every grade level, each of them ranked in the top of their class. Like my mother, I was a controlling, overprotective father, particularly of my two daughters, putting academic achievement above all other pursuits and interests, an emphasis that eventually created tension between Karen and me. Like I had done with my mother, she exerted her individuality and independence of thought in her own time and way. And as my mother and I had done, she and I eventually found the mutual love that was always there and that nothing could ever divide or separate.

Lessons Learned from a Teenage Daughter
For Karen

> Once, while riding with you into the horizon,
> I saw a dab of light on the tip of a fine brush,
> long and handless. In the blink of an eye,
> the brush, with a single stroke, painted
> a yellow sickle perfect in its arc
> across a plain of purplish hues.
>
> I had always known a time would come
> when you would not need my permission
> to follow the voice that answers
> whether you should go here or there.
> I had hoped that in whatever hour or season
> a dim light spoke you would discern
> right from wrong. Like the tale told
> of children who stood before the old, wise
> blind woman with a bird in their hands,
> the voice you found was your own.
>
> On a day that would have been perfect
> but for your discontent with my sternness,
> I recollected those fire-breath moments
> when your grandmother and I argued
> petty rightness as you and I often did.
>
> In wiser years, how nice that we grow

together to watch chameleon, mosaic skies
and let pains die that we might have cried
and hidden in raindrops sprinkling
on a starless night without a kiss surrendered.
God knows those nights are long.

Later in his life, when Patrick had become a father of two sons, he very lovingly and honestly told me, that despite his appreciation of my love and discipline, there were times in his childhood when he felt that I wasn't taking the time to get to know him and teach him the ways of manhood. There were moments, he said, when he felt that I didn't seem interested in having a family at all. They were bitter words for me to swallow as a father and grandfather, but truthful, nonetheless. Even now, as I think of his words, I shed tears. In retrospect, I wish those words had been said to me when I was a young father, and I wish that all young, black fathers would heed those words, even when they are not spoken to them.

Feeling very strongly that I needed a master's degree for professional growth, I decided to go back to college in 1983 to get a Master of Business Administration degree. The University of Southwestern Louisiana (now University of Louisiana at Lafayette) offered an executive MBA program that would allow me to work and pursue my degree on a part-time basis and complete it in three years. The City of Lafayette would pay my tuition through its employee development program. I refinished an old oak desk that I had stored inside an outdoor utility building and moved it to our bedroom. For three years, I went to work, came home, and studied business administration, graduating with honors in May 1986.

I remained very close to the employees of SCDF and Southern Consumers Cooperative while working at City Hall, often having lunch with several of them to socialize and keep my finger on the pulse of the local black community. Every Wednesday we ate *healthy* at the cafeteria of a local hospital. On Thursday I joined them for lunch at the home of Mrs. Taylor's. Lorita Taylor was a black widow in her early 70s who lived on Jackson Street, near the downtown area, in a small wooden frame house. Every Thursday, she cooked and set her dining room table for guests. She didn't charge a fee, but she kept a flip-top metal canister on the kitchen counter that collected payments that guests voluntarily made. She had started the tradition years before for a group of men who worked at a black-owned insurance company located a block from her home. Eventually, several employees of SCDF and Southern Consumers Cooperative, including Alfred "Mac" McZeal, the manager of Southern Consumers and her next-door neighbor, joined them. In time, there were two groups, the insurance agents eating at 11:30 and our group eating at noon. The second group grew so large that "Mrs. T" set up two tables, one in the living room and one in the dining room.

We went to Mrs. Taylor's to eat her Creole cooking, but the stimulating political talk proved to be the main course. Jessie joined me every week and Phil attended regularly. Word soon spread among political circles that Thursday at Mrs. Taylor's was when and where the *movers and shakers* of the black community had lunch. Before long, white elected officials and aspiring politicians showed up, but only at the invitation of a member of the group. Several Republicans, including the mayor and a right-wing member of the school board, made occasional visits. The president of a major bank that was planning to close branches in the black community showed up to gauge the black community's response to the branch closings. I invited Merilyn Istre, a staff member of State Representative Kathleen Blanco. When Merilyn became a regular, she invited Mrs. Blanco, who joined us regularly.

Friday after work always started with a visit to Mac's office, where five of us, all black men, met to eat boudin and sip wine or whiskey while wrangling about local, state, and national politics. The walls of Mac's office, lined with African artifacts and framed prints of Nelson Mandela, Malcolm X, and Reverend Martin Luther King Jr., provided the perfect backdrop. One Friday evening in April 1984, Je'Nelle Chargois, the manager of a local black-owned radio station and a former employee of the coop, showed up at Mac's office with a cassette tape player. She had been working on a project for a special Lafayette Centennial edition of the *Southern Consumer Times,* in which she orally captured the stories of old black residents of the city, who gave accounts of the black history of Lafayette. We listened to a few of the recordings.

Mr. Jeanlouis, a man in his mid-eighties, told the story of the 1922 trial Emile Hebert, a young black man who was accused of killing a white man and seriously injuring the Lafayette Parish Sheriff in a shooting that took place in Youngsville, Louisiana. I vaguely remembered hearing my mother tell that story years before about an older brother of my grandfather. "I think that's my great-uncle," I said excitedly. Soon after hearing the recording, I visited Mr. Jeanlouis and gathered more facts. He had known Emile Hebert and gone to the trial. He even remembered the names of Hebert's attorneys. I delved into newspaper articles and court records, and eventually wrote a story of the trial for the newspaper's centennial issue.

Twenty-five years later, as a creative writing graduate student, I looked deeper into my great uncle's case and learned of Louisiana Governor John M. Parker's relentless efforts to stop the dominance of the Ku Klux Klan in the early 1920s. Only then did I fully appreciate the historical significance of the trial.

In late 1985, Jessie approached me with the idea of the City sponsoring the first celebration of the Martin Luther King Jr. Holiday to coincide with the first national holiday in January 1986. She knew that she could use the power of her office to get it done. She invited a half-dozen black women to form a planning committee and begin meeting at her home on Sunday afternoon. I would get there at least a half-hour early and sit with Jessie to pre-plan, always with both of us having a couple of glasses of whiskey, an indulgence that she only partook in the privacy of her home. The planning committee created the organizational framework and membership of Lafayette's first MLK, Jr. Holiday Committee, which would plan and carry out the inaugural program. Jessie felt very strongly that the program should be ecumenical and led by local black ministers, so she recruited every black minister in Lafayette to join the committee.

With Phil's help in securing non-federal funds to cover expenses, the City became the lead sponsor of the event. In December 1985, Jessie and I worked nearly full-time on the project, coordinating committee planning meetings and implementing tasks that needed completion. We partnered with the Department of Recreation and Parks to hold the event at the MLK Center and got the City's print shop to print the program. We secured funding from local churches to purchase and erect a flagpole for the inaugural flag-raising ceremony on the morning of the event. After the flag-raising, we had a full day of activities, including a film festival, a community luncheon forum, and a student quiz bowl. The celebration culminated with an evening commemorative program with a community choir of local churches and a local minister giving an inspiring keynote address. Of all the projects I undertook as a city employee, none gave me more gratification than being a part of the first MLK Holiday Celebration. To this day, I don't think that the black and white residents of Lafayette fully appreciate the great contribution that Jessie Taylor made in that endeavor.

In March 1988, Buddy Roemer was sworn in as the 52nd Governor of Louisiana, having placed first in the primary election and won the election when former two-term Governor Edwin Edwards, who ran second, conceded the race to Roemer on election night. During the transition period, Mary Lib Guercio, a local public education advocate whose work I was supporting, suggested that I submit an application to the Roemer transition team for a position in his administration. She arranged an interview and I drove to Baton Rouge on a cold, rainy day with my resume. After sitting for two hours in the lobby of the transition headquarters waiting to be called in, watching what seemed like a human jungle of applicants streaming in and out, I got discouraged and left.

Two weeks later, while sitting in my office, I got a phone call from a cousin who asked if I would contact Phyllis Mouton and recommend him for a job. Governor-elect Roemer had just announced the appointment of Phyllis as his Secretary of Labor. I had developed a working relationship with Phyllis when she became the first black and first woman to be President of the Greater Lafayette Chamber of Commerce, and I was a next-door neighbor of her sister and brother-in-law, Gwen and Joe Lewis.

Between the time of receiving my cousin's phone call and my calling Phyllis, I gave more thought to the idea of working in state government. I was a civil service employee, and even though my job was federally funded, I felt a sense of security. The state job would be unclassified. I would work at the pleasure of the department head and governor and could be fired on any given day. But job security wasn't something that concerned me. I instinctively felt that I had more to offer and that I could rise to bigger and greater challenges. The words of Robert Kennedy, "Only those who dare to fail greatly can ever achieve greatly," had always rung in my heart. Like the move to Natchitoches, I was ready to take another leap of faith. Instinctively, I felt that taking an unclassified job would widen my path to success.

I knew very little about the Department of Labor and had no idea what unclassified positions were available, but I asked Phyllis if she had a position that might fit my qualifications and experience. Much to my surprise, she felt that my experience and qualifications seemed to be a good fit for the Undersecretary of Management and Finance position, which would direct the administrative arm of the department. She knew that I had an MBA and was aware of the work that I had done as the City's economic development manager. I sent her a resume, we met, and two weeks later she hired me for the job. That quickly, without me having to jump through hoops or sit for hours in the clutter of Roemer's transition headquarters, I was the Undersecretary of the Louisiana Department of Labor. At the age of thirty-five, less than nine years after losing my job at NEDC, I became a high-ranking state official.

As Undersecretary, I directed the administrative functions of the agency, including budgeting, accounting, human resources, information services, building maintenance, the print shop, and the mail room. I was also responsible for fiscally managing a $1.3 billion trust fund for the state's unemployment insurance program. The job required that I interact with assistant secretaries who headed the programmatic offices of the department. I had a staff of several hundred civil service employees, six of whom reported directly to me as division managers. I quickly won the support of my staff with a people-focused, listening style of management.

In Democrat administrations, including the eight years of former governor Edwin Edwards, the AFL-CIO played a dominant role in the appointment of key executives and major policy decisions of the Labor Department. Under Governor Buddy Roemer's "pro-business" policy agenda, the state's leading union organization was virtually absent in the management affairs of the agency. One of Phyllis' first directives was to not honor the agency's employee union contract, a decision that ultimately ended in a court battle. In other reform initiatives in workers' compensation and workforce development, we were at war with the AFL-CIO and with senior managers who were long-standing classified employees with strong allegiances to the AFL-CIO.

Instigated by senior employees who were union members, the state Inspector General launched an investigation into the Secretary's alleged misuse of state travel regulations, which my fiscal division administered. I found myself "in the middle," having to support the Secretary's decisions and maintain a positive working relationship with her while supporting my staff's recommendations to address irregularities and improprieties in our administration of state regulations and policies. I had to navigate and negotiate our way through accusations of regulatory violations. Phyllis, on the other hand, was confident that her authority superseded and was not in violation of state regulations.

I was in a very unpleasant situation, that of being loyal to my boss while maintaining an effective working relationship with employees who strongly disagreed with her policy initiatives. Senior managers respected the Secretary's authority but the constant disagreement in policy direction created constant tension, which spilled over into my relationships with all employees, particularly my staff. My commitment to Phyllis was deeper and more heartfelt. I had great respect for her courage and self-confidence. She was a strong black woman who wasn't intimidated by powerful white men who disagreed with her. She had given me an opportunity to grow professionally, and I would always feel indebted to her.

In time, the management atmosphere became one of distrust. At the point in which I sensed that Phyllis was growing distrustful of me and my close working relationship with my own team, I knew that I could not continue to work there. I was stressed and unhappy. It was time to move on. As in the case of NEDC, I had stepped out on faith and left a secure job only to find that I might have made a mistake.

By then, the daily sixty-five-mile commute from Lafayette to Baton Rouge had begun to tire me. Phyllis and I carpooled for a while, but when she took an apartment in Baton Rouge, I shared rides with other state employees, including Phyllis' top executive assistant, who was a target in the travel irregularities that we were being cited for. Eventually, I drove alone. Secretly, I began to search for another job.

One of the many positive outcomes of my experience as Labor Undersecretary was meeting and building lasting relationships with some of Baton Rouge's most talented professionals, black and white. Among them were Leo Hamilton, an attorney who headed the Office of Workforce Development, and Stephen W. Cavanaugh, Assistant Secretary for the Office of Workers' Compensation. Leo left the agency to practice law and would eventually become a partner in one of the city's largest firms. While at the department, Steve co-wrote and championed legislation to privatize the state-funded workers' compensation insurance fund. He went on to found and head the Louisiana Workers' Compensation Corporation. He would grow LWCC into a highly successful enterprise until leaving the CEO post to take another job shortly before his untimely death in 2006. When he was planning the startup of LWCC, Steve offered me the job of heading his finance division. It would have required me to relocate to Baton Rouge, which I was reluctant to do. I graciously declined the offer, but I have often joked that if had taken the job I would have retired as a millionaire many years ago.

On Friday, April 14, 1989, I drove to Morgan City to deliver a speech at the invitation of the director of the area's community action agency. What I mostly remember about that night was the drive back to Lafayette. By the time I left Morgan City, dense fog had started to set in. About halfway home, the visibility was zero. I could not see the road. I wanted to pull over but I couldn't see the shoulder and the fog was growing thicker. There are a number of bridges on Highway 90 between Morgan City and Lafayette. I felt myself climbing them but I couldn't see where they were taking me. I prayed the entire trip. Eventually, an 18-wheeler passed me, and I sped up to get behind it, letting its rear lights take me home.

My natural father, John Douglas Smith, was in the audience of that event. I had not seen him since the summer of 1960, but I had not forgotten the telephone conversation we had years later when I asked him to help me pay for college expenses. After I gave my speech, he came over and complimented me. To my recollection, not much else was said by either of us. Three days later, I received a letter.

A Letter from John D.

This is something I haven't done in many years,
write a letter. I guess you can see by my penmanship
I never was much good at writing. This one is long overdue.
It was very rewarding to get to talk to you

after all these years. You are a very fine young man.
Any man should be proud to call you his son.
Your mother and her husband did one fine job
of rearing you. I can only claim the biological part.

I regret not being able to have been there
when you needed someone to lean and depend on
when you were growing up. That may have been my loss
as well as yours. Sometimes foolish pride
can cause you to cut off your nose to spite your face.
All I am sure of now is that I want to know you better,
to meet my grandchildren and their mother.

I hope God grants me enough life to try and make up
for some of my mistakes. One thing you may not know
is that I have kept abreast of your progress
and I am very proud that we wear the same first
and last name. I hope you overlook all these mistakes.
I am a little out of practice. Take care of yourself
and in between your busy schedule let me hear from you.

I remain your father,
John D.

One evening in early June 1989, I saw an evening news report
that Andrew Duhon, the Chief Administrative Officer for Lafayette
Parish Government, was resigning to return to the city's utility system
in a management position. I knew Andrew and had developed a
professional relationship with him when I worked in city government.
I called him the next day and inquired about the job. He said that the
Parish President had asked him to develop a short list of prospective
applicants and that my name was on his list to contact.

I had two interviews for the Parish CAO job, the first with Jeff
Moss, the Parish Attorney, and the second with Walter S. Comeaux,
the Parish President. I knew absolutely nothing about Walter and
wondered why he would even consider hiring a black man as his top
administrator. I later learned that he was a seasoned politician who
had served many years on the Police Jury, which later adopted a home
rule charter to establish a president-council form of government.
He was Lafayette Parish's first Parish President. He had also been

a successful real estate developer who declared bankruptcy during the severe economic downtown of the mid-eighties. Andrew talked about Walter's leadership style. He was an artful politician, but he generally left the administration of the government to his CAO. He wasn't totally hands-off, but he wasn't a micro-manager. I liked him before I met him.

During the interview, the issue of race came up in a rather indirect way. Walter asked if I would be able to handle the perceptions and attitudes that people, including several of my own directors, might have of me as a black man in charge—people who might question my ability solely based on my skin color. My reply was that if I knew that I had his confidence and support, the problem would not be mine, but theirs. As long as he backed my decisions and my exercise of authority in those situations, I would see that as an opportunity, not as a problem. That meeting proved to be the beginning of an eight-year relationship. Walter Comeaux was more than a change agent in my life. I credit him for giving me the opportunity to grow as a public administrator. Phil and Jessie had given me breath and wings. Walter was the wind.

Unfortunately, several members of the seven-member Parish Council thought differently. In my first meetings with them individually, it was apparent that three of them clearly did not agree with Walter's way of running the government. They had been in a legal battle with him over contracting authority, which ended in a compromise, but there was clearly a lack of trust in his integrity. One of them told me privately that I had gone to work for "the devil." I saw their opposition to Walter as a challenge. Despite their differences with him, which I perceived to be personal and political, I had to maintain a positive working relationship with them.

The other challenge that I immediately faced was the airing of Council meetings on live television broadcasted later in the week. Every mannerism I displayed and word I spoke was captured on live television. There was no room for error, misjudgment, or inappropriate displays of emotions, especially by a *black* top administrator. I was confident in my public speaking ability but the contention between Walter and three members of the Council would test my composer under pressure. Walter attended most Council meetings, but my job was to carry the agenda, to defend policies that we recommended through proposed ordinances, and to oppose Council-recommended policies that we disagreed with. On some occasions, as a way of speaking *silently* to the Council, Walter sat in his office a few feet away from the meeting room and watched the meeting on television. I became the Council's target, but my best weapon was understanding that and being prepared. I prayed before the start of every meeting that God would give me the knowledge and confidence to do my job well and represent the black community to the best of my ability.

My first major administrative policy initiative, which would require the Council's approval, was a new classification and pay plan for the two hundred government employees. Unfortunately, I didn't have a personnel director who, in my opinion, had the knowledge to get the job done. Worse than that, my sense was that many employees didn't trust him to be fair. Rudy Bourg, the only director who didn't have a college degree, was one of Walter's political *lieutenants*. As a Viet Nam veteran, he carried significant influence, but his professional skills and abilities were not strong. Without being named, he had been one of the directors whom Walter had spoken about during my interview. Whatever Rudy might have thought about me personally was going to be his problem, not mine. I was focused on getting the classification and pay plan done with or without his support and expertise. I retained an outside consultant to provide technical assistance, and I put employees on the appeals review committee. I was closely engaged in the entire project from start to finish and presented a plan to the Council that secured their unanimous approval.

The other director who I intuitively felt would pose a challenge working with was Jim Dorton, the Finance Director. A CPA, Jim was a competent financial manager but lacked strong *people skills*. My accounting knowledge proved invaluable in working with him, but my willingness to lead by example, with core values that I expected all employees to exemplify, particularly my directors, enabled us to build a strong, trustful relationship. He and I worked closely together for seven years, effectively managing a very difficult fiscal environment of dwindling tax revenues, while maintaining and in some cases expanding basic services and occasionally giving parish employees a pay raise.

My most difficult decision as CAO was firing the manager of our job training program. Evidence gathered by our finance and legal staff revealed that he corroborated with another employee in falsifying travel reimbursement reports of the other employee. It was difficult because he was black and because he had once served on the board of LNEDC. Although I intuitively felt that the impropriety should warrant less severe disciplinary action, he failed to convince me of his complete innocence during our private meeting on the matter. He wasn't the first black employee I had terminated in public service, but he was a respected member of the black community, and my somewhat personal relationship with him before and outside of parish government made it difficult.

In going into public service, I had again taken a giant leap of faith, risking job security while raising a young family. After six years in city government, I left with a clear understanding of the risks and knowing the possibility of failure. I had accomplished much as a city employee, but I had also calculated my limits of staying there and knew that I didn't want to be constrained by them. I felt compelled to seize the opportunity to work as an unclassified appointee in state government. Maybe it was purely ambition, but it wasn't blind. The silent voice I heard told me to go and assured me that I had made the right decision. Something in me was daring to fail in order to realize a greater purpose.

I've given little thought to how different my life and career would have turned out had I stayed at the Department of Labor. I might have eventually taken the job at LWCC and moved to Baton Rouge. I'll never know. But I do know that if I had not become the CAO of Lafayette Parish Government, all that was unseen and unknown of what lay ahead in doing that work and discovering my passion for poetry, would not have been manifested and realized. Poetry had not begun its tug. I had long ago pushed aside an interest in literature and teaching English, and despite the hints and signs along the way that pointed toward my becoming a writer, I hadn't given them an ounce of thought. My only focus was being a successful public administrator and rising to the challenges that I now faced.

Double Consciousness

The Parish CAO position was more *public* than any job that I had previously held in government. I had what W. E. B. Du Bois called a "double consciousness." I was always conscious of my public persona and what was expected of me professionally, but I was equally conscious of my blackness—the importance of representing the black community and being sensitive and responsive to its needs and concerns. I had to be careful not to be *too black or not black enough*. At times, the two faces clashed. When the local NAACP launched a "Buy Black" campaign, I agreed to put a bumper sticker on my car. Walter pulled me aside one day and tactfully suggested that I take it off. When he said that it would be just as inappropriate if he had a "Buy White" bumper sticker on his vehicle, I understood the political position that I had put him in. I removed the sticker.

When then U. S. Senator John Breaux, Walter's close friend and strong political supporter, convened a dozen local black leaders to explain his support of the nomination of Clarence Thomas to the U. S. Supreme Court, I sat silently, knowing that I was opposed to Thomas' appointment and felt very strongly that he should not be nominated to the high court. Mr. Breaux said that he had sought the advice of a group of black politicians and ministers in New Orleans, who strongly supported his position. I intuitively felt, and was quite correct in my assessment, that showing my "blackness" and expressing disapproval of Mr. Breaux's vote would not have made an ounce of difference in his political decision to support Mr. Thomas, but it clearly would have strained my relationship with Walter at a time when he needed Mr. Breaux's political support. It was a judgment call and I didn't feel that I had sacrificed principle in making it.

I had many memorable experiences working with my directors. I went out of my way to bond with them, but I never shied from exercising my authority when it was necessary, especially in times when we disagreed. My relationship with Jeff Moss, the Parish Attorney, was always like walking on eggshells. He worked on a contract with the government but was one of Walter's closest confidants. He or Steve Jankower, an Assistant Parish Attorney, sat beside me at every Council meeting. I had tremendous respect for Jeff's legal knowledge, and we generally enjoyed a positive working relationship, but I suspected that he held racially biased views but wouldn't dare compromise his professionalism or his relationship with Walter by displaying them overtly. My first sign of it was at a birthday party that several staff members held for me in my office shortly before a Council meeting. In my own silly, humorous way, I sent invitations to them to join the party. Moss showed up with watermelon and moon pies…a not-so-subtle stereotypical jester. I went with the flow of it, giving him the poker face that I had long since mastered, but I knew the day would come when our worlds would clash in a much more serious way and I would have to confront him directly.

After being on the job for a year, I attended a retreat hosted by the Greater Lafayette Chamber of Commerce. It was a joint City and Parish retreat attended by all local elected officials. The top agenda item was the consolidation of the City of Lafayette and Lafayette Parish Government into a single entity. Walter made it clear that he supported the initiative. Given the Parish Government's dwindling tax base, the state's imposition of "mandated" judicial and correctional services on the Parish, and the aggressive annexation policy of the City, consolidation was clearly in the Parish's best interest. City officials, on the other hand, had serious concerns, particularly about the impact that the proposed measure would have on its municipally-owned utilities system, which provided a significant sum of in-lieu-of -tax revenue to the City's general fund.

Eventually, the two councils agreed to form a "technical committee" comprised of the CAOs of the City and Parish and the independent auditor who served both governments. The committee would write a feasibility report outlining the major issues and concerns of merging the two governments. The City and Parish Councils would then review the report and vote on whether to create a joint, nine-member charter commission to develop a charter for the new government that would be put to a parish-wide vote. I seized the opportunity to showcase my analytical and composition skills in writing my section of the technical report, which comprised the departments of recreation, planning, grants management, and personnel. The report resulted in both governments agreeing to the formation of a charter commission, which would undertake a nearly year-long study of the governance structure for the consolidated government and the development of a home-rule charter to put before the voters.

Chaired by Ed Abell, a local attorney, the charter commission hired an outside consultant to provide technical expertise and help guide the process. I was never more excited about working in government. It was a rare opportunity for a public administrator, black or white, to help create the framework for the formation of a new local government. I attended every meeting of the commission and willingly provided information and offered advice on important policy issues. City officials and administrators were usually absent, attending only when their testimony was required or requested.

When the election was called and the campaign got underway, the Lafayette Chamber of Commerce commissioned a fiscal impact study by a local CPA that concluded that consolidation would save the parish taxpayers at least $6 million annually by the elimination of duplicate jobs. Jim Dorton and I refuted the findings, but on Walter's advice, we were careful not to speak against the consolidation proposal itself. Except for the Chamber's informational propaganda, there was virtually no campaign for or against the proposition to merge the two governments. The singular print advertisement against the referendum appeared in the *Quick Quarters* weekly flyer, in which a voter voiced opposition while personally attacking the City's housing manager for demolishing abandoned property. Voters of the parish approved the charter for the new government in 1992. The consolidated government would become effective in June 1996, giving us nearly four years to plan the transition.

Shortly after voters approved the consolidation referendum, I took the initiative to organize a transition planning team comprised of City and Parish administrators. I wrote transition planning guidelines that won the approval of City executives. Kenneth Bowen, the Mayor of Lafayette, later issued a directive to his department heads that they don't participate in any transition planning meetings. Despite the Mayor's opposition, we met, mostly clandestine, and got the job done. The development of a transition plan was largely driven by Parish administrators, and I personally wrote most of the text. The plan was later approved by a Transition Planning Committee comprised of local citizens and headed by Barry Berthelot, a former finance chief of the City who had become a senior vice president at a leading bank.

One morning, while at home on vacation, Walter called to tell me that Mayor Bowen, who was vehemently opposed to consolidation and had tried to thwart the transition planning process, had gotten a freshly printed copy of the transition plan and was calling a press conference in several hours to announce the release of the document and praise the work of his executive team in developing it. No Parish officials, including me, had been invited. I quickly cleaned up, got dressed, and went to City Hall, finding Mayor Bowen sitting behind a backdrop of American flags with his directors seated around the conference table, and a local television reporter and camera man present. The mayor had the appearance of someone who had not bathed or shaved in several days. He was surprised that I showed up and had to give me the opportunity to speak. It was one of my most memorable moments working in local government.

When I turned forty years old in December 1992, I quit smoking and started jogging. Within a year, it became an obsession. I had at least five or six pairs of new tennis shoes, and I'd cancel meetings during the day to go to Girard Park and run when I felt the rush. I'd awake before dawn, lace up, put headsets of a cassette player in my ears, and run four or five miles in the dark before Narva left for work and the kids went to school…and do it again after work. Smooth jazz was my Jesus in those days, especially mornings. In stride with the jazz, and with cool, dark air in my lungs, the morning jog lifted me as high as the rising sun, and I felt that I could go wherever my dreams would take me.

After finishing a run one very hot late July morning, I got a call from Uncle Andrew, my mother's oldest brother, saying that Victor had suddenly died of a heart attack. He was thirty-nine years old. I don't recall what went through my mind at that moment. I was in a state of shock and cried all the way home. I quickly showered and drove to pick up Uncle Andrew to visit Grandmother, who had moved to Lafayette several years before, to tell her the news. "Don't tell me," she said upon seeing both of us walking in at that time of morning. "Victor is dead." She had had a premonition. No words can describe a mother's cry over the death of her child.

In the days after Vic's passing, I put Bette Midler songs in my ears while jogging, listening to "The Rose," which I rewound for miles and days around the jogging path. I was mourning and felt depressed. I could not get over the suddenness of Vic's death at such a young age. I recalled his big laugh and optimistic spirit, and the day he stopped by dressed dapper as always but took time to fix the washing machine that needed repairing. I recalled that very sad, painful moment when he visited and asked why I had not attended the funeral of my natural father's mother. She had been buried a week before and no one called to tell me she had died. The day Vic said those words to me I cried in my sleep. If there was any chance of forgiving my father for his abandonment of me as a child, that moment destroyed it.

I am certain that it was Vic's death that drew me to poetry. I'd sit in my rocking chair in the living room, sip bourbon, play my favorite songs, and think of him. One night, I picked up a pencil and writing tablet and wrote my first poem, "Last Christmas," in which I reflected on Christmases of our boyhood days and about the last time I had seen him alive, a week after the Christmas of 1993. Vic had moved to Houston and remarried. His air conditioning and heating maintenance business was doing well and he was feeling blessed. Looking like Black Santa with his thick beard and burly stature, he stood at the front door holding a bag of Christmas gifts for Narva, the children, and me. It was the first time that Vic had given me a gift. As was my habit and still is today, I didn't open the gift immediately. I placed the small, neatly wrapped package at the top of my dresser mirror, eventually forgetting that I had put it there. Shortly after Vic's death, I opened it, finding a set of handkerchiefs, as if he knew that I would one day need them to wipe the many tears I shed. I loved Vic. Although he was an uncle two years younger, he was closer to me than a brother. Years later, I reflected on his adventurousness and the nights he confided in me about his relationships in and out of wedlock.

My Brother's Flowers
(FOR VICTOR HEBERT)

> I wasn't there the night
> he shattered the glass door
> and set Mr. Bob's bike shop on fire,
> but I knew he was burning hate

and not the steel wool and oil
that turned our rims into rhinestones.
And I wasn't there the night
he sped through the whorish fields
into all the years he hadn't lived,
playing chase with a trooper
as he swallowed white pills
and a half ounce of redbud,
or when his lover's husband
snapped a .38 at his head
and the barrel swallowed air.
I didn't stand with him
on the steep, jagged cliffs,
in closets he entered
before looking inside.
But I listened to him
reasoning in his obsessions,
moaning midnight blues
by quiet fires he lit
of letters from Debbie, ashes
settling like dust in his soul,
lilies blooming where he cried.

In the days and months that followed, I read poetry. I can't explain why, except that Vic's passing awakened something inside me that was latent, needed to be found, and helped me to deal with the grief of losing him. Browsing the poetry section of a bookstore, I stumbled upon Jean Wagner's *Black Poets of the United States*. I do not know with certainty if what lured me to turn the book's pages was my longstanding interest in literature or simply the book's evocative title and striking black and white cover. I read the poetry of Langston Hughes and other writers of the Harlem Renaissance. In addition to poetry, I read Frederick Douglass, Malcolm X, Carter G. Woodson, E. Franklin Frazier, James Baldwin, and other black scholars and protest writers. I started writing poems, most of which were introspective or dealt with themes of black history and the suffering of black children.

Several poems of *A Mandala of Hands*, my first collection, were among the earliest poems I wrote. They included "Rosa's Winter," "Hand Sewn Dolls," "Letter to the Oaks," and "Hunting Dragonflies." At the University of Louisiana at Lafayette, I attended my first poetry workshop, which resulted in seeing my first poem in print—an early version of "Rosa's Winter" that I had titled "Soul Too Tired to Move." I grew totally obsessed with a long poem that I wrote titled "Medgar, Malcolm, and Martin," and was so proud of it that I framed three copies and gave them to my children to hang on their bedroom walls. Of course, they had no idea what I was saying and probably thought of the prints as a total waste of a frame. Twenty-five years later, I made a version of the poem part of my second collection, *Soul Be A Witness.*

In time, I moved away from my fixation on Hughes and Renaissance poets. Convinced that being a poet was a personal calling of sorts, I read every black poetry anthology in print and discovered a great love for the poetry of Gwendolyn Brooks, Lucille Clifton, Nikki Giovanni, Etheridge Knight, and Robert Hayden. By then, I had also discovered the nature poems of Mary Oliver and had grown quite fond of her work. Hayden's "Those Winter Sundays" remains one of my favorite poems. Every reading of the poem stirs a remembrance of Grandfather Andrew and how I'd awaken before dawn on some mornings and watch him pull his tall rubber boots up to his knees. Those memories are the source of inspiration for poems that I would later write about my stepfather.

Sometime during the mid-1990s, I stumbled upon an article in *Newsweek Magazine* about the new renaissance emerging in black poetry—a flowering of expression by contemporary black poets such as Rita Dove and Yusef Komunyakaa, who had received literary acclaim not as black poets but as poets in the mainstream literary community. That was a major turning point in my writing experience. Reading Komunyakaa's *Magic City* and Dove's *Thomas and Beulah* inspired a different realm of literary possibilities. But reading and writing African American literature was something that I did sitting in a rocking chair late at night. During the day, I was a top public administrator of a majority-white community. I gave no thought to why I was reading and writing poetry but it seemed to fill a void, a hunger in me that I needed to feed.

There were moments in the months following Victor's death when I was deeply depressed and flirted with the thought of suicide. I use the term "flirt" because I knew for certain that there was much more of me that could not end my life than the part of me that entertained the idea of doing it. They were strange thoughts that were not constant and consuming but would surface in moments of depression. I was not fully aware of their coming and going or of their cause and effects, but there were clearly moments when I felt the ground beneath me slipping away. It was as though I had two minds, one that projected a persona of confidence and success and would awaken every day eager to go into the world and do the work that I thoroughly enjoyed, and another that didn't feel the joy of life and felt lost about life's true meaning.

On occasion, those thoughts spilled over into my marriage life. I would lash out at Narva in angry bursts of dissatisfaction about something she did or wasn't doing, as if she was the cause of my discontent. Narva grew concerned and probably felt unsafe. One morning, I got a phone call from her church pastor while sitting at my desk, in which he said that she had spoken to him and was concerned about my well-being. I don't think I ever talked to her about that conversation, but it was clearly a wake-up call that I needed to be more sensitive to how my moods affected the loved ones around me. I wonder sometimes whether that, too, was poetry's way of calling me. Without my conscious awareness of the deep, swirling currents, poetry was a lifejacket that kept me afloat.

In November 1995, the election for the City-Parish President and Council of the new government would be held. Walter announced his candidacy, as did a large field of other contenders. After leading in the primary, we ended up in a runoff with Ed Roy, a former television weather reporter and former Parish Council Member. It would be the first and only political campaign that I would be actively engaged in. I became the door to the black vote and the target of black opposition to Walter's candidacy. Although we had the majority support of the black community, several black politicians, for whatever reasons, quietly supported Ed Roy.

One day, I went to the mailbox and pulled out a red flyer, which had the appearance of not being professionally developed, on which statements were made that Walter's father, the former Parish Sheriff, had deputies that terrorized and beat black people. Without naming me, the flyer stated that Walter had "one Negro," whose job it was to block other blacks from getting jobs and contracts. The flyer, which had been sent to every registered black voter in the parish, called me an Uncle Tom. It was painful, to say the least, and planted the seed that at some point in my public life I needed to leave Lafayette. I had seen and become the brunt of the ugliest side of politics, and I didn't want to experience it again. Two weeks later, a red, makeshift ballot was mailed to black voters endorsing former Congressman Cleo Fields, a black candidate for Governor, and Ed Roy for City-Parish President. Photographs of both candidates appeared on the ballot side by side. Walter's campaign later traced the source of the mailings to a white law firm that supported the Ed Roy campaign.

We immediately retaliated with advertisements on black-owned radio stations. Several of the ads were endorsement statements of influential black ministers. My favorite was a cleverly produced radio ad done in hip-hop style that dubbed statements made by Ed Roy himself that he employed "no blacks" at his meteorologist business. It solidified our support of black voters, but in the last two weeks of the campaign, Roy went on the personal attack in a direct appeal to white Republican voters, in which he used newspaper, radio, and television advertisements to expose Walter's bankruptcy as a real estate developer many years before. Polling showed our lead dwindling rapidly. Had the election been held two weeks later, we might have lost it, but we won by three-thousand votes.

The stage was now set for my realization of a dream that I had intuitively felt would come many years before—my becoming the first CAO of the consolidated government, and a black one at that. At the age of 43, fourteen years after sitting in a small, partitioned cubicle in City Hall, I would be the top administrator of city-parish government, leading the implementation of a new government of one of Louisiana's major cities. I was never more comfortable in my ability and welcomed the challenge with enthusiasm. I assembled a strong team of executives, mostly composed of current City department heads, and began to tackle the task of merging city and parish departments into one workforce. In less than a month, we secured the Council's approval of a major bond proposition for capital improvements that had been deferred by previous City administrations. The bond proposition, which at the time was the largest undertaken by the local government, won voter approval.

Through a contract with Phil Lank, my former City department head who by then was a private consultant, we launched Rebuild

Lafayette North, a major civic engagement campaign to revitalize the northern part of the parish. Walter had already conceived the anchor project of the northern strategy. When he lost his push to locate a new police headquarters on city-owned property that had been a former elementary school in north Lafayette, he proposed the development of a comprehensive, multi-service community center at the location. Rebuild Lafayette North would go on to become a strong catalyst for redevelopment of that section of the parish.

In preparing for a $200 million bond proposition that we would put before the voters for capital projects, Jerry Osborn, the city-parish bond attorney, arranged a meeting for a group of consolidated government officials to meet with bond analysts in New York. The objective was to present information that would result in an improved rating on city-issued bonds and ensure favorable pricing in the market. The group included Walter, Jeff Moss, Finance Director Becky Fontenot, Assistant Finance Director Jim Dorton, Assistant Director of Public Works Robert Benoit, Utilities Director Terry Huval, Councilman Daryl Schouest, and me. Our agenda for the three-day trip included meetings on Wall Street but much of it was social, including lunches and dinners at some of New York's most popular restaurants. We had lunch at Windows of the World atop the World Trade Center and dinner at Tavern on the Green. We did some sightseeing but time was too limited to catch attractions other than the Statue of Liberty and the Empire State Building.

On the final day of the trip, a group of us decided to rent a limousine to take a short tour of other sites before heading out to the airport. I suggested a ride through Central Park, but several others, namely Jeff Moss and Daryl Schouest, who sat near me in the rear of the limo, insisted on a tour of Harlem. As we rode through Harlem, Moss and Schouest made racially tainted jokes *around me*, not nigger jokes, but the kind that educated, so-called liberal white people who wrap themselves in the robe of Jesus say when they put down black people without calling them niggers or when they disguise their racism in subtle stereotypes that, in their opinion, don't quite cross the line. Their words were not said *to me* but in my presence and clearly with the intent of aggravating me, if not outright reminding me that I was no different from all black people, including those who were homelessly wandering the streets of Harlem, New York. Not wanting to become part of a sideshow that they undoubtedly thought was entertaining, I thought it best to not display emotion and respond. I *pretended* to ignore them.

Many years had passed since I first stepped foot into the white world. I had grown to be the top administrator of Lafayette City-Parish Government. But sitting in that limousine I found myself back in ninth grade, standing in a lunch line in front of Hugh Morton and his pals, and feeling globs of spit hitting the back of my head. I was in the car with Terry riding through downtown Beaumont on our way back to the plush office of my corporate job and hearing him call a black man a *nigger*. I was shelving library books with silly college boys who had tried to tell me a nigger joke. I was the Uncle Tom that white and black men had labeled me to get the support of black voters after all I had sacrificed and done to help and represent *my people*. I had grown. Everything had changed except the color of my skin. It hurt, so much so that, a quarter of a century later, tears flow as I write these words.

As I was writing this chapter of the memoir, I called Schouest to talk about the Harlem incident. He didn't recall the words he spoke that afternoon, but he apologized for any words he said that offended me. I accepted his apology.

I was particularly disturbed by comments that Moss made as we rode through Harlem. In my opinion, they crossed the line. At the airport, when I had a moment alone with him, I told them that his remarks were insensitive, inappropriate, and racist. He denied any strand of racism in his body and went on to make the case of how fair and impartial he had always been to black people. In November 2021, I sat beside Moss at a banquet and award ceremony honoring Barry Berthelot for his many years of civic work. It was the first time since August 1997 that Jeff and I had been face-to-face. We talked about public service and the good work that we and others did. I didn't bring up the watermelon and limousine incidents. That was not the time and place to dig up buried bones, but like all racial experiences that I encountered, the memory of them were haunting.

Jeff and I crossed paths again in December 2024 at a local fundraising gala for the arts. We exchanged cordial greetings and joked about how I managed to keep my weight down. I had remained deeply appreciative, not only for Jeff's support of my candidacy for the CAO position but for the exemplary legal guidance he provided in our service to the people of Lafayette Parish. As I had done with former Councilman Daryl Schouest, I felt the need to tell Jeff about the words that I had written and why I wrote them. More than anything, I wanted him to know that my accounts and reflections of those incidents were honest, well-intentioned, and deeply personal.

Several days after the gala we had a long telephone conversation. He said that he felt bad that I had felt offended by his words and actions and that his intention was not to be disrespectful in either of those incidents. That was good enough for me, and I was thankful to resolve, at least internally, a tension that stood in the way of my fully appreciating the amicable relationship that we enjoyed in the eight years we worked together. He, too, was thankful that we had talked.

When I became the Parish CAO, I joined the National Forum for Black Public Administrators (NFBPA) and started attending its annual conference. Through NFBPA, I networked with black city and county administrators across the country and established relationships that proved invaluable, personally and professionally. It was through NFBPA that I met Sam Davis, a native of Louisiana and the director of gas utilities for the City of Tallahassee, Florida. Sam called to inform me that Anita Favors, a black woman and the newly appointed City Manager of Tallahassee, was seeking an Assistant City Manager for her executive team. I was intrigued by the idea of working in a city manager form of government, in which a Council-appointed manager, not the mayor, ran the city. In fact, I had previously been one of two finalists for an assistant city manager job in Austin, Texas, and didn't get the job. The more I looked at the Tallahassee job opportunity, the more interested I grew. By then, Narva and I had been living in Lafayette for nearly seventeen years. I had experienced the best and ugliest of them and was ready to move on to another challenge.

The day before the job interview, our bond attorney had arranged a planning session at his office in New Orleans. I secretly made plans to fly to Tallahassee directly after the meeting. Anita Favors offered me the job two weeks later. As one of three Assistant City Managers, I would head the development arm of the city, including the departments of public works, planning, growth management, airport, transit, and economic development. It was a promising opportunity to spread my wings in a different city and state, but I agonized over the decision to leave Lafayette and Louisiana. I would be leaving the city where we raised our children, and where I had grown professionally. My grandparents were natives of Lafayette Parish. I would be leaving those deeply planted roots. I would leave my parents who lived an hour's drive away and an aging grandmother who depended upon my support. Narva would again have to find a new teaching job and Patrick would leave his high school senior class. I prayed to God that he would make the choice between Lafayette and Tallahassee his decision and not mine.

One of my three job references that the City of Tallahassee would contact was Barry Berthelot. Upon hearing about my interest in leaving Lafayette, he offered me a position in the public funds division of the bank. He arranged a breakfast meeting with the bank CEO, who assured me that I could succeed as a banker. He also assured me that his bank would not be bought and that my future with them would be secure. I graciously declined the offer and accepted the Tallahassee job offer.

On the first day of the job, I was given a windowless office that was considerably smaller than the spacious office that I had in Lafayette City Hall, the office that I had not long ago renovated and added one of the few windows in a building that had originally been a Sears department store. Two gifts awaited me, a house plant sent by the local Chamber of Commerce and a book on environmentalism left by the local Sierra Club. In time, I understood why both groups were eager to welcome me. Tallahassee was a city of trees, lakes, and rolling hills. As the policy chief for growth management, I quickly found myself in the middle of a war. The Chamber wanted commercial development and the environmentalists wanted to preserve trees and green space.

Narva took a teaching job in Thomasville, Georgia, twenty-five miles north of Tallahassee, so we rented a townhouse in the northernmost part of Leon County. My daily commute to downtown Tallahassee was forty-five minutes long, in traffic that was congested nearly the entire drive. Soon after we settled in we began house hunting, eventually deciding to purchase a lot and build a home in the city's most exclusive gated community.

One workday afternoon, I left work to drive out to our lot. On the way back, for reasons that I can't explain, I decided to stop at the townhouse where we lived. As I approached the subdivision, I saw smoke billowing from one of the buildings. It turned out to be our home. Patrick had come home from school, decided to cook, and fallen asleep with a pot on the burner. By the time the fire department had arrived, he had gone back into the burning building with a fire extinguisher and put the fire out, saving all but the kitchen but preventing the entire house and the adjourning townhouse from burning down. When I pulled into the driveway, he was coming out of the house with a smoking skillet in his hand. Fortunately, he was not injured. My leaving work, driving to the house that time of day, and being there with my son when he risked his life to save our burning home was another one of those inexplicable moments when someone or something outside of me was in control.

Culturally, Tallahassee required quite an adjustment. The food was neither Creole nor Cajun, even when the restaurant signs said it was. I missed hearing and dancing Zydeco, and I especially missed seeing Grandmother Rose. We took the nearly eight-hour drive back to Lafayette at least once a month. I continued jogging but found the hills hurtful for my knees, eventually settling on a flat but boring one-mile jogging path at one of the lakes. On Saturdays, we'd drive to Panama Beach over an hour away, or take the scenic drive south to the white, sandy beach of Saint George Island, stopping at one of the many seafood restaurants along Hwy 98 on our return.

The weekend nighthawk that I was frequented one of the neighborhood bars or found myself drifting miles across town, past the downtown area, into a "hole-in-the-wall" bar near the campus of Florida A & M University. I relished the anonymity and the idea of being a stranger in a city where I worked as one of its top executives. A downtown bar held open-mic poetry readings and played jazz on Thursdays, and I soon found myself there every week, though never getting up the courage to read a poem. No one in Tallahassee, including my co-workers, was aware of my love for poetry.

My work as an assistant city manager was both challenging and boring. I was in the middle of policies shaping the growth and development of the city. Planning and Growth Management were especially challenging in a city that was divided between commercial and environmental interests. My first directive from the city manager was to fire the Growth Management Director. She needed the department to go in a difficult direction and he was not the guy

112

to do it. In Lafayette, the director of every department had reported to me. I oversaw the administration of the entire government and thought strategically about policies that would improve the lives of an entire city and parish. In Tallahassee, I had oversight over one-third of the departments. Although I oversaw the development arm of the city, my department directors were extremely self-directed, and the city manager, still somewhat new on the job, was very hands-on. I had great respect for Anita Favors and wanted so badly to be a part of her executive team, but I soon found myself feeling unchallenged, and, quite frankly, bored.

My grandmother, a still attractive, light-skinned woman with long, silky, white hair, was living in Lafayette but had gone to live with my Aunt Nancy. I'd visit her often when she lived alone, never missing a day when she baked homemade bread. She was an excellent writer, and we exchanged many letters over the years before she moved to Lafayette. One day, she gave me every letter that I had written to her, including the one I wrote on June 2, 1962. She loved to watch Perry Mason television shows and was an avid reader of *Reader's Digest* and Danielle Steel novels. She also kept up with current events, reading the daily newspaper, and watching the evening news. She had been wheelchair bound for several years, and Narva and I took turns driving her to doctor and hospital visits. Before moving to Tallahassee, I noticed that the newspapers, which I was paying for, were starting to pile up on the front porch. Not long after starting the job of Assistant City Manager, I had the subscription canceled. One morning, as I sat preparing for a staff meeting, she called me on my office phone, complaining in a rather fussy tone that the newspaper had stopped coming. I had the subscription reinstated.

After being on the job for eight months, I began to question whether I had made the right decision. I contacted Stephen Cavanaugh, who knew the chairman of the state's group health benefits program, which was searching for a CEO, a position that would be based in Baton Rouge and appointed by Louisiana Governor Mike Foster. I contacted Barry Berthelot and asked if the bank position was still available. Surprisingly, the bank had been bought but Barry assured me that he could find a way to bring me on. Several days before I was scheduled to attend the job interview for the group benefits position, Barry called and said that he had worked it out. He offered me a Vice-President position at what would be Bank One. The only catch was that I'd have to move to Baton Rouge, where Bank One was headquartered. I would also have to work the Alexandria market, a two-hour drive away, which would mean regular travel. The bank was most generous in nearly matching my City of Tallahassee salary, providing a hiring bonus, and paying for moving expenses.

On our first trip to Baton Rouge, Narva secured a teaching job with the East Baton Rouge School System. Patrick, who had graduated with honors at Leon High School, had been offered a full-tuition-paid scholarship to Morehouse College. The stars were aligned. Baton Rouge was clearly where I was meant to be. In early August 1998, after being on the job for a year, I resigned from the position of Assistant City Manager to return to Louisiana as a banker.

I started a banking career in the middle of a conversion from one banking system to another one. I had the title of Vice-President, but so did all the bankers who managed relationships with commercial and not-for-profit clients. I knew how government operated and felt comfortable talking to governmental clients about their financial management product needs, but I knew little about the products I was selling. Like a fish out of water, I felt lost. Everything I learned in the First Commerce system was changing in real time to the Bank One system. After two years, I caught on and grew more confident. In time, I was given three geographic markets to work: Baton Rouge, Alexandria, and Lake Charles, requiring extensive weekly travel. Barry Berthelot, my direct supervisor, worked sixty miles away in Lafayette. Most of the governmental clients in Baton Rouge, including the State of Louisiana, were handled by another banker. My largest client was the historically black Southern University. The bank had closed a branch on the edge of Southern University's campus, and I was tasked with the challenge of managing, maintaining, and growing the relationship.

There were no black commercial loan officers at Bank One in Louisiana. I was one of two black officers in the government/nonprofit banking division and the only black officer in Baton Rouge. I had no misgivings about being the black face. It had its benefits, like having the front row center table at a bank-sponsored banquet honoring Nelson Mandala or introducing Nancy Wilson, Dionne Warwick, and Roberta Flack at outdoor concerts that Bank One sponsored to raise funds for the Baton Rouge Symphony Orchestra. The one time that I felt "black" was when the executive vice president of finance at Southern University told me that in his opinion the bank had assigned a black officer to manage the university's accounts because it had closed the branch and didn't want to lose the business. I told him that I was insulted and offended by his remarks, and he apologized. Of course, away from the bank, racism reared its ugly head.

The Black Man in Mayberry
Not Seen on Television

That day, I drove a sporty new rental, something no black man
would ever be seen driving in that town of 1,500 people.
A bank vice-president, I had spent the day calling on clients,
including the sheriff of a city an hour away. A long day.
I was tired, but my starched, bright-white shirt looked crisp
as morning and my black shoes stilled sparkled like stars.

Passed up a gas station, then backed up a few feet. Suddenly,
Barney Fife pulled up. You know Barney, the only deputy
in Mayberry, where Andy Griffith is sheriff. Jerking nervously
like a twig in the wind, with a hand on the pistol in his holster,
the hand I remember more than a face and a pointing finger,
Barney loudly yelled, "Get out of the car; let me see your hands."

With a prayer my silence spoke, I quickly stepped out of the car,
raised both hands high, and showed a face that asked, "why,"
with an unspoken thought that begged, "Please don't shoot."
Thank God, Barney didn't, but speaking in a tone that said,
Do or say something stupid, so I can cuff your ass and lock you up,
he wrote a ticket on me for reckless driving and took my license.

"Is there a mayor in this town?" I politely asked with eyes
fixed on Barney's badge. He kindly escorted me to City Hall,
just past the barber shop, knowing I hadn't committed a crime,
knowing I wanted to file a complaint, and knowing damn well
the mayor wasn't there. But he was Barney, a cop with a gun.
I was just a well-dressed black man driving a sporty new car.

Sometime around 2002, I discovered the Baton Rouge poetry scene. A bar downtown sponsored a weekly open-mic slam competition. Judges held up cards after each performance that scored the performer on a scale of 1 to 10. After several visits, I decided to read, not perform, a poem. It was my first public reading of a poem that I had written, and I was scared and nervous as hell. My voice cracked, my hands trembled, and I'm pretty sure my knees buckled a little. My performance got good scores but not enough to win. It was one of my earliest poems and had grown out of memorable boyhood experiences of chasing dragonflies. Somehow the poem had evolved into the dragonfly being a metaphor for a young victim of child abuse. Years later, while studying under Tracy K. Smith at a Callaloo Creative Workshop, she suggested that I say what was in the mind of the predator.

Hunting Dragonflies

If you got lucky you would swat a big one
with a stick that had no other purpose
just after the sun dropped,
when twilight hid the slow pitch.
You would hurry too late
to pinch her thin translucent wings
before she recovered and fluttered,
darting the ghostly plain
even your thoughts would not enter.

One day, when a warm beam sealed
the mud pond, you held your breath
and crept through the cattails
to sneak up on a little one
with wings like brittle leaves.
She wilted in the weight of your hand
until you sighed and let go.
Yet, sooner than you blinked
she crisscrossed the sky,
taking your breath with her,
leaving your scent
dangling like a jingling chime.

If you got lucky, she'd flit right by
your hawk-eyed stare
and tangle in the sweet-briar.
You could reach in, free her,
and hold her like a morning breeze
swaying a robin's nest. Instead,
you put her in your darkened room,
cluttered with the memory
of your father's heavy coarse hands
and the thump you felt
while swatting a drowning light.

After being at Bank One for two and a half years, Narva and I moved into our newly built home in Santa Maria Subdivision, a golfing community that was one of Baton Rouge's most upscale developments. Although our home met the minimum size requirements, it was one of the smaller homes in that section of the subdivision. All of our neighbors were white. In fact, at that time we were one of only a half-dozen black families living in the entire subdivision, which was fairly large. It was the third home we had purchased, but the first time that we lived near upper-income white people. Within a year, several neighbors, next door and across the street, sold and moved. Two fences went up, one on the left and another on the rear of our lot.

Many years later, one of the neighbors described us as "quiet." We generally kept to ourselves, seldom walking past our front yard to exchange small talk and not accepting their invitations to sip wine on their courtyards. I'm sure some were curious about what work we did and how we could afford to pay the mortgage, but they seldom asked. As time passed, I had occasional conversations with some of them while doing yard work and at least got to know their names, but I wasn't particularly interested in getting to know them personally. To me, the house was just a home and a good investment, and they just happened to be my neighbors. No one there had even the faintest clue that I was a poor black boy from Dixie Homes housing project who had been spat on, called a nigger, and been treated like one, and had been carried by enough soft, gentle winds to end up being their neighbor.

Not long after Narva and I settled into our new home, the Hebert family was struck with three unexpected deaths in less than a year.

In May 2000, Donette, a 27-year-old first cousin and daughter of my Aunt Antoinette died in an automobile accident. Five months later, my Grandmother Rose passed away at the age of 82. Antoinette, my grandmother's third youngest child, died in early March of 2001.

Antoinette and I were born seven months apart. She is the little girl sitting on the front row in the photograph of my kindergarten class with her sister's Sunday-worn socks and her hanky balled tightly in her hand. Antoinette dropped out of school at a young age. When I studied psychology in pursuit of my first undergraduate degree, she often called me at odd hours of the night for "coping" advice. She was experiencing some life challenges that had her feeling that she was losing her mind. After marrying and having two children, she lived the life of a homemaker. When Narva and I moved to Lafayette in August 1980, she provided childcare for our two youngest children. I have many fond memories of Antoinette, mostly for her sense of humor and how she poked fun at my proper pronunciations of words. To her, I was always "Jay," the boy she grew up with in Dixie Homes. Being around her made me not take myself too seriously, no matter how much education I had or what I had accomplished. After her husband divorced her, she lived in a low-income apartment. Always a heavy smoker, she eventually developed bronchitis. When her health seriously declined and she could barely talk, she was moved to a nursing home. She died at the age of 47.

Ballerina
(For Antoinette Ruffin)

> The last time we talked,
> you wanted to feel the crocheting rays,
> so I wheeled you outdoors,
> a short distance from the cinder block walls
> you were given to live your last days.
> It seemed a pity you had to lift
> your un-blooming burden out of bed
> and carry it with the lush asters
> you plucked from memory.
>
> I watched you indulge fragilely,
> awkwardly in the breath-giving air,
> whirling and flouncing
> your ponytail and prong hands

as if you needed to feel
that your tattered bones
were still attached to earth.
And the struggle was as much mine,
to settle the restless prattle
that your tongue-slurred wit
and long, shivering pauses stirred in me.

Thinking about you now,
and the playhouse moments we shared
years ago, when we picked clovers
for bees we trapped in a Mason jar
and dressed the dolls we made
out of Nehi bottles, wooden clothespins
and braided rope, it seems
you were always like crystal,
kept on a mantel, wanting
and needing to dance in the sun.

Despite my job title and income and the cordialness my white neighbors showed, I had no illusions about being seen any different than how they saw black people in general. Despite having a black mayor, I was living in a very racially and politically polarized city, in which few if any of my neighbors drove near and cared anything about the side of town where most black folks lived. But I had reached a stage of life when I felt free to be whatever I wanted to be. There was no longer a "double consciousness." I didn't feel the least bit constrained or limited by how white people saw me or what they thought of me, and I surely did not feel the need to not act and think black. I sensed a quiet militancy brewing inside me but I didn't quite know where it was going or how it would be acted out.

During my years in public service and banking, I read and wrote poetry. On many road trips to see bank clients, I composed poetry behind the steering wheel. The creative demon was constantly stirring. The passion to write had possessed me, and I wrote because something in me was making me create. The thought of publishing poems in journals crossed my mind, but every submission to a literary journal was rejected. Undeterred, I continued to write, but becoming a poet and publishing a book was still the farthest thought from my mind.

In several ways, moving to Tallahassee was like the move to Natchitoches. Both were at least partly driven by experiences with racial prejudice and by the desire to fulfill an unmet although not fully understood need for change and growth. Both were short-lived, but they were necessary turns in my journey and resulted in my being where I had to be to fulfill purposes that were completely unknown. When I walked into a cubicle at Lafayette City Hall in early 1982 and unpacked a writing tablet and pen, nothing in my wildest imagination would have thought that fourteen years later I would be the top administrator of the local government. Had I not left Lafayette at what appeared to be the peak of my professional career and gone to Tallahassee, I would not have become a banker.

Although I had grown confident in my ability to sell bank products and manage client relationships, the work required no conviction to political, social, and economic ideals that I had grown passionate about. My analytical, organizational, and written communication skills were not being used or tested. The sole objective in everything I did was earning income and profits for the bank with the expectation of a good enough performance evaluation to stay employed and earn a year-end bonus check. Nothing in me thought or felt that I would be a banker for the rest of my working life. I felt hollow and incomplete, as if I were standing near a deep crevice of complacency, and I was going to either step back, fall inside, or jump to the other side, not knowing where any of those plots of ground would lead me. I had yet to realize that being a banker in Baton Rouge would lead to the discovery of a part of the wholeness of me that was just beginning to evolve. Only the still, silent voice—the knowledge of who I had become and the sense of who I was becoming—could point the way toward it.

SELF

In November 2003, Lieutenant Governor Kathleen Blanco defeated Congressman Bobby Jindal in a race for Governor of Louisiana. I personally knew Kathleen from my days at Lafayette City Hall when she served as a State Representative and later as a Public Service Commissioner. I gave no thought to working in her administration until I got a call from a friend in February 2004, asking me to submit his resume to Jimmie Clark, who headed Governor Blanco's transition team. Clark asked if I had given any thought to applying for a position myself.

The only cabinet level position that I felt would be of interest to me was Secretary of the Department of Revenue, a job that I had declined at the start of the second term of Republican Governor Mike Foster, who in 1995 had paid $150,000 for the mailing list of Ku Klux Klansman David Duke, who later endorsed then Senator Foster in his first successful bid for governor.[1] In fairness to Governor Foster, I declined his offer not solely because of his no doubt regretful political affiliation with David Duke during the campaign. I had made a career change to the private sector just several years before and felt that I needed to give my work as a banker time to develop.

After giving the opportunity of working in the Blanco administration some thought, I sent my resume and was invited to an interview, where I discovered that another candidate for the position was the current Secretary of Revenue, a black woman who was exceptionally talented and qualified. Not wanting to compete with her, I walked out of the interview regretting that I had applied. As I was leaving the room, one of the governor's top aides said that the governor wanted me to consider interviewing for the position of Secretary of Labor, which I did several weeks later. The Chief of Staff recommended my appointment, and during a personal interview with Governor Blanco,

[1]https://www.cbsnews.com/news/duke-deal-costs-governor/

she offered me the job. The first words she spoke in that meeting were how much she missed those Thursday lunches at Mrs. Taylor's.

The Governor asked me to meet with officials of the AFL-CIO, who had strongly supported her, but she had not appointed the candidate of their choice for the Labor Secretary position. We met several days later, where they questioned my sensitivity to the plight of working-class people and had the audacity to offer me the Deputy Secretary position. I told them that I was the governor's choice and had absolutely no interest in being *their* deputy. I talked about my upbringing and my commitment to social and economic justice, and I pledged my strong support of their programs and policies. Of course, I had an equally uphill battle to climb in gaining the confidence of the Louisiana Association of Business & Industry, the state's largest business lobby group, which had not endorsed the governor during the campaign. I made it a priority to involve both organizations in every major decision regarding the Unemployment Insurance Trust Fund and the business-funded Incumbent Worker Training Program.

I resigned from Bank One in early March of 2004, a week before it was bought by Chase Bank, and started the position of Secretary of Labor a week later. It was euphoric and seemed unreal that I would be leading an agency that I had worked at fifteen years before. I would be Louisiana's Secretary of Labor, a black boy who had grown up in a public housing project, met racial prejudice at every stage of his development, and had risen to the top executive level of state government. I couldn't be happier and feel more blessed.

My first challenge as Labor Secretary was assembling an executive staff that would report directly to me and oversee the administrative and programmatic work of the agency. My team was competent but had some weaknesses that I either had to get rid of due to politics or lack of competence or be forced to keep and manage for political reasons. I decided to keep Raj Jindal, the mother of Congressman Bobby Jindal, who had served as Assistant Secretary of Information Services under former Governor Mike Foster. I had worked with Raj in my brief stint as Undersecretary of Management and Finance and had great respect for her abilities. Not only was she the mother of the candidate that the governor had defeated, but she had also been active in the campaign. Eventually, I got a call from the Chief of Staff directing me to fire Raj and send her back to her classified job. I interviewed candidates to replace her but never hired an Assistant Secretary for that office. She continued to direct the Office of Information Services as a classified employee.

No one at the Department of Labor knew that I read and wrote poetry. In May 2003, due to my mother's illness, I had passed up the Callaloo Creative Writing Workshop, a two-week workshop in which I would be taught by award-winning black poets, but I applied again and was accepted in 2005. I can't imagine what my executive team thought when I told them that I would be taking a vacation to go to Texas A&M, where Callaloo was based, to study poetry. I am indebted to Andy Kopplin, the governor's chief of staff, for approving the leave of absence. That summer at Callaloo, I was taught by Forrest Hamer and I discovered the work of Tracy K. Smith. I would return to Callaloo in 2007 and 2008, when I studied under Tracy K. Smith and Terrance Hayes.

The Callaloo workshop of 2005 was held several months before I met my biggest tests as Labor Secretary: Hurricane Katrina and Hurricane Rita. Fortunately, I had exceptionally competent executive support in the areas that mattered most. Two of my most trusted confidants were Gwen Fabre, my executive assistant, who kept my ear to the grapevine and told me what no one else had the courage to say about what other employees thought or said about my job performance, and Alicia Wilkerson, an attorney and our Deputy Secretary. I respected and appreciated her quiet counsel and sound judgment.

I credit Marianne Sullivan, who headed the Office of Regulatory Services, for steering us in the massive undertaking of handling over 250,000 unemployment insurance claims. She set up call centers and partnered with other states to handle the massive flow of claims. Raj Jindal teamed with Desire Honoré, Undersecretary of the Office of Management and Finance, to establish a debit card program in partnership with Chase Bank that enabled us to issue paperless unemployment insurance checks to any address in the country. Benny Soulier, whom I had worked with in Lafayette government, headed the Office of Workforce Development and competently led the programming and administration of the large sums of federal training dollars that were flowing in to rebuild the state's workforce.

Except for Marianne and Benny, my executive team and administrative support staff were black. Raj, of course, was Indian

American, but you wouldn't know it by the color of her skin. Labor Secretary was the first public job I held in which I seldom thought of being a *black* administrator. As much "black power" as there was in our executive meetings, I thought of myself simply as a leader with a job to do, and I'd like to think that most of the employees of the agency viewed us in that light, but I never lost sight of how being in that position could make a difference in the lives of black Louisianans. I was one of only three black department heads on the governor's cabinet, and I knew that in many ways I was doing more than leading. I was *representing*.

There were times when the business of government and the politics of government were not congruent, situations when I had to walk a fine line between my sensitivity to the needs of the black community and the exercise of my fiduciary responsibility as an agency head, such as when influential black legislators made requests that would benefit their constituents but in the professional judgment of our team were not an effective or appropriate use of state resources. As a seasoned administrator who had been tried and tested, there were clearly times when I questioned my own judgement, but I never wavered on ethical or moral standards and didn't hesitate to say "no" when I felt that it was the *right* thing to do. Nor did I hesitate to at least voice my opinion to the governor's office when the politics of a decision could not be justified on sound management principles. Every day was a day of decisions, particularly after the storms. I am certain that I made mistakes, but in the moment, history would have to be the judge.

In the aftermath of the storms, I had major disagreements with Ed Pratt, my public relations officer, and with the governor's communication staff about how much and how frequently we reported information to news outlets. Like every state agency, the Labor Department was in a constant state of flux and change. In my opinion, we needed to achieve results before talking about them. I personally felt that the governor was overexposed publicly, and I didn't want to add fuel to the communication fire. I repeatedly stressed that the governor's cabinet meet to share information and collaborate on strategies to better serve the public in the recovery process. One of my biggest disappointments was the first cabinet meeting held after the devasting storms, which turned out to be more of a public relations show than a meeting. There was essentially no business agenda. We were told to remove coffee and donuts from the table to look "professional." The governor walked into the room, and with flags as the backdrop, made a statement about the progress of the recovery efforts, doing a photo and camera shot for news reporters with the Adjutant General of the National Guard and Superintendent of State Police at her side. The Chief of Staff made a brief statement and the meeting was adjourned.

When Andy Koplin left the Chief of Staff post to head the Louisiana Recovery Authority and Jimmie Clark resumed the duties, I differed with Clark on the allocation of executive staff pay raises for my department. I offered to forego my usual 4% annual raise and apportion it to my assistant secretaries, who were paid less than the assistant secretaries of most of the other state agencies and who clearly had deserved a larger increase for their performance in the aftermath of the storms. Clark declined my request based on it setting precedence for other agency heads. I could not allocate the pay raise among my top executives and had to accept the increase whether I wanted it or not. That made absolutely no business sense to me, but I had no choice but to live and manage with it.

From day one, I had been a proponent of applying systems theory in the management of the agency. Our work depended upon a system of many public and private stakeholders effectively working together in partnership with the federal government. The storms had clearly taken us off that course, despite our internal efforts to reshape our mission from being an "unemployment" agency to a workforce development agency. Sometime in 2006, I began to press Clark to allow me to reconvene a Task Force on Workforce Development that the governor had established before the hurricanes to reimagine and reinvent the mission of the department with a stronger focus on business engagement. I had been working with the business-led Workforce Investment Council to develop a new strategic plan for the workforce system, but the effort was at a stalemate because of the unwillingness of the partners in secondary education to come to the planning table. Despite my repeated requests, the task force was not reconvened.

Notwithstanding those differences and disagreements, I was thoroughly enjoying my work. Standing up, pulling back, pushing forward, and sometimes falling down were all part of the job. Not a day passed when I didn't feel privileged to serve, and I took great pride in the good that we were doing to rebuild Louisiana. I was fully committed to serving Kathleen Blanco for as long as she was governor, but in the summer of 2007, she announced that she would not seek reelection. The announcement was not surprising or unexpected. The hurricanes, particularly Katrina, and the negative publicity the governor had suffered during and after the storm, had taken too great a toll. I started thinking about the next chapter of my professional career.

While at the Department of Labor, I had begun to focus on the root problem of Louisiana's labor challenges. The storms had caused a severe shortage of skilled labor, but my research uncovered a more basic problem: Louisiana public schools and post-secondary institutions were failing far too many students. The high school graduation and college retention rates were woefully and embarrassingly low. I kept research publications about the problem on the left corner of my desk, all of which proved to me that spending hundreds of millions of federal dollars to rebuild the workforce would not solve the root problem, which clearly was that the public education system of Louisiana was failing to effectively educate and prepare students, particularly those of color, for success beyond school.

Shortly after the governor's announcement, I received an email from Greg Davis, a former co-worker at SCDF, about the establishment of a new nonprofit organization dedicated to improving outcomes in PreK-12 public education. As a Board member, he was leading their search for a chief executive officer. Without being consciously aware of preparing myself for the job, I had done just that while studying the workforce challenges facing our state. I would also bring the expertise and experience of establishing and managing non-profit organizations, having done that work in Lafayette city government. I applied, was offered the job, and began working in mid-November 2007.

I resigned from the Secretary of Labor job in early October 2007. Shortly after receiving my letter of resignation, the governor called me at home to thank me for my service. It was an unexpected call late one Friday evening. Although we talked for nearly an hour, the governor did most of the talking, the longest one-on-one conversation we had in my three and a half years of service to her. During the conversation, she expressed her frustration about how badly the Bush administration had treated her administration during and after the hurricanes for purely political purposes. She felt certain that Bobby Jindal would be the next governor, and she expressed grave concern that he could not feel the pain of disadvantaged people of our state. She also said that, notwithstanding the good work that her communication staff did, her team had been overwhelmed, and if she could do it all over again, she would have suffered the criticism of hiring a professional public relations firm to manage communication after the storms. History will be kind to Governor Blanco. Despite the criticism she suffered after Karina and Rita, she was a woman of strong faith and character who led Louisiana through one of its most difficult periods.

Rebuilding
FOR GOVERNOR KATHLEEN BLANCO

> The city's blood had been her air,
> her sounds and smells in crowded squares,
> a murky river asleep beside her.
> The storm made her breathless.
> When the sun died and was reborn
> we were not there, only the brown pelicans.
> Spreading their candelabrum wings,
> the pelicans raised their giant jaws
> and began the long journey home.
> Deep in the marsh, miles away
> from the unraveling sky, mangrove roots
> lay torn and twisted, branches tossed.
> Twig by twig the mandibles and bills
> weaved their cross-stitches
> and rebuilt their breeding nests.

The next several pages were written after much of this manuscript was completed. They were withheld until the end because I hesitated to publicly speak about the darkest period of my life—and the most painful and regretful. As much as one bears the soul in a memoir, there is a reluctance to talk about dark secrets. They are difficult to confess. In retrospect, those experiences were all part of my journey toward wholeness and might well have been the most significant and impactful. To be true to myself and to those who read this book in expectation or search of some insight into humanness and spirituality,

I cannot omit the experience of my unfaithfulness to Narva.

As common as it might be in marital relationships, no man wants it remembered that he cheated on his wife. He doesn't want his grandchildren to know the shameful, adulterous side of their grandfather, and he certainly doesn't want to be remembered that way when he is laid to his final rest. The lives of *public* men with "feet of clay" are replete with such stories, although most of them go to the grave untold.

I didn't break a law in the legal sense, but in the eyes of God, I broke a commandment that is no less of a sin than theft or murder. In fact, during that experience, I had a recurring dream in which I had secretly killed my stepfather and buried him in a hill of rocks in the backyard of my childhood home on Gelpi Drive, always fearful that his body would one day be discovered and knowing for certain that one day I would bear the consequences.

During the affair, I struggled to maintain a sense of normalcy, but I was clearly living two lives, torn between a lie and truth, and waking up every day to gaze into the face of a phantom. I was unhappy and hated the person I had become. As much as I couldn't bring myself to leave Narva for another woman, I felt that I was in the grip of something out of my control, as if I were being swept along by another kind of wind. Unlike the soft, gentle breeze that had carried me when life was threatened by the forces of man and nature, I knew, at least from a psychological point of view, that the source of the spell that had taken hold of me was internal, not external. The darkness that I slipped into on weekends had completely engulfed me and spun me the way drunkenness makes one forget.

Carl G. Jung would call the other woman of my marriage my "anima," an archetype of the collective unconcious—the inherited image of "woman" embedded in the psyche of every man and projected onto women in the physical world. She is the cause of many human triangles that result in broken marriages. I had always felt the presence of my anima, from my contentious relationship with my mother during my teenage years to my first physical and emotional attraction to girls and women. Although she is purely an unconscious entity, her projections are often manifested in the form of sexual fantasies and attractions, oftentimes leading to negative consequences. Unaware that she is an inherited, "collective" unconscious representation of "woman," men act on the belief and feeling that the woman they have fallen in love with or the flesh and beauty that aroused them is actually a physical being, thus causing the spell to be spun and the relationship damage to be done. There are times, however, when the positive projection of the anima occurs and she becomes the source of insight, inspiration, and creativity. In a poem written for *Spirits of the Gods*, my fourth collection, I spoke of the anima from the viewpoint of the male psyche.

Legion

When he was a young man
    believing he was falling in and out of love,
        their trust in him drowned in his hollowness.
Even in guilt and regret, he yearned for more
of the wild, intoxicating spell they spun.

In his old age, they grow younger, paler,
        and appear everywhere he goes.
He searches their angelic eyes, the silence
between their polite and kind words,
for answers to questions still burning.

He might never know

    they are not the flesh he sees,

        not a legion of beauty
            stalking his dreams and conscience,

    but one spirit, inside him,
        life lived long before his life,
        mind deep below
        the well of his mind,

        raising pillars of cloud and fire,
    bearing imagination, pointing his way
to inner peace and wholeness.

Tuesday before Thanksgiving Day of 2008, I went home after work to find Narva gone. I pushed the message button on the answering machine and heard a message from her, saying that she had had enough and was moving on. I went to her closet to find clothes missing. She didn't answer my phone calls. I went to the bank and discovered that large withdrawals had been made. I called the kids and got no answers or clues as to where their mother was. I panicked and cried. Suddenly, my life became a long blues song that I was living instead of listening to.

Narva had moved into an apartment and was resolved to start a new life without me. We went to counseling but she saw that as something I needed more than she did. Eventually, she stopped going. On the advice of the counselor, I read several books on making faith in God the center of a marriage. *Sacred Marriage* by Gary Thomas opened my eyes to the sanctity of that union. In addition to the broken-heartedness and guilt, I had to deal with the persona that the world had seen and known of me, much of which was now a masquerade shielding my shattered ego. I told several family members about the breakup but said nothing about it at the office, to close neighbors, and in my small circle of friends. Outwardly I displayed collectiveness and normality while inwardly I was nervously breaking down. The face that I wore publicly became more of a mask than the one I had worn in my infidelity. I was embarrassed to admit that I cheated on my wife and dreaded the thought of having failed in the one area of my life that I had the most control over. The mental strain took a toll on my health. I couldn't sleep, had no appetite for food, and lost a considerable amount of weight.

Less than two months after our breakup, I took my first creative writing courses in the University of New Orleans MFA Program, a pursuit that was born on the last day of Callaloo workshops the prior summer. The semester-long assignment of my first poetry course was to write one poem a week on a common theme and compile a chapbook of the poems at the end of the course. Written in third person, the thirteen sonnets that I wrote were about the experience of my separation from Narva. I wrote poems about my pain and loneliness, about moments we spent together while living apart, and about our reconciliation and reunion.

Under the title, "Between After and Before (The House of Ernest and Mathilda)," nine of the sonnets found their way into *A Mandala of Hands*, my first collection, which was published six years later. As it had done after my Uncle Victor's sudden death in the summer of 1994, poetry became my life raft when I was drowning in pain and sorrow. This time, however, poetry was there to stay. It had taken hold of me and was not letting go. My anima was repurposed to become my inspiration and source of creative expression. Narva and I reunited on the eve of Valentine's Day in 2009. The years that followed produced most of the poems of *A Mandala of Hands*. Jung might say that I had begun to tap into the positive unconscious depth of me, the "mandala" or wholeness that I might ultimately discover.

*

Ever since he saw the golden fan petals of a ginkgo,
he's been struck by flowers blooming high above ground.
He had hoped for a day in February when they'd catch
the lavender of Japanese Magnolia before it fell.

That day, they buried his Aunt Sally less than a mile
from where he and the boys of Dixie Homes hopped a fence
and stole pears and he slit his left kneecap on a broken
sandlot bottle. The morning drive took them across
the steep Sunshine Bridge through cypress swampland
and towns girded by dirt levees holding the Atchafalaya River.

It was Friday, the eve of Valentine's Day. Pink roses,
white gold, lobster at Chelsie's. Before dinner, he prayed
questions. He was at the front door and didn't hear her at
first, until she sat him down, folding answers into his hands.

*

She went home in February, the dying days
of winter. Now they wake to sounds of silence,

they listen and touch, and every moment
inside them passes between after and before,

the time when lavender blooms, cardinals feed,
and seedlings sow where earth is bare and frost.

Years will pass. They will see ponds and trees
and unfinished houses around the corner, an old

wooden chapel in the woods. They will pray,
gather leaves and spread flowers, drive into

a gray horizon with sunset peeping behind.
Like memory and dawn, death will come to heal,

wheat will be born and birdsongs will make
sounds for their house. Time will love.

The separation of our marriage was an awakening that literally brought me to my knees. It pushed me toward an awareness of what really mattered in life and awakened me to the realization that the road I was traveling was not just morally wrong, it was self-destructive. Reality had to be shattered for me to see the pieces of me that needed to be made whole. Had that not happened, I would always be in search of something that had the appearance of "self" but was undiscoverable.

After healing our marriage, Narva and I joined Living Faith Christian Center, a Full Gospel church and one of the largest black churches in Baton Rouge. I had attended the church at the suggestion of our daughter Joy. Narva had been a member of Shiloh Baptist Church for many years but the only time I saw the inside of a church was during funerals. We had not worshipped together regularly since 1978, when we were members of Refuge Temple in Lake Charles. At Living Faith, we paid tithes, attended church every Sunday, and went to Bible study on Wednesday evenings. Narva joined the bereavement ministry. I didn't volunteer for any ministry and knew the names of only a handful of church members. Just as I had been at Refuge Temple, I was very much an outsider who was called "Brother Smith" yet acted more like a first-time church visitor.

I have been skeptical of organized religion my entire life and have always felt a great distance between the societal practices of religious belief and my personal conceptualization of God. That probably dates back to my early years growing up in the Catholic church, when the mass was spoken in a foreign language that I didn't speak or understand, the congregation was mostly light-skin black people who looked foreign, and priests were white men who sat behind the shutters of confession booths that frightened me. I find it baffling and disgusting that one hundred sixty years after the abolishment of slavery the ideology of white supremacy is still embedded in the psyche and soul of America, a nation that purports to be religious. The epitome of hypocrisy is church-going white people who give time and money to programs designed to lessen the pain and suffering of poverty, then vote for politicians whose policy agendas only widen social divisiveness and exacerbate the impacts of economic disparities.

Despite the fervent prayer, praising, and singing that takes place in the "house of worship," I also can't help but see it as an organization. Notwithstanding the spiritual enrichment that I get out of the experience, I struggle to get beyond the thought of a church being a "business," especially when it is founded and directed by the pastor and his wife and is grossing at least several million dollars in revenue. Something in me refuses to accept or conform to the structure, rhetoric, and ritualistic practices of religious organizations and not also see them as not-for-profit enterprises that collect a lot of money from their members, pay no taxes, file no tax returns, and provide little information to their members about how collections are spent.

Although I never doubted the sincerity and integrity of the pastor of Living Faith and that he was a man called by God to be a minister, I had concerns about how church revenue was being spent, not the least of which was the large billboard that I saw of the pastor and his wife while enroute to church services. The church was also supporting ministries in Africa and other parts of the world, all worthy causes, but I felt that not enough was being invested in the impoverished neighborhood where the church was located and where many of the tithe-paying members lived. In our first annual meeting of the church in which the year-end financial statements were presented, I was the only member who raised questions about expenses, and the answers I got did not fully satisfy me.

In the twelve years that Narva and I worshipped at Living Faith, the only church member with whom I had regular conversations with was Darrel Smith, the youngest brother of my natural father. A member of the church long before we joined, Darrel was part of the routine of Sunday services. He attended the service immediately after ours and stood in the same spot in the church lobby every Sunday. We chatted with him as we exited. When we hadn't seen him for several weeks, we learned that Darrel was seriously ill and had been hospitalized. In a twist of irony of John D's refusal to help pay tuition for my first semester in college, I later paid a portion of Darrel's funeral expenses with a family burial fund that my sister Tracie and I had established with money that my stepfather had hidden in a dresser drawer. I was deeply moved by the dignified manner in which the church handled Darrel's funeral service. It was the only funeral of a Living Faith member that I attended.

On most Sunday mornings, Narva and I drove separate cars to church. After the service, she went home and I drove seventeen miles to Port Allen to read the Bible to residents of a nursing home there. Even though I feared crossing bridges, especially tall ones, the drive took me across the Mississippi River. I made three stops along the way to buy canned sodas, ice, and several dozen doughnuts. I didn't give much thought to what the residents or nursing home employees thought of me. They called me "Rev," which I surely wasn't and had no desire to be. Most of the residents had mental illnesses that compounded their physical health problems. Strangely, they all seemed very normal to me, and I genuinely enjoyed the time I spent with them.

I don't know why I went to the nursing home those Sundays, except for feelings of guilt for not visiting Aunt Sally when she lived so close to me. She had been a resident of the facility in the late years of her life, but when her health seriously declined she was moved to a respiratory rehabilitation facility and was later admitted to a hospital. Because her nearest child lived two hours away, I was the last family member to see her alive. I will never forget standing alone at her bedside under a dimly glowing light and gazing into the face of her dead body.

Bird Nests
(FOR SALLY BARTLEY)

> One Sunday, when Oriental Magnolia bloomed
> high above the garden, I visited Aunt Sally
> in Room 60, her new home. Like bird nests,
> her lifelong belongings had been tossed to the floor.
>
> From one of the two bundles, I lifted

a blue hooded shirt and pulled it over her head
and shoulders. I slipped a pair of wool clogs
on her feet, then lifted her arms to a walker.

The scars of madness had faded in her face,
shrunken now with thick manly brows, her body
frail as a broken-winged sparrow, weightless
as the air she struggled to breathe in the pain

she could not speak of. I imagine she slept
the way I saw her the following Friday,
lying on her back, mouth open wide and gasping,
her forehead cool as spring water, hair soft

as hand-sewn silk. After the cup-shaped petals
had fallen, I would see her once more. Again
I gathered the straws of her wind-torn nests,
one nof them still bundled, strewn to the floor.

Perhaps my visits to the nursing home were a manifestation
of my longstanding interest in human behavior and study of the
psyche, particularly that of the mentally ill. For certain our marital
reconciliation and my recommitment to live a more Christ-centered
life had much to do with it. Regardless of the reason, my visits there
were blessings that I will always cherish. I befriended many of the
residents who came to the dining hall those Sunday mornings—Mr.
Biddings, Bernadette, Mr. Scott, and Lucy, to name a few, all of whom
died during the years of my visits. They were the only people I knew
whose company I enjoyed enough to want to be with every week,
not to mention crossing a bridge to be there. My visits always ended
with a humbling feeling of humanness. Sometimes I drove away with
a heavy heart for the suffering I had witnessed, bringing me to tears
and prayer as I drove away.

That Sunday routine lasted about seven years, ending after the
great flood of 2016 in Baton Rouge and several years before the
outbreak of the Covid pandemic. They were important moments
and a phase of my life when I grew to appreciate the innocence,
frailty, and vulnerability of the human spirit that we so often ignore
or never see, and I discovered it among the most unassuming people

whom I had ever met and known. I can't say that I really knew them, but if nothing else I saw them. To the rest of the world, they were invisible.

Women of Rose Hill

They could be scarecrows
in their torn ragged clothes
reeking of urine and sweat,
or bronze sculptures, posing stiffly
until their arms nimbly jerk and sway.
You might never see them
melting in the quiet stir of morning coffee,
not even their cupped hands
and slurred, fragmented sentences
with commas of saliva dripping
from the corners of their mouths.

If you lean close, you'll hear
their hallelujah-hellos,
as when Bernadette says:
Things got real bad, so I came here.
Dogs walking down the sidewalk
in broad daylight,
going into the stores and banks,
and nobody gave a damn—
snakes and rats crawling everywhere,
even in church. So I came here.
Or out of the blue Lucy blurts:
You're a nice fellow.
That your wife? Where you from?
Hey, got a dollar for a soda pop?
Pay you back. I promise.

Hold on long enough
and you'll climb the steep slope
beyond your centered self
to the sweet, jagged ledge
where they dance.

I purposely did not connect my service at the nursing home to Living Faith and I did not tell the leaders of the church that I was doing it. I have never measured up to the standards of virtue that people preach or teach of the Gospel, surely not enough to be a church leader or volunteer. My relationship with Jesus Christ matters to me. It is a deeply personal, spiritual relationship that has little if anything to do with membership in a church organization. God is a big, almighty, divine spirit whom I seek to know intimately and not through the structure and hierarchy of churchly affiliation. Still, I understand the importance of church membership to Narva and of us being a part of a community of worshippers, and, quite frankly, I am a better person because of it. It was not by coincidence that after decades of blindness to the creative demon that had been stalking me I bravely turned and stood face to face with it, but only after mending the brokenness of my marriage and becoming more grounded in my Christian faith. My journey toward a realization of self had weathered the biggest storm. Sunlight began to peek through the clouds.

NEXT HORIZON

Education's Next Horizon had been founded by a group of business leaders from every region of the state. Their aim was to develop a non-profit organization whose work would transcend politics and be a strong voice for education reform that would improve academic outcomes. Several of them had personally committed donations of $50,000 per year for three years, but by the time I started working, only one of the commitments had been disbursed, and the money sat in a Shreveport bank. Starting the business with only a personal cell phone and a writing tablet, I immediately set out to establish an office in downtown Baton Rouge within walking distance of the State Capitol. I hired Frances Farlow as my executive assistant, developed operating policies and procedures, and began the work of planning our policy agenda. By the time we started up, one of the incorporators had been appointed Superintendent of the Louisiana Department of Education. The most engaging member of the first Board of Directors was Dr. Phillip A. Rozeman, a Shreveport cardiologist who was a founder and initial funder. A visionary and passionate supporter of public education, Dr. Rozeman was more than our first President and Board Chair. He was like a voluntary co-CEO, who not only developed our initial policy agenda but provided a tremendous amount of guidance to me in our implementation of it.

We could not have gotten off to a better start, establishing a Stakeholder Council comprised of business, education, and community leaders across the state, who came together to undertake a year-long study of early childhood education and workforce skills policies. In 2008, we partnered with the Louisiana Department of Education to launch Louisiana's first-ever conference on dropout prevention. America's Promise Alliance, an organization founded by Retired General Colin Powell and his wife Alma, who was the conference keynote speaker, provided major funding for the initiative, along with the Louisiana Association of United Way and other supporters. The conference was attended by over 800 participants, with leadership representation from every school district. Education's Next Horizon soon became one of the state's leading advocates for increasing high school graduation rates, providing high-quality early childhood education, and bridging the skills gap in the workforce.

In 2010, we established the Louisiana Center for Afterschool Learning (LACAL) in partnership with a national foundation. LACAL would go on to be the leading advocate and network of afterschool programs in Louisiana. A year later we launched a local program of Communities in School (CIS), requiring a staff of social workers who worked in two middle schools and a high school to prepare at-risk students for school success.

Knowing that our work was making a difference in the lives of disadvantaged families and children, I never felt more excited about going to work. In addition to managing the day-to-day operations, I built relationships with key business, education, political, and community partners across the state. I became a member of the Columbia Group, a group of statewide public education advocacy organizations in the Southeast that met several times a year to share information and best practices in education reform. All the knowledge and every skill that I had acquired and developed as a professional was being practiced. I felt a sense of wholeness, a sense of "self."

In the summer of 2007, I attended my second Callaloo Creative Writing Workshop at Texas A&M University. There, I was taught by Tracy K. Smith and Terrance Hayes. Poetry had discovered me, and I was convinced that part of my life's calling was to write poetry. Still, I felt ill-equipped with the skills of technical craftsmanship. I attended my third Callaloo Workshop in 2008 on the campus of the University of Missouri, where I again studied under Tracy K. Smith. On the last day of class, a young workshop participant, who couldn't have been more than nineteen years old, encouraged me to think about pursuing a Master of Fine Arts degree in creative writing. Knowing that I had financial obligations and held a full-time job, I thought it was unthinkable. She suggested that I look at the Low-Residency MFA Program at the University of New Orleans, which would enable me to study online and attend summer residencies abroad. I applied and started the program in January 2009.

I attended my first summer residency in San Miquel, Mexico, in the summer of 2010. A year later, I studied in Edinburgh, Scotland. Narva joined me, and we made it one of the most unforgettable experiences of our marriage, touring the castles, monuments, and countryside of Scotland and taking a train for a weekend excursion to London. While I studied many poets during the MFA program, including Mexican and Scottish writers, as well as British and American romanticist writers, I was closely drawn to Robert Frost. In Frost, I saw reflections of my own poetics, at least regarding the meaning of poetry and the figurative power of symbols and nature. Like Frost, I believe that a poem must run its own course and discover its meaning out of the infinite possibilities of meaning. Frost likened this mystique of poetry to a "piece of ice on a hot stove." He believed that the meaning of the poem must spring spontaneously as a revelation not necessarily intended by the poet but discovered by him or her and ultimately felt by the reader. In writing poetry, I strived to remain open to that element of surprise.

During my studies in Edinburgh, I approached one of my instructors, Dr. John Gery, about chairing my thesis committee. After giving it some thought, he agreed, and my real education in writing poetry began. Two other professors, Kay Murphy and Shelley Puhak, agreed to serve. Although I had probably written at least fifty poems by then, my manuscript would consist of twenty-five poems. Dr. Gery literally dissected every poem and provided invaluable advice on syntax, line breaks, imagery, and sound. There were times when I dreaded pulling the packet of his comments from the mailbox, knowing that I would see his marks on the pages and would have to submit more revisions. In the Spring of 2012, when Dr. Gery called to say that my thesis was approved and I had passed my oral exam, I fell to my knees and cried.

In many poems of my thesis manuscript, and in others that I had not included, I chose natural settings with objects such as trees, birds, flowers, ponds, rivers, stars, sun, and moon as backdrops. Additionally, as with Frost, many of the poems engaged the changing force and variability of the four seasons. Like Frost, I viewed nature as apart and indifferent to human struggles, and I often depicted nature as a metaphor for human vulnerability and adversity. While I saw nature in that context, I also believed that human interaction with and passage through nature can represent the individual's journey toward self-actualization.

The title of my thesis manuscript, *A Mandala of Hands*, was taken from a poem written in the vigil of my mother's illness in May 2003 and became the title of my first collection.

Vigil
FOR MOTHER

You spent your last days tangled
in the tributaries that drowned
every movement and sound.
No bird song lulled
your wind-borne leaves,
but I knew by the candy red
gloss of your nails that you
had come to die.

The walls of your room paled
like frostbit ground.
A calendar had stopped turning.
Like the tulips Akemie sent
FedEx from Gainsville, the balloon
Auriana brought refused to die.
Sermons and songs stayed muted
in the television hanging above
your bundle of belongings.

I could never tell
what your jaundiced stare saw,
whether my words folded
halves of your heart
or colored the portraits
you might have seen
in kisses to your sweat-beading brow.

In days that went too long
without rain
to keep your gladiolas alive,
the May sun locked
a mandala of hands.
Like the Magnolia grove
blooming outside your window,
we circled your bed.

The title figuratively signified the collection's theme. "Mandala" is a Hindu word for "circle." In Jungian psychology, the mandala symbolizes wholeness of the individual self. The imagery of "hand" or "hands" appears in fifteen of the twenty-five poems of my thesis manuscript and in many other poems that eventually comprised the final collection. The "hands" imagery takes on a dual symbolism, conveying the vulnerability to hardship, suffering, and death, and the more positive imagery of healing. In time, the mandala unfolds through the individual and collective trials and strengths of black Americans as woven into history, but in essence comprising a collective journey toward wholeness and liberation.

The poems of my first collection are primarily narrative. Several were composed as dramatic monologues. Six of the forty-four poems of the collection are written about my stepfather during his journey with Alzheimer's. Nine of the poems deal with the suffering of black children, a theme that would be a part of several collections that followed.

"All history," Emerson wrote, "becomes subjective…there is properly no History, only Biography."[2] So it is with the experiences I meant to portray in *A Mandala of Hands*. As is often seen in the poetry of contemporary black poets, the experiences depicted in the manuscript are real, not imagined. Some are biographical, but many happened in another time, long before I was born, and in distant places to people I've never met. But in an important way, I lived these experiences, grew with them, and passed through them in heart and spirit, if not physically in time and place.

As I wrote in my thesis manuscript, each of the experiences portrayed in *A Mandala of Hands* had moved me to feel, think, or act in some way that might bend toward light or virtue, at least as I defined it. Each had in some way shaped the limits and possibilities of my own personal journey—even when I wasn't conscious of their influence. But the poetry of my first collection did more than recount experiences as history. I believe that whether one lives inside or outside those events, knowing or encountering them through poetry draws an individual nearer to the experience, so much so that the poem

[2]https://archive.vcu.edu/english/engweb/transcendentalism/authors/emerson/essays/history.html

becomes a window to the heart, enabling one to see and remember what might otherwise be overlooked, ignored, or forgotten. I was blessed that Karen Kelsay, owner of Kelsay Books / Aldrich Press agreed to publish my first book. She was only a handful of publishers that I had queried.

My mother was the oldest of ten girls who were born a year or two apart. "Sisters Mourning," one of my favorite poems of the collection, grew out of my reflection of sisters growing old and dying, and how universal that experience is for large black families.

Sisters Mourning

That year, the old sisters wore black in every season,
emptying hope chests like a roof-tearing twister—
so much to keep, so little to pass on. They must have sensed
fear flashing in their uteruses and wondered

what locust larvae lay dormant beneath the goldenrod,
boring their tender limbs, reminding them
of limpid skies, how bound they were to things living.
Some days they gathered to celebrate the family—

Sundays in the sun, young lovers with nests
full of babies, old lovers with memories cradled
in their brows. Circled beneath a canopy of oaks,
they boiled blue crabs and crawfish in an open flame.

They told their stories with songs and black-and-white
photographs, between shuffled cards and dots counted
on small ivory stones. Now, four hand fans later,
the sisters speak of fallen branches. They take refuge

in beveled mirrors, in quiet times with questions
dangling in a slipknot. From their necks hang
hand-knitted scarves and the albatrosses
of pain not forgiven, salutations written but not sent.

Still, they wait to see patterns quilted for the spring
bazaar, the evergreens blooming in their winters.
Through the lives of their great grandchildren unborn,
they wait, silent about their steep climbs and falls.

Although I would not receive my MFA degree until May 2012, I had already started teaching English as an adjunct at Southern University in Baton Rouge. Shortly before being told of the approval of my thesis and oral exam, I was accepted to Cave Canem, the prestigious and highly competitive program for black poets founded by Toi Derricotte and Cornelius Eady. My application for acceptance to Cave Canem had been rejected twice. In December 2011, several days before the submission deadline, I decided to apply again. When I received the acceptance letter in April 2012, I did cartwheels across the floor. I graduated from UNO with honors in May 2012. A month later, I began the three-year writing program that literally changed my life as a poet. I attended the Cave Canem one-week writing retreat in 2012, 2013, and 2014.

In the Spring of 2013, I was blessed to be published in *Ploughshares*, the second top literary journal in the country, with a poem that I felt was a long shot to be published anywhere. In the summer of 2012, the editor of the journal informed me that my poem, "Zydeco on Dog Hill," would be sent to Major Jackson, the guest editor for a future issue of the journal. I didn't get the final answer until December, but it was worth waiting for. When I opened the Spring issue of *Ploughshares*, I discovered that I was doubly blessed to be on a page opposite of a poem by Tracy K. Smith, who by then had been awarded the Pulitzer Prize for *Life on Mars*. Being on the opposite page of Tracy K. Smith in *Ploughshares* was *my* Pulitzer. I would have the added pleasure of socializing with her and Major Jackson at a reception held at Emerson College in March 2013 to launch the issue in conjunction with the Association of Writers and Publishers Conference in Boston, Massachusetts.

Zydeco on Dog Hill

Before they put Cousin Gladys
inside the ground in a cornrow
of fair-skinned Creole men, I sat
in her funeral mass imagining
two shadows dancing in the swish
of a swift moving blade
that slit her dreams in half
and sent her father strolling

across the cane field
like a land-bending river, turning
a page she could never turn back:
news that a man had been killed,
her husband had been jailed.
I heard spoons scratching
a washboard, and a zydeco
accordion pump a groove
through a sweat-dripping rumble
of fast-shuffling feet. I felt
the wooden floor turn to water
and tasted the salty wave
as Jo Jo, her lover, swung out,
flaunting his gabardine
in two tones, his wide brim
fedora suddenly seen
whirling in a herd of flamingos
and a pool of whiskey-warm blood.

At Cave Canem, I was taught by some of America's award-winning poets and was in the company of many writers who would go on to literary stardom. In addition to Toi and Cornelius, my instructors at Cave Canem included Terrance Hayes, Harryette Mullen, Patricia Smith, Chris Abani, Nikky Finney, Thomas Sayers Ellis, Angela Jackson, and others. In 2012, the legendary Amiri Baraka and Nikki Giovanna were guest lecturers.

Upon graduating from Cave Canem, I grew more committed to the advice that Langston Hughes spoke to black writers in his 1926 essay, "The Negro Artist and the Racial Mountain," that black writers should not strive to write "white" but should let their art reflect the beauty, ugliness, and struggles of ordinary black people. I was determined to write "black," especially in light of the struggles that I had experienced growing up and living in the Jim Crow South. I was also determined to publish my first book, and immediately began assembling poems to include in the manuscript.

One Sunday morning in July 2013, I got a call from a hospital in Jennings, Louisiana, telling me that my father had gone into cardiac arrest. I was shocked, because of all the health problems Daddy had, the condition of his heart was never a concern. But I knew that he was at a stage of Alzheimer's when his body and vital systems would begin to break down. Knowing that I was two hours away, they said that they would do whatever they could to keep him alive until I got there, but I had to hurry. I sped down I-10 driving 100 miles an hour, but I got there just after Daddy took his last breath. Our journey had ended. I spent the night at a hotel in Lake Charles and went to the funeral home and his church the following morning to arrange for his funeral mass and burial. Parting was painful.

While waiting for my first book to be published, the theme or concept of my second collection was born. In June 2014, while waiting to board an airplane in Charlotte, North Carolina, en route to Pittsburg for a Cave Canem Retreat, I opened an email from my son Patrick. It was Father's Day, and the email was Patrick's gift to me, a rather long letter in which he mostly expressed praise and gratitude but also mentioned moments when he felt my shortcomings as a father. He was speaking from a different point of view than a son to a father. As a father of two young boys, he now had the experience of being a father and understanding the challenges of that responsibility.

I read that email many times in the first two days at Cave Canem, struggling with a response. Should I apologize to him for not being a perfect father? Should I express regrets as my natural father did in a letter that he had written to me twenty-five years ago? What advice can I offer him as a father of two black boys growing up in Chicago? Should I write another *Fire Next Time, Notes of a Native Son*, or *Between the World and Me*, and make my reply to him a pivoting point on a discourse about the race problem in America and how black men suffer because of the color of their skin?

On the first or second day at Cave Canem, I attended a workshop in which the poetry of the young British poet Warsan Shire was presented. Within several hours of reading her poem "Ugly," I had written a draft of "Dumb," which spoke to the shortcomings of a black father and the inherent capacity of his son to overcome adversity and "take back his soul."

Dumb
(AFTER WARSAN SHIRE)

> Your son is dumb, a nobody,
> without honor, country, or history.

Talk to him.
The books he reads do not.

Have you not told him
life is mean but fair,
God created the stars, wind, and sea
and slave ships passed,
God parted the sea
and slave masters drowned?

So what, that your son's belly
bears the marks of your teeth
and blunt edges of your fist.
So what that his father is a ravaging wolf.
Your son is a shark
with no reverence for life,
not even his own.
Does he not know
that no loving outstretched arms,
no prayer, salt, or grail will save him?

Fathers tell their daughters
to not go near him,
not let his words be pomegranates
or the soft-drip thaw of ice on the myrtles.
They tell their daughters
your son grows like a reed in the wind
and dreams only when he sleeps.
Talk to your son.
Tell him what it means to be a man.

Why the blindfolding fog
between his hand on a trigger
and the barb-wired walls
that will bend his knees?
Why the gorge
between his head and heart?
Can you not fill *that* hole in him?

Have you not told him
how *he* could sail the ship

that bounds and carries him,
and he needs no stars, moon, or lighthouse
for the rogue waves
and swirling forked strait?
Does he not know
he can bend rivers, storm the palisade
and take back his soul?

The following day I wrote "Hands," a two-part poem about my Grandfather Andrew's imprisonment for killing a man when he was 27 years old and about my own close encounter with imprisonment when I was a teenage boy. After writing those poems, I decided how I would respond to Patrick's letter. I would write a collection of poetry dedicated to him that spoke to the heart and soul of black boys and young black men. That week, while continuing to reflect on Patrick's letter, I felt compelled to respond to the letter that my natural father had written me and that I had never replied to, so I wrote a reply to him, eleven years after his death.

Reply to the Letter from John D.

One night, nearly two decades before you wrote,
I drove a few miles from home and called you

from a roadside pay phone, needing help
for my college tuition. My memory has grown

kinder over the years but in plain truth you said
no. Slowly, the sound grew faint then silent

but the wound of your words never healed.
That was the first and last time I asked

anything of you. And then, one day I heard
that my grandmother, your mother, had died.

She had always made me feel loved, like one
of her children. I learned of her death

incidentally, a week after she had been buried.
It has taken me twenty-five years to reply

to your letter. My hurt buried you long before
we laid you inside those narrow, tunneled

walls. There can be no reconciliation,
only your loss and regret, but I forgive you.

Patrick's letter had become a mirror, not only of the good and bad of my fatherhood, but of the pain that I had not let go as a son, and of my need to heal the wound that was now in my power to heal. Writing "Reply to the Letter from John D." was a redeeming, liberating experience, to finally forgive my father for choosing not to be a part of my life. As an eighteen-year-old, my father was as much a "native son" of America in the Jim Crow Era as I would eventually become. His country did not cause him to abandon me, but as a young black man who suddenly and unexpectedly found himself in fatherhood, and with dreams of success deferred and shattered, his country offered no other way but for him to escape the reality and weight of that responsibility. That doesn't explain or compensate for his absence in later years, when he had remarried and raised five other children, but I now knew, even long after his death, that I had the power to bridge the gulf through love and forgiveness. Through poetry, I was finally able to say what a hardened, unforgiving heart couldn't say when I read my father's letter twenty-five years before and tucked it away in a chest on the shelf of my bedroom closet.

All the poems composed during my final retreat at Cave Canem, and several that I wrote in prior retreats, were eventually published in literary journals. Spending an entire week in the company of black poets for three summers was an indescribably uplifting experience. The Cave Canem workshops caused me to be more deeply introspective and to see and speak as much to my inner self as to the outer world. After completing three retreats and graduating as a CC fellow, I felt that, more than anything else, I was a poet, and I had a poetic voice that was uniquely *me*. I credit Cave Canem for igniting the fire that I had been kindling for two decades.

The title of my second collection, *Soul Be A Witness*, was taken from the longest poem of the collection, a dramatization of the 1922 murder trial of my Uncle Emile, in which I spoke in the voice of ten people who were figures in the actual trial. Years before, while studying at the Callaloo Writing Workshop, I had presented my first version of the poem to A. Van Jordan, a workshop instructor. His feedback was that as a history poem, the piece was too rhetorical and lacked poetic style and imagery. Armed with knowledge acquired in graduate school and with the experiences of Cave Canem, I revised the poem and made it the centerpiece of the collection.

Focused on a theme that I had lived as a black boy and young man growing up in the Jim Crow and Civil Rights eras, the other poems of the collection easily followed. As native sons of America, boys of color have had to bear a unique burden, that of the history of slavery and Jim Crow and the timeless burden of their darker skin, which never ceases to shape the perception that others have of their intellect, worth, and sense of morality. But the struggle has not been entirely racial. Like all males, black and brown boys are pulled and swayed between the "I" and the "Not I" on a journey of choices. *Soul Be A Witness* attempts to go beyond history, biography, and contemporary influences to capture the inner, spiritual struggles and possibilities— archetypal forces—that shape and ultimately define the individual and collective journey toward manhood and selfhood. The poems of the collection call upon the inner self, the soul if you will, to be a witness to itself…to witness its good and evil, its weaknesses, shortcomings, and vulnerabilities, but invariably, to know its abiding strength and power to overcome adversity.

I am especially fond of "Stars," a poem selected by Tupelo Quarterly as a finalist for the TQ5 Poetry Contest in 2014. MadHat Press accepted the final manuscript of *Soul Be A Witness* for publication, and the book was released in 2016.

Stars

New Orleans, a Tuesday, 7:30 A.M.
I'm sipping coffee at a McDonald's on Canal
when two young black men, early twenties perhaps,
walk in, buying nothing. Suddenly,
I'm aboard a mother ship,
streaking toward the farthest stars.

One, like a fly, bobs the aisles, sweaty
in his *Crown Royal* muscle shirt.
Gym shorts hanging off his ass,
headset in his ears, he pantomimes
a singer and dances a Mardi Gras mambo
in July, with himself, second lining
silky-smoothly across the floor, out the door,
onto the parking lot—his own block party
without the block.

The other, well-groomed, small backpack,
talks loudly, eloquently to himself
about home, what it is, isn't, and should be; then,
facing the faces, he launches a soliloquy
of senseless babble,
and you sense the other—
the voices, a stage, curtain, and cast,
his fans and followers looking on,
inside his head.

I'm gazing stars. Drawn to the glow
of their wayward worlds,
I can't help
but pause, watch, and listen.
I'm entertained,
but scared, because they're black men
and I'm one, too,
with a son and grandsons of my own,
and I can't help
but ponder: what's loose,
what's broken, what's gone wrong,
what's the fix?

Despite having published two collections of poetry, I felt invisible in the vastness of the literary world. I was an unknown entity, writing in the quietness and aloneness of my personal spaces, but not destined to be an award-winning writer whose poetry the world would take note of. There were many moments of disappointment and rejection that lurked like demons to discourage the creative self, but I kept writing and submitting, finding encouragement in occasional acceptances of work by journals and in invitations to read publicly. Intuitively, I felt that my poetry was perhaps too "black" or too much about race to warrant any serious attention or accolades. I knew that except for *Callaloo* and *Ellipsis*, a journal based at UNO, literary journals below the "Mason-Dixon" line had not accepted my work for publication. Still, I continued to write, more out of necessity to let the creative demon in me breathe and speak.

In early 2016, I approached Dennis Paul Williams, a long-time friend, about undertaking a project that he and I had talked about doing from time to time. Dennis was a visual artist whom I had known since the early 1980s. I loved his art and bought some of it on layaway while working in a cubicle at Lafayette City Hall and struggling to support a wife and three young children. I had purchased my latest piece of art from him in 1997 for $2,400, before he became unaffordable. We discussed doing a collaboration of his art and my poetry, a project that was inspired by a book by Chris Abani, an award-winning poet and novelist and one of the workshop instructors in my last year at Cave Canem. Chris had teamed with the renowned artist Percival Everett to produce *There Are No Names for Red* (Red Hen Press 2010), a collection of Abani's poems inspired by pieces of Everett's art.

Spirits of the Gods (UL Press 2017) has thirty-two paintings and thirty-two poems. Over six months, Dennis texted me photographs of his art. As I stated in my personal notes to the collection, I would print the images and begin the writing process, studying and meditating on the art in search of poetry. The creation of each poem was always spontaneous, made in the moment of my contact with the painting itself. I would scribble notes on the back of each printed image… thoughts, feelings, symbols, metaphors…whatever the image conjured or inspired. Eventually, a poem was found and created. I wrote one poem at a time and did not move on to another one until I felt that the poem was finished.

Dennis' work is very spiritually grounded. In musing over his work, I returned to Carl Jung's psychoanalytic theories of the unconscious and archetypes and found parallels in Dennis' work. As in Dennis' art, the poems focus on inner, unconscious forces, "gods" if you will, that influence how we respond to the outer world and who we ultimately become, individually and collectively. Some poems were born out of my faith in religious belief, some out of myth. Some simply grew out of reflections on history and personal experiences or were inspired by local, national, and global events that happened that summer. Each painting and poem is unique, but there is a definite spiritual and psychoanalytical underpinning to what was imagined. While meditating on Madonna figures in several pieces of the art, the fictional character Hannah was born.

Silhouette

My cousin Hannah sleeps in the dungeon of a castle
with men whose hands and words
make her sing with her mouth closed.
Others make her mouth their music
and sear their names into her flesh.

She doesn't feel the pincers pulling, pecking
on her brokenness. Her mother thinks
it began when Hannah started lighting candles,
rooms full of them, or the day her Magic Mirror
shattered in a prayer she sang morning to morning,
as if she weren't a flower blooming only in the night,
peddled on street corners, as if she weren't a bird
feeding on wild mushrooms
while her babies were dying of starvation.

With Hannah the portrait and silhouette
do the posing. Her makeup doesn't wash off.
It's the shadow of her soul that breathes,
walks the alleys, sells the body to gain a world.

Hannah's Epiphany

She doesn't see them anymore:
her crimson petals wilting,
the masquerading personas,
all the faces appearing in her mirrors
and outwardly to a world
indifferent to her pain.

All she sees now is that crystal night
she once dreamt, when she gathered

her beauty and sure-footedness,
folded them into the hem of her dress,
jumped off a steep cliff
and went tumbling,
careening into the abyss.

She can't see or hear
what lies beneath or ahead:
ocean, ground, dark deep ravine,
Sunday sermons echoing,
but she knows she must go there.

In June of that year, 2016, Muhammad Ali died. That weekend, while studying a piece of Dennis' art, I was inspired to write my first poem about Ali, originally published in *MockingHeart Review*.

In the Wake

Rain pouring all day.
Tributes, photo shots, film footage.

He floats.
He jabs.
He whups ass.
He mouths off.
He rhymes.
He defies.
He lights a torch.

The Greatest is dead.

I can't stop the rain.

Can't stop remembering a boy
dreaming, shadowboxing,
shuffling feet—me
pretending to be
Ali.

That summer, two other events which gained national attention became subjects of poems inspired by Dennis's art: the Orlando nightclub shooting and the killing of Alton Sterling in Baton Rouge. The Alton Sterling poem, "Why Being a Black Father in America Today Frightens and Angers Me," was selected for publication in *Black Lives Have Always Mattered, A Collection of Essays, Poems, and Personal Narratives* (2Leaf Press 2017), edited by the legendary poet, Abiodun Oyewole.

Why Being a Black Father in America Today Frightens and Angers Me

> FOR IT IS NOT LIGHT THAT IS NEEDED, BUT FIRE;
> IT IS NOT THE GENTLE SHOWER, BUT THUNDER.
> WE NEED THE STORM, THE WHIRLWIND, AND THE EARTHQUAKE.
> —FREDERICK DOUGLASS, 1852

I am an American, a descendant of an African boy
who was stolen from his family, brought
to America, and sold into slavery.
I am a father and grandfather of black boys
born and living in America,
doing honest work,
not committing crimes,
not hurting people.

> We walk and drive down city streets,
> get stopped by flashing blue lights, cars
> emblazoned with the word POLICE.
> White men who stop us step out of their cars,
> pull their guns, shoot, and kill us.

Twice this week, when I closed my eyes
to sleep, the rat-a-tat-tat of gunfire
and the screaming cries of mothers
rang in my ears. I saw blood
pouring out of a man's body, two men:
> Alton Sterling and Philando Castile,
> black, young—shot and killed
> by white police officers in two American cities.
In Baton Rouge, Alton Sterling was shot multiple times
at execution range after he was wrestled

to the ground and pinned down on his back
like a man being nailed to a cross.

Too often the purveyors of justice have seen
   such horrifying images and viral afterimages,
   far too many, but not enough for them
to see the guilt and dishonor
of militarized police officers
   who kill innocent African American boys and men.

I consider the Alton Sterling poem a giant step up the racial mountain, not because it was published in the anthology and in my third collection, but because I had held true to myself as a black writer in speaking on what is debatably the most controversial racial problem plaguing American society. It was a poem that no white poet could have written and with a message that could only be spoken by a black father and grandfather.

Several months after the killing of Alton Sterling, Baton Rouge experienced a disastrous flood caused by days of rain. One morning, I looked out of a front window and saw a foot of water in the street. I went outdoors and saw neighbors scrambling to lay sandbags. A coulee bordering the back of the golf course overtopped with backwater. I rode with a neighbor and his sons to fill sandbags for our front porch. By the end of the day, the entrance to the subdivision was unpassable and we were wading in the street with water up to our knees. The entire parish of East Baton Rouge was experiencing one of the worst floods in its history. Water continued to rise. Homes directly across the street from us that bordered the golf course started receiving water. Everyone scrambled to help them. By the third day of the flood, water reached my chest as I walked from my front door to the neighbors across the street. Fortunately, the homes on our side of the street dodged a bullet and did not flood.

The disaster brought out both the worst and best of some neighbors. It brought us together, and for the first time, I got to know the names of people whom I had lived near for fifteen years. One neighbor, who moved in many years after Narva and I, asked me how it was playing professional football. "Football?" I responded. "Yeah, I heard you retired from the Denver Broncos." I have no idea how that rumor started, but I understood why it was necessary that some white people, unable to see the *invisible man*, had to make me a black man who could afford to live that close to them and who they felt comfortable living near.

A week later, when the high water had finally subsided and things were somewhat back to normal, I heard music in the backyard of a neighbor who lived adjacent to us and whose yard was the least kept lawn of the entire block. Wanting to get information about a rumor I had heard about the bayou starting to rise again, I grabbed a ladder and peeped over the fence to ask if he had heard the rumor. I saw a group of people huddled around each other. The next day I learned quite surprisingly that he had held a "hamburger party" with all the close neighbors to celebrate the end of the flood. Narva and I hadn't been invited. We had lived next door to him, his wife, and their three large dogs for sixteen years. That incident caused me to reflect on what is needed for me to be invited to walk through the front door, through the house, and into the backyard of a white neighbor's home. In Santa Maria, there were moments when I felt like an enslaved black man living inside his own home.

Through Unsettling Mist

Two burglaries late one night
in a so-called up-scale neighborhood,
where you might see one black guy
at his mailbox, tending his lawn,
or pulling out of the driveway.

That night, I peeped out a front window
after seeing police lights flashing.

A half hour later, more blue lights,
then more, then flashlights shining
inside the homes of two white neighbors
vacationing on Memorial Day.

Still wearing yard clothes,
I thought of opening my front door
and stepping out to the porch,
but a silent voice reminded me
that I was a black man.

So, I kept the door shut,
and gazed through unsettling mist,

>   thinking about the arrest
>   of Dr. Henry Louis Gates Jr.
>   after he entered his own home,

and pondering the frightening question
of why any black man in America today
would hesitate to stand on his front porch,
not for fear of being a victim of a crime
but a suspect of committing one.

LATER WORKS

I didn't set out to write a collection of poems about Muhammad Ali. Still stunned by his death and feeling the loss of him, I sat at a computer one day in the summer 2017, nearly a year after he died, wondering what poems had been written about him. The thought entered my head that a good book concept would be an anthology of those poems. Searching the Internet, and much to my surprise, I found only a handful. At that moment, the idea of the collection was born. I immediately began my research, downloading articles and ordering books and DVDs. I became completely immersed in every detail of Ali's life, from his boyhood days in Louisville to his career as a boxer, and ultimately his work as an ambassador for peace while being stricken with Parkinson's. I read extensively, watched every documentary of him that I could find, and repeatedly watched his major fights. My research had to extend beyond Ali's personal and professional life to capture the social and political climate of the American half-century when Ali stood on the world stage.

The collection would be biographical but poetic. Structurally, I wanted it to chronologically highlight the important events and moments of Ali's journey. In the beginning, my research and reading didn't follow that order. I simply allowed myself to delve into every facet of his life, making notes as I went along. Before I started writing poems, I developed an outline of how the manuscript would be structured, noting timeframes and turning points in Ali's life. The original outline was simply a framework. I regularly revised it to note milestones, people, and events of Ali's life that needed to be put into the manuscript. But I didn't let poetry be constrained by structure. If a poem started to speak, I listened and let it "float like a butterfly." In a big way, I reflected through a personal lens.

Big Brother Muhammad

> I never had the pleasure of meeting Muhammad Ali
> or seeing him in person, but I've always admired him

as an athlete and a person who had the courage
to stand up for what he thought was right.
Muhammad was ten years older than me.
In some way, I saw him as the big brother
that I didn't have. Like all the boys my age,
I thought he was exactly what he proclaimed
himself to be—The Greatest. I recited
his silly rhymes and shadowboxed,
pretending I was him, never any other fighter.

In April of 1967, when Muhammad refused
to be inducted, I was 14 years old.
That fall, I became a ninth-grade student
at a white junior high school in the first year
of public school integration in my community.
I was one of only five black students there,
and one of two black males. I was the darker
skin Negro boy. That year was without a doubt
the loneliest and most depressing experience
of my life up to that point. A school day rarely
ended when I hadn't been treated in the most
degrading way, and hadn't felt humiliated
just because of the color of my skin.

My father was a great fan of boxing, especially
of Sugar Ray Robinson and Muhammad Ali.
Watching Friday night boxing on television
was like being in church on Sunday morning.
Except for home, I was seldom in places
where I heard grown people talk about Ali,
but I heard his story on the evening news.
Strangely, I felt a kinship: like me,
Muhammad was alone.

Of course, I knew we were different.
I was an ordinary, poor black boy
and he was heavyweight champ of the world.
I understood that our circumstances
and experiences were different. Still,
I felt that we had something in common.
We were black and living in a world

in which we were misunderstood
or not understood at all. People hated us
just for being ourselves. We weren't trying
to pretend or be somebody we weren't.
People just hated us for being who we were.
I felt proud that he was black
and had taken a stand against the Army,
and although I didn't understand
the Muslim religion or the Viet Nam war,
I admired Muhammad
for what he did and why he did it.
I never doubted his sincerity.

That was the cement of my bond
with Muhammad, then and over the years
that followed. My admiration for him grew
as I grew older. He is my greatest hero.

Several publishers accepted the manuscript, but I contracted with Lavender Ink, a New Orleans-based press owned by Bill Lavender, a former professor and advisor of mine at UNO. The editing process proved to be challenging for both of us, largely due to my meticulous attention to detail. I wanted the collection to not only be factually and grammatically correct but to be a poetic product worthy of homage to The Greatest.

For a modest fee, Getty Images allowed me to use the most iconic photograph of Ali for the front cover, the photograph taken by sports photographer Neil Liefer of Ali standing over Sonny Liston and taunting him after knocking him out in the first round of the May 1965 rematch in which Ali retained his crown as the heavyweight boxing champion of the world. I wanted the buyers of the collection, many of whom would no doubt be fans and admirers of Ali, to have that photograph.

The poems of the book were widely accepted by literary journals. By the time the manuscript went to print, 22 of the 43 poems had been accepted for publication. *The Missouri Review* asked for six poems. Unfortunately, only "The Torch" was still available, which they agreed to feature as Poem of the Week in the June 04, 2018, issue of their online journal, commemorating the second anniversary of the death of Ali on June 3, 2016.

The Torch

Muhammad, twenty years before you left us,
we saw you appear out of pitch-black darkness

on a mountainside and watched you step
slowly toward a blooming bush. Your hands,

trembling like a man twice your age, held
a lit torch and raised it high above your head,

as if you were saluting your maker, the first
and only lasting spirit of humankind.

You reached down and touched the bush
with your torch until an all-consuming fire

lit the midnight sky. Through tears, joy,
and adulation, through history and your life

flashing before us, we watched you stand
straight and strong until you became

our lives, our torch, our flaming, blooming
cauldron for dark, unsettling days.

For the back cover, I was blessed to have the words of Hana Ali, the third youngest child of Ali and the author of several books about him; Charles deGravelles, a Baton Rouge-based writer who had published a book on the legendary football star Billy Cannon; and renowned poet Nikki Giovanni.

I discovered Giovanni's long-term friendship with Ali during my research. I had met her when she was a guest lecturer at the Cave Canem Retreat of 2012, took a picture with her, and gave her a writing pen that I cherished dearly. Knowing that it would be a long shot, I found her email address on the website of Virginia Tech University, where she served as the University Distinguished Professor of English, and sent her a copy of the manuscript, asking that she consider reading it and providing a blurb for the book. When she didn't respond after two weeks, I decided to call the phone number of her office. To my complete surprise, she answered the phone. "I don't do email," she said, "but if you mail me a copy I would gladly read it." Several weeks later, the blurb arrived in an envelope containing her handwritten note. I was ecstatic.

Every poem in the collection is a favorite of mine. One that I am particularly fond of celebrates Ali's invisibility as a young heavyweight champ.

Renaissance Man

After Liston, they fell like dominoes:
Folley, Terrell, Williams, Mildenberger,
London, Cooper, Chuvalo, and Patterson,
dizzied by his lightning quick jabs
and the waltz of his dazzling white shoes,
sparkling like chrome
as he bicycled across the canvas.

We stood witness to the creation
of modern-day myth—Black Superman
from Krypton, Kentucky,
undefeated god of the ring,
clairvoyant and charismatic,
denigrating and taunting challengers

while staring into his crystal ball.

He wanted to go to heaven so I beat him in seven.
It ain't no jive, he'll go in five.
He might be great but he'll fall in eight.

Ali vernacular.
Ali meter.
Ali rhyme.
Ali renaissance:
     black beauty,
     black ballet,
     black poetry
on the wings of a butterfly,

with foot work, hand speed, and power
that whupped ass.

In the summer of 2018, I reached out to the Ali Center in Louisville, Kentucky, about selling *Muhammad's Mountain* at the museum's bookstore. Although they didn't agree to stock the book, they invited me to attend the annual Muhammad Ali Humanitarian Awards Gala scheduled to be held in September 2018. They also agreed to my doing three readings of the poems the morning after the Gala in conjunction with the premier showing of the *City of Ali*, a documentary sponsored by the City of Louisville that chronicled events of the week immediately following Ali's death. It was a dream come true. Before the Gala started, I was photographed on the Red Carpet and had individual photographs taken with Ali's wife Lonnie and me, and with Martin Luther King, III. During the banquet, I sat as a guest of the table of Muhammad Ali's younger brother Rahman Ali and his wife, along with several close relatives and friends of The Greatest.

The next morning, I stood at a podium in the auditorium of the Ali Center with *Muhammad's Mountain* in my hand and did three readings, one preceding each showing of the documentary. During one of the readings, I gazed at the audience and saw Martin Luther King III sitting there. One of the poems I read was "Black Power," a poem about Ali's first fight after being in exile for over three years. Coretta Scott King was at ringside of that fight, and I'm sure that Dr. King would have been there had he been alive.

Black Power

>October 1970. Jackson 5 tops the charts.
>>Ali three years without a fight. Like a buzzard,
>>>jail time hovers over his head. Tonight,

>the ring is his stage again, black drama
>>on the big screen in badass, blaxploitation fashion.
>>>Ali coming back. Quarry, the latest Great White Hope,

>a hired dream killer. But this is Muhammad Ali
>>after three years in exile. This is Atlanta, GA, where
>>>black dreams come true, on a night

>when blackness steps out dressed to kill. Black actors,
>>athletes, singers, pimps, preachers, prostitutes,
>>>and politicians – all panache, all here to see

The Greatest, cheer him on, hear his mouth,
    watch him float, duck, and jab. Ringside sideshows
        decked in mink, fur, diamonds, and pearls.

This is Nation Time, Civil Rights, Black Power Time.
    And tonight, no one is blacker, prettier,
        more right and powerful than The Champ.

That moment was a poem to be written. I didn't sell books at the reading. Every one of them was a signed gift to someone, including King and several of Ali's children. Still, I returned to Baton Rouge inspired and uplifted. Unfortunately, without an agent and being published by a small press that does little to market its books nationally, *Muhammad's Mountain* didn't win praise beyond the Muhammad Ali Center and the borders of Louisiana. It didn't win a prize or a nomination for one. Despite the publication of half the poems by literary journals, it was just another ordinary book of poetry.

But such is my life as a poet. Although it is nice to have work recognized and to see one's name in the company of award-winning writers, I had long ago abandoned those yearnings. There was a phase of my life as a public administrator when I collected news clippings of my name in print. I felt a deep sense of accomplishment, especially as a black public administrator, to reach what I had worked hard and made many sacrifices to achieve, and to be at the pinnacle of my profession. It was equally gratifying to be in a small number of black officers in a large bank. I hadn't been an undergraduate college student of creative writing. I didn't attend workshops and formally study creative writing late in life to write poetry for recognition or acclaim, and I certainly didn't publish books to make money.

Fortunately, the realization that I am a poet came long after I had achieved professional success, and at a stage of life when financial security was not as critical of a motivating factor as it had been while struggling to realize the American dream of material success. As an older writer and teacher, and especially a black artist, I write out of a sense of obligation and responsibility to express feelings or reflections of truth in the hope that my poetry will shine a little light on darkness. That carries no price or expectation for reward. I never question the purpose or outcome of creating art, knowing that I create for the sake of art and humankind, not me. I am content to leave the fate of what I create to the world that finds it.

Art

> I never had a racial encounter
> that didn't anger me,
> even while I stooped
> to cast down a bucket.
> Those words say nothing
> about my pain,
> a native son of America
> struggling to find work,
> pay some bills,
> keep a roof over my head,
> and feed my family.
> I'm standing alone
> on a street corner
> that has no signs,
> peddling my soul
> and singing the blues
> to icy-cold air.
> My shoes barely got soles
> and I have no coat.
> I've got two dollars
> on my government card.
> So if you find my verse
> too void of verve
> or my painting
> of raised fists
> in broken chains
> too racial and black,
> hell, light a fire, let art burn.

In some ways, I think, that was part of Muhammad Ali's legacy. He did what no boxer will ever do in the history of the sport. But in the end, Ali was much more than that. While battling Parkinson's disease, he didn't have to seek God. God had always been with him and he knew that. What he sought and found was his higher purpose, not as a fighter but as a humanitarian and champion of world peace.

By 2016, as initial funding commitments supporting the core advocacy work of Education's Next Horizon fell off, we began to downsize. CIS, which had lost funding support from its national CIS partner, could no longer sustain operations and was reduced from five to two employees. The program was later absorbed by a CIS organization in New Orleans. LACAL, which had only one employee, was moved to Louisiana Tech University. By 2018, the staff of Education's Next Horizon had gone back to its original size with a CEO and an executive assistant. Revenue constraints necessitated that I eliminate the executive assistant position in early 2019, leaving me as the only employee. I moved to a two-room office and went there every day to do research and advocacy work that justified my salary, but our impact as a statewide education policy advocate had greatly diminished.

Major funders of the organization had either left or made significant cutbacks in financial support, but the Board of Directors showed no interest in fundraising. I felt that I was only writing grant applications to keep a job. Sensing our inevitable closure, I reached out to large, organizational stakeholders about establishing strategic partnerships that at best would provide enough funding to buy time, knowing that without a significant infusion of cash, the bank balance would not sustain the organization beyond 2020. The strategic partnership opportunities failed to materialize, and at the start of 2020 we began the process of dissolution. We officially shut down on December 31st. By the end of our thirteen-year life as an education policy advocate, Louisiana had reformed its early care and education system and begun to see significant improvement in both the quality of preschool care and the readiness of children to enter kindergarten. The state's graduation rate had risen from 67% in 2007 to over 80. Education's Next Horizon can take little credit for those improvements, but we clearly had a voice that contributed, at a time when advocacy for change was sorely needed.

At that point in my career, I had little interest in working for anyone, public or private. Although I sent several emails under the subject of "transitioning" to trusted colleagues, after having directed organizations most of my career, I had no burning desire to be somebody's subordinate employee. At worst, I could teach parttime, write, and draw Social Security until I began withdrawing from my

IRA. Narva and I started talking about selling the house and moving closer to family members in Lake Charles or Lafayette.

In early 2019, an email appeared in my inbox about the applications and selection process for selection of the next Poet Laureate of Louisiana. The appointment would be made by Governor John Bel Edwards in July or August 2019. The idea of being the Poet Laureate of Louisiana had entered my head at one point and vanished just as quickly. Although I felt as qualified and capable as any of the recently named state poet laureates, I knew that there were poets much more qualified than me who deserved consideration. While there had been two African American women named to the office, there had never been a black male. I thought, "Why not me?" With no encouragement from anyone, I decided to apply.

I reached out to Patrice Melnick, a former professor at UNO and the founder of Festival of Words, a cultural arts organization that had provided strong support of every collection that I published. She agreed to write the nomination letter. I asked several other individuals, including Bill Lavender and Nicole Sealy, the then executive director of Cave Canem, to write letters in support of my nomination. I called on a few colleagues who were serving in "high places" in state government to write letters as well. I hadn't intended to make it a campaign, but knowing that it would be a political appointment, I knew that I had some due diligence to do and at least let my interest be known among several of Governor Edwards' strong supporters.

I had strongly supported Edwards in his first successful bid for governor. Later, I applied to work in his administration as Secretary of Labor. I felt that I had a good shot at getting the job, and eventually learned that I was under consideration, along with several other candidates. As fate would have it, I got a phone call one morning from the president of the AFL-CIO informing me that the governor "decided to go in a different direction." It was a great disappointment, but after later being appointed the Poet Laureate of Louisiana, I understood the fate that I had felt so badly about. Had I become the Secretary of Labor, "politics" would have dictated that I not become the first black male Poet Laureate of Louisiana, at least not as an appointee of Governor Edwards. It was that simple and clear. There was a purpose in my failure that was much larger than me.

When I got the call from Erin Greenwald, Vice President of Public Programs for the Louisiana Endowment for the Humanities (LEH) informing me of the appointment, I could hardly speak through my tears. The hours and days that immediately followed were surreal. When the Governor's Office made the official announcement in August 2019, my life changed. I was no longer *me*. I was the Poet Laureate of Louisiana, an office that had not been held by a black man since its inception in 1944. Emails and phone calls of congratulations were constant. Suddenly, I was a news story and, strangely, some sort of "black" achiever. It felt strange but good. Requests for interviews from radio stations and newspapers came, as well as requests to do poetry readings. I gladly obliged all of them.

My inaugural reading would be held in mid-October at the LEH office in New Orleans, but my first reading as the Poet Laureate of Louisiana was held at my college alma mater, McNeese State University, in September. The McNeese event had been planned long before my appointment. I was scheduled to do a public reading one evening and have individual creative writing sessions the following day. The public reading was well attended, but what was most gratifying was seeing former high school classmates walk through the door. When Martin and Garston, my two best pals from elementary and middle school showed up with their wives, I felt my feet rise above the floor. Wayne Lemelle, another childhood friend who had lived in my first neighborhood in Lake Charles, also came with his wife. After selling a few books, Narva and I treated them all to dinner.

By the time the date of the inaugural reading was decided, I had accepted several public invitations to read. On November 13, 2019, I did a reading at Nicholls State University as a fundraiser for CROWN, a mentorship program for African American male students. Several days later, I did a reading for the Iberia African American Historical Society (IAAHS). Its work began in 2017 to teach the true and inclusive history of New Iberia through research and recognition of the history, heritage, and culture of African Americans of the area. Dr. Phebe Hayes, the organization's founder, had asked me to compose an original poem to read at an event that would commemorate the 75th anniversary of the expulsion of eight black leaders in Iberia Parish who had been advocators for vocational education for black residents of the parish. I worked on "Sermon of the Dreamers" for nearly a month. To stand before an audience of several hundred attendees and read the poem was one of the highlights of my service as Poet Laureate. I later recorded a reading of the poem for a podcast by Southern Hollows and paid for the graphic layout of the poem on a brochure that the IAAHS was to print and sell as a fundraiser. The poem appears in *Our Shut Eyes*, my fifth collection.

Several months later, at the inauguration of the second term of Governor John Bel Edwards on January 13, 2020. Shortly after the governor's reelection on November 16, 2019, I approached a key member of his executive staff about the idea of the Poet Laureate of Louisiana reading an inaugural poem written for the occasion. After doing some research on the First Family's personal interests and religious beliefs, I started composing a poem in anticipation of a positive response. On or around December 20th, I was informed that the governor had approved the request and that the First Lady wanted it to be a poem about children. I was further told that in addition to my reading the poem as part of the inaugural ceremony, a copy of it would be inserted in the official program.

The poem that I had drafted, "Faith of Children," had already gone in the direction that the First Lady requested. I sent a draft on December 20th. When I got no reply by the end of December, I started making inquiries but got no response. I sent my final inquiry on January 6th, a week before the event. A day or two later, I got a phone call stating that there must have been a breakdown in communication between the Governor's Office and the inaugural planning committee. Still, I got no final answer on whether I would be in the program. By then, I had received an invitation to the event, in a seating area that was clearly not meant for someone who would be a part of the program. I knew that the program had been finalized and was probably being printed.

On the day of the inauguration, with the poem in my hand, Narva and I went to the ceremony and sat in drizzling rain. I opened the program to find that actress Lynn Whitfield, a native of Baton Rouge, would read a poem written by Maya Angelou. A copy of the poem was inserted into the program. When I returned home from the event, I tossed the printed program in the garbage can and sent an email to the Governor's Office, expressing my disappointment, not for being denied the opportunity to read a poem, but for the unprofessional way I had been treated. To this day, I have no idea why I didn't get a final, official response. I can only guess and hope that the decision was more political than personal. Still, it was a great disappointment that I will always remember.

As the pandemic of Covid-19 began to spread in March 2020, "Faith of Children," seemed more relevant. I went back to it, made revisions, and dedicated it to Louisiana. It appears in my fifth collection.

By March 2020, I had confirmed my participation in three major events for the next three months, including two readings in New Orleans. All of them were canceled due to the pandemic. Over the next fourteen months, I did many virtual events that I enjoyed immensely, but the pandemic had taken the wind out of my sails. I was the first Poet Laureate of Louisiana who was not "public." Despite the constraints of Covid-19, there were moments to celebrate. In April 2020, I was awarded a Poet Laureates fellowship by the Academy of American Poets, which came with a $50,000 prize. My project was to conduct workshops for economically disadvantaged students at four high schools in the Delta parishes of northeast Louisiana. Although I couldn't get the schools to finalize scheduling the workshops, I did virtual workshops with students in St. Parish and Calcasieu Parish.

The pandemic also impacted my work at Education's Next Horizon and as an English instructor at Southern University. To be safe, I spent as little time as possible in the office. At the mid-term of the Spring 2020 semester, the university shifted to online instruction, which proved challenging for both the students and me. I literally spent the entire day and a great part of every evening working with a computer on my lap on my home's back courtyard. Somewhere during that shift, I stopped writing poetry. I needed a hiatus and felt the need to explore other genres of creative writing.

While waiting on the publication of my fifth collection, I continued to do virtual poetry readings and maintain a strong presence on social media, posting video recordings of poems that would appear in my forthcoming collection. *Our Shut Eyes* was released in April 2021. The original concept of the collection was a book of selected and new poems on the theme of race in America. After writing the "new" poems for the collection over the course of a year, it occurred to me that 2021 would mark the 40th anniversary of the Atlanta Child Murders. I decided to devote nearly half of the collection to poems that would memorialize the victims of those killings. The other thirty-one poems of the collection touch on a range of "racial" issues plaguing contemporary America. Some, like "American Portrait" and "Artifacts" give historical context. Several follow the theme of my second collection, *Soul Be A Witness*, and speak to the continuing problem of stereotyping, under-educating, and having low achievement expectations for black boys.

After seeing the body camera of the police officer who shot and killed Alton Sterling in June 2016, a recording released one year after the shooting, I wrote the longest poem of the collection.

I first learned of the Atlanta Child Murders in July 1979 while living in Natchitoches, Louisiana. All the twenty-eight victims (thirty by some sources) were poor and black. All but two were boys. The news story haunted me for two years. For reasons that I can't rationally explain, I became obsessed with the ordeal. I had nightmares of being personally stalked and murdered as a young boy. I visited a hypnotist to decipher the symbolism in the dreams and started collecting news and magazine articles about the murders. Little did I know, that 40 years later, I would be a poet writing poems about the murders.

I devote the remainder of this chapter to poems of *Our shut Eyes* that I have done the most reading of publicly.

Our Shut Eyes

1979 – Four Victims

We speak of horror as numbers:
black children murdered and missing,
mothers hurting and waiting—days
weeks, months without answers.

With eyes shut, we wander
a labyrinth of emptiness,
smothering in hope of finding
what time has given and taken back.

1980 – Thirteen Victims

Like sky caves of silence,
mornings never dawn.

Rumors loom of shadows
lurking hooded nights.

Trees walk with men
searching the moribund woods,
where snakes slither to the crackle
of twigs, scattering the quails.

1981- Thirteen Victims

Children hustle, squint
at the sun, or lay pretending
to dream, until sleep comes
coldly and unawares.

Like baptism, someone is washed,
someone chants a freedom song
of slaves lost to seawater
with only the past to gaze.

Darron Glass

I am one of the innocents
slaughtered by a world
that never heard stories we told
and songs we sang.

I know the rage of night,
but you needn't wonder or worry.
I am safe and strong,
not a black boy shattered
by the weight of hate,
the one who became vapor
in the twilight of day.

I am sounds stirring
cool, spring air, the ones
you can never name.
I am a mist of blinding fog,

faces of clouds,
and the whir of birds soaring.

I am not a memory or phantom.
I am not flesh, bone, or dust.
I am invisible but real,
like a bud in the garden
of your children's dreams.

I don't remember
my mother and father,
how I became Glass,
but I know that I am Darron,
broken yet whole.

Note: Darron Glass, a foster child, is the only victim of the
Atlanta Child Murders whose body was never found.

Face

Curtis was a Mama's boy.
He mostly stayed home, helping me
care for his younger brothers.
His favorite show was *Sanford and Son*.
He loved to draw and would say, "Mama,
one day I'm going to make you rich."

I told him not to leave the house,
but he left anyway. When he didn't come home,
I went down the road looking for him,
praying, "Please God,
don't let nobody have my child.
Please, please God."

I was watching television,
and saw them pull my baby out of the river.
He had been missing for two weeks.
When the mayor came to say Curtis was dead,
I ran out the front door.

I couldn't go to see my baby's dead body.
My sister said he couldn't be recognized
by his face. That night, I cut off all my hair,
and I put a razor blade to my wrist,
until I heard a deep voice say,
"You've got to live for your other children."

At the funeral, all I could do was close my eyes
and picture Curtis the last time I saw him,
when he left to go down the street
and carry groceries to earn a few dollars.
All I could do was close my eyes
and imagine his smile and laughter.

I only have one photograph of Curtis.
My kids took the others away
to help me deal with the pain.
For years, I slept with that photograph.
Woke up holding it.
Cooked with it in my bosom.
Curtis will always be in my heart.

For the past thirty-six years, I have
dreamt of him. In the dream,
he's smiling and laughing,
as if he's in the room playing with his brothers,
but I can't see or remember his face.
He's there but not there,
and I wake up praying,
"God, show me his face."
I go walking down the road in tears, praying
"God, show me his face."

Note: This poem was found in statements made by Catherine
Leach-Bell, the mother of Curtis Walker, during various
media interviews.

At the beginning of the Covid pandemc, I began writing a novel.
The story, a big part of it at least, had its genesis during the mid-1980s,
when I lived and worked in Lafayette. I had carried it in my head
with the idea of one day writing the novel, a decade before poetry

discovered me. Totally consumed and absorbed, I completed the novel in three months, losing countless hours of sleep writing late at night and into the morning.

Spanning nearly a century, *Sisters of Gavinville* chronicles the lives of Jesse and Ella Hayes and their seven daughters, an African American family living in Gavinville, a small fisheries town in southeast Louisiana. Four of the daughters move to South Side Chicago in their early twenties. Another, who had remained in Gavinville, becomes involved in a murder, the true details of which are not revealed until seventy years later. The sisters in Chicago become successful in the women's clothing business and become part of the wealthy, black elite community of Chicago. For over fifty years, they are also actively involved in Chicago and Illinois politics, supporting candidates to address racist laws and policies that confine black residents to slums and ghettos.

In time, all the sisters, having grown much older, live together again in Gavinville, where they continue their political activism and use their wealth and influence to address the education and housing problems in Gavinville's poor neighborhoods. Aside from their wealth and political activism, what is most unusual about the sisters is their longevity. None of them dies before the age of 99.

The sisters' journey depicts the significant racial, political, and economic events of the second half of the 20th century and first sixteen years of the 21st, as African Americans struggled for civil rights and equal opportunity. The novel was published in December 2024 by Between the Lines Publishing.

In April 2019, I contacted UL Press about publishing a play that I had written ten years before about the 1922 murder trial of Emile Hebert. UL Press suggested that I consider converting the play to a novella, which I did. I finished the novella in early July 2020 and sent it to the press. After making a number of structural revisions that the press recommended, they agreed to publish the book. It was released in early 2022.

For All Those Men narratively recreates Hebert's trial, but also chronicles the rise and fall of the Ku Klux Klan in Louisiana during the early 1920s, a period known as "the second coming of the KKK." Louisiana Governor John M. Parker, who practically led a one-man crusade to end the KKK's dominance in north Louisiana and its expansion into the southern parishes, is a central figure of the story.

Parker ordered the National Guard to guard the parish courthouse during Hebert's trial in October 1922, marking the first time in the history of the parish that the National Guard was used in connection with a trial.

Two months after Hebert was arrested, two white men in Morehouse Parish, who had reportedly spoken against the KKK, disappeared. In December of that year, with the aid of federal crime investigators that Parker had requested, the mutilated bodies of the men were found in a river.

Although no one was ever convicted for the deaths of the two men, the "Mer Rouge Murders" gained national attention and are largely attributed to the decline of the second KKK nationally. The trial of Emile Hebert ended in a hung jury. The State never retried Hebert, and while on bail he left and hid out in Ames, Texas, where he lived until his death at the age of 95, having not set foot on Louisiana soil since moving away. *For All Those Men* was released by UL Press in November 2022.

The Shadows

Narva and I sold our Baton Rouge home in May 2021 and moved to Lafayette. Several months later, a staff member of the Urban League of Louisiana contacted me about doing consulting work on the development of a policy brief on disparities in the Louisiana workforce. While trying to keep Education's Next Horizon afloat, I had met with Judy Reese Morse, the President & CEO of the League, about building a strategic partnership between our organizations to advance equity in public schools and develop a more skilled workforce. She had recommended me for the equity study. My task was to compile the research data, analyze it, and write the report. As that work was winding down in early 2022, the League asked me to consider applying for a full-time position as their education policy director, work that would entail conducting research on inequities in education outcomes and advocating policies and practices to improve the academic achievement levels of African American students. It was a natural transition from the education policy advocacy work that I had led at Education's Next Horizon for thirteen years. I gladly accepted the job offer and began the work in mid-March, working remotely from home.

The League's approach to education equity was to gather and report data on key academic metrics by race in order to shine a bright light on inequity, while partnering with school district leaders and local residents to identify policies and practices that would close the equity gaps. An outside consultant conducted the research and drafted the report. My job was to provide input to recommended policies and practices and to build community partnerships and engage them in the process. Baton Rouge education and community leaders embraced the approach and agreed to be a partner. Lafayette school officials decided not to participate, but we managed to enlist the participation of a half dozen community leaders and education advocates.

In the months that followed my start at the Urban League, my evenings were consumed with research of a more personal nature.

The chief editor of UL Press had sent edits of my novella that I needed to address, requiring me to become immersed in research on political events leading up to the arrest and trial of Emile Hebert in 1922. The reading included extensive study on Reconstruction, the disenfranchisement of black voting rights in the post-Reconstruction period, and the rise of the Second Ku Klux Klan in the parishes of North Louisiana in 1922. I had taught African American Literature at Southern University in the context of American history for eleven years, but I had not delved as deeply into the racial history of Louisiana.

What I found most shocking in my research of these events was that few people in my circle of friends and acquaintances knew much about them. Few Louisianans know that in 1922 North Louisiana was controlled by the KKK. Were it not for the public backlash to the Mer Rouge murders and the one-man war that Governor John M. Parker had waged against the Klan, they might have succeeded in taking control of the entire state.

Reconstruction and post-Reconstruction are misunderstood and seldom taught periods of American history, yet the events of those periods have had a profound generational effect on the well-being of African American society, particularly in the South. One cannot overlook or take lightly the fact that the Louisiana Constitution of 1898 stripped blacks of all political influence, causing the number of black voters in Louisiana to fall from 130,444 to 5,320 by the turn of the twentieth century. One cannot ignore or take lightly the generational impacts of racism and racial segregation in every facet of American society, not to mention the violence and terror that was inflicted on black people from the post-Reconstruction era well into the Civil Rights Movement.

As I stated in the workforce policy brief, assessments of the root causes of poverty, education inequity, and healthcare disparities, and the development of solutions to those problems, must take into account our country's long history of economic and social injustice, not the least of which has been the history of disenfranchisement, Jim Crow laws, and the systemic denial of equal and fair access to education, housing, and jobs. In American society today, many conservative politicians view this acknowledgement and teaching of historical fact as an attempt to delegitimize American democracy and values. Choosing to not remember and teach the history of enslavement and white supremacy does not stop their ghosts from stalking and haunting every generation of Americans. The criticism of "critical race theory" and "woke" activism is nothing more than a rebirth of the myth of the "lost cause" and a laminated version of the "race card" that subtly plays on the fears and anxieties of white voters under the guise of preserving traditional family values and remaking the greatness of America.

Denialism is easy to propagate, but its ultimate cost is the price of human ignorance and the widening of schisms of ideology, race, and caste that have plagued our nation for four hundred years. As America approaches the eve of its 250th Anniversary, it is even more fitting that we remember and reflect on all of its history.

In April 2022, our Uncle Harvey, the last surviving brother of Narva's mother, came to live with us to get better treatment for his legs. They were badly infected from complications of diabetes and he feared that one of them might have to be amputated. In August, Narva fell in our apartment bathroom and broke her kneecap, requiring surgery and four months of physical rehabilitation. Fortunately, I was working from home and was able to care for both of them. Shortly before Narva's accident, I enrolled in a screenwriting course at the University of Louisiana at Lafayette with the goal of writing a screenplay of *For All Those Men*. I finished the course with a full-length script of the story. My workdays were spent juggling work, Narva's and Uncle Harvey's home care, and school.

By the time I submitted my final edits of the novella to UL Press, the history of America and Louisiana of the past one-hundred fifty years was stirring my gut. As Richard Wright had experienced in the books he read by H. L. Mencken with the use of the infamous "Dear Madam" notes that he forged to check the books out at a Memphis library, "a vague hunger" had come over me. As Wright later wrote, "My reading had created a sense of distance between me and the world in which I lived and tried to make a living." That distance was not new to me. I had seen it between me and the snickering faces of white ninth-grade students. I had seen it while driving out of Sundown Town for the last time with the sun setting in my rearview mirror. I saw it from the rear seat of a limousine cruising through Harlem while white city officials spoke as if I were a "nigger" standing on a street corner. I saw it in the eyes of white neighbors who never got past the thought of a Negro living next door. I had experienced it in reading Jung, Thoreau, Emerson, Robert F. Kennedy, and other writers whose words pulled me inward and challenged my sense of reality and self. History tugged me that way, but with a push, not a pull. I was a native son of America who had seen and felt the brunt of racial hatred and injustice, but for the first time in my life, I was seeing purpose in all of it.

I was relieved to have gotten the edits done and eagerly awaited the book to be printed in November 2022. As the year moved toward a close, my teaching duties at Southern University wound down, and the community engagement work of the ULLA slowed down considerably due to the holiday season. With the time and freedom to think creatively, I started planning my next collection, which would consist of new poems and selected poems from my previous collections. One of the first of the new poems, later published in *Hole in the Head Review*, recounted one of my most painful and unforgettable experiences of racial hatred.

Spit

> In ninth grade, while standing
> in a lunch line, a white student spat
>
> on me, a quiet, shy boy, the darkest
> of five Negroes in the school.
>
> I felt the thick, slimy glob
> stinging the back of my neck.
>
> I felt the sticky wetness
> when I reached back to wipe it.
>
> I saw white faces smiling like clowns,
> some snickering with a dare.
>
> I wiped my hand on my shirt,
> put my hand to my mouth and tasted spit.
>
> I put my hand to my nose
> and sniffed the pungent odor of spit.

I didn't go to the principal's office
to say what happened.

I didn't tell my white teachers
or my parents or neighborhood friends.

I swallowed white spit in every breath
and silent cry. Racial hatred:

never more bitter, never forgotten,
still haunting, piercing, scarring.

In January 2023, I received a phone call from Dr. Phebe Hayes. We talked about the brochure of "Sermon of the Dreamers" and how the Covid pandemic had prevented any public promotion and sale of it. We discussed the idea of me going to New Iberia to do another reading of the poem at one of the programs that she was planning for the spring. She mentioned the partnership that the IAAHS has with the National Trust for Historic Preservation and its historic site, Shadows-on-the-Teche, a plantation museum located in New Iberia, Louisiana.

She also said that the executive director of the site was retiring in six months and that the National Trust was seeking candidates for the replacement. A big part of the job was leading a new interpretative framework that would tell a more complete history of the site, inclusive of a wealthy family who built and owned the site and the people they enslaved. I knew nothing about the Shadows, but the idea of telling a true and inclusive history of the site immediately piqued my interest. Phebe followed up with a copy of the job announcement describing the duties and responsibilities of the position. After reading it, I felt a strong urge to apply, and the inner voice told me to give it some thought.

Around that same time, I got a phone call from Judge Jules Edwards, a longtime friend and colleague who had retired as a District Court Judge and had recently been elected to a City Court judgeship. He said that *The Current*, a local online journal, was inviting individuals to contribute to a series of essays that the journal was publishing on the topic of racial reconciliation. He had been asked to contribute but felt that I would be better suited to the task. I agreed to write an essay, which was published in *The Current* on February 8, 2023. In the essay, I wrote about my understanding of the cause of racial hatred and injustice and how we as one nation can eradicate it. I spoke about the importance of embracing and teaching the full history of America and how necessary that is in achieving racial reconciliation. The essay immediately follows this chapter.

While living the changes that occurred in my life from 2019 to 2022, it did not occur to me that they were connected in any way. I was following my dreams, passions, judgment, and intuition, but not with any thought of a grand design for the change that was unfolding. I saw no guideposts on the road on those nights. In contrast to the work-related or personal disappointments and failures that had oftentimes altered my course, I had only experienced good fortune—blessings that had come without my asking or expectation. Oddly, I didn't view the closure of Education's Next Horizon as a setback. It prompted our move to Lafayette, not knowing what fate lay ahead but knowing in my heart that Narva and I had made the right decision. Even Narva's surgery and rehabilitation were taken in stride, never triggering doubt that Lafayette was where we needed to be but still not knowing the reason or purpose of our being there.

Pondering the Shadows job opportunity in the still hours of late nights, an inner voice whispered that it was not by chance that the opportunity coincided with my increased study of American history and the crystallization of my appreciation of the power of that history being told. The direction that I had to go was clear. Even clearer were the purposes that had been hidden in all the successes and failures of life that had brought me to that point. I was beginning to see the oak tree that had sprung from seed and had not fallen or been cut down. Confidently, I submitted my job application to the National Trust and was offered the job three interviews later. I started work on March 1, 2023. Narva and I moved to nearby Youngsville, a smaller city in the southern tip of Lafayette Parish, which was less than a half-hour drive from the Shadows.

Built in 1834 by wealthy sugar cane planters, the Shadows is located on Main Street of New Iberia, in the heart of the city's downtown district. Twenty enslaved people worked at the main house and nearly two hundred enslaved people worked in the Weeks family sugar cane plantations located fifteen miles away on Weeks Island. Modeling Greek Revival architecture, the main house is a majestic three-story, 16-room townhouse, the rear of which sits on the Bayou Teche, a 125-mile waterway meandering through central and southeast Louisiana. The site's most distinctive appearance is its six tall, stately white concrete columns, a front and rear second-floor balcony, and the shadowing canopies of its towering, two-hundred-plus-year-old Spanish moss-draped oaks. William Weeks Hall, the last of the four generations of Weeks family members who occupied the house and who later donated the property to the National Trust for Historic Preservation, lined the front perimeters of the site with bamboo, adding to its mystique.

The administrative offices of the Shadows are located in its Visitor Center across the street from the mansion. The Research & Learning Center of The African American Historical Society is housed on the second floor at no cost. At the time I came aboard, the Shadows was in a transition. It had shut down in March 2020 at the outbreak of the Covid pandemic and reopened for visitor tours in October 2021. Eleven months later it closed again to conduct more research on the site's history of enslavement and to prepare for a new visitor experience that would uniquely tell the site's full history. The major challenges I faced were hiring a senior manager to lead the full development of the new interpretive framework, building public understanding and support of the new visitor experience, and shoring up the organization's financial condition. On May 6, 2023, I stood beneath the shading canopies of the Shadows with National Trust staff and community leaders to cut the ribbon of a grand reopening ceremony. I recited a poem composed especially for the occasion and dedicated it to Pat Kahle, the outgoing executive director who was retiring after working forty years at the site, twenty-seven of which as executive director.

Dreams of the Shadows
FOR PAT KAHLE

> Bayou water, sugar land,
> letters, ledgers,
> photographs and paintings,
> furnishings, clothing, and knickknacks,
> histories told and untold
>
> Here, in the South, in Iberia,
> at the mansion on the bayou,

we bear witness to the beauty and brokenness of humans,
    the free ones who traded and profited
    and the captive, chattel ones
    who sweetened the salty earth beyond us,
    all hidden in the canopies
    of our draping moss and beckoning boughs.

In the whirling winds of centuries and seasons,
we bore seeds wing-borne and carried far away,
in air
whispering the *coo-woo* calls of mourning doves
and shouting the holy-danced *hallelujah*s of
of freedom songs.

When twilight dimmed the cabins
and patterns were cut and stitched,
    we dreamt patches
    of fine lace and coarse cloth,
    a collage of crystal and glass,
    porcelain and cracked pottery,
    carved wood and bleeding hands.

Now, as sunbeams pierce the clouds,
    we dream the mosaicked and unpainted,
    the marbled and bare,
    the privileged and poor, disparate, yet
    forever bound together by love.

When truth slumbers and dies
in the deep, dark well of memory,
we live, we remember, we tell.

See.   Listen. Dream with us!

History is Our Witness
The Current
February 8, 2023

To me, a seventy-year-old African American who lived through the Jim Crow and Civil Rights eras of the 1950s and 1960s, race has been like a prescribed pill swallowed with a glass of tap water. I am what some might call an educated, enlightened, and successful Black man, a native son of America who is a victim and product of racial hatred, but who long ago learned to mask his bitterness toward racial prejudice by relishing the sweetness of knowing both the person he is and the person people see or think they know.

I have grown to understand hatred and oppression, not as a consciously contrived emotion, thought, or act, but as a deep spiritual hollowness in many Americans, and a byproduct of a complex web of unconscious forces that religion, history, and politics do little to explain or untangle. Still, the more I grow to understand racism, the less tolerant I am of it, and the more determined I am to fight it.

What I didn't know, for many years at least, and what many white people don't know or understand or refuse to accept, is that, like Tar Baby in the briar patch, I am stuck to them, and it is their task, not mine, to learn that they cannot be free until I am free.

Thirty-four-year-old Martin Luther King Jr. understood that fact, and he never said it more plainly and eloquently than when he faced a quarter of a million people at the Lincoln Memorial Reflecting Pool on that hot August day in 1963 and spoke to America about the unfulfilled promises of its democracy. His words were just beginning to ascend toward the "dream" and had not reached the crescendo that would later soar the clouds when, suddenly, like a birdsong, his cadence caught a crosswind, and the words struck a chord that sent the crowd into its first thunderous applause:

> *Many of our white brothers*
> *as evidenced by their presence*
> *here today have come to realize*
> *that their destiny is tied up with our destiny.*
> *And they have come to realize that their freedom*
> *is inextricably bound to our freedom.*

That personal transformation of white Americans, caused not by reasoning or law or physical force, but through compassion and a sense of spiritual identity and moral purpose, did much to ignite and fuel the national movement for Civil Rights. Our becoming a "more perfect union" will only be within reach when each of us, white and Black, discovers that common bond and interdependence.

Even when a Black man led America and the free world, discourses on race relations bordered on benign neglect and did little to address the grave disparities and injustices of our present situation. Not surprisingly, the election of America's first Black President awoke and galvanized some of the very same prejudices that the Civil Rights movement fought to eradicate.

Measured against the indignity and degradation suffered by generations before me and by many of my own generation, my personal experiences with racial prejudice are hardly worth mentioning. But if, as James Baldwin suggests, one's forgetfulness is the serpent in the garden of one's dreams, Americans of all races must surely watch and witness, not to indict the past or present, but to never lose sight of the race-molded shadow of our beloved country, however long it persists.

A young white man in his early twenties once said to me, "You seem to know a lot about the race problem, but I don't get it. What's the solution? How can or will the country ever be free of prejudice, injustice, and inequality?" To him, I replied:

"Let us, *you and I*, climb a high bridge. Admittedly, I am afraid of heights, and I dread crossing tall bridges. They're one of my worst fears. I can't really explain why, except that crossing them makes me very uncomfortable. I feel a loss of control. When I approach a tall bridge, I see more than steel beams and concrete. I see fear, a fear of being too high above the ground, climbing into the clouds, falling from the sky, and careening into the river below, or maybe it's the fear of not being on solid ground, or losing gravity and my surefooted grip on the world.

"The problem is personal but has everything to do with you, because if you and I can both believe that together we can climb and cross any tall bridge, even in my fear; if *you and I* can get beyond history, accept our differences in age, ancestry, race, and culture, and genuinely care about each other's life and well-being as if it were his own; if you will sit beside me and believe that I can hold on to the wheel and not faint but keep straight ahead toward that bridge with my heart pounding as my body climbs, tilts, and loses ground; and if I, with you by my side, have the courage and faith to stay the course, conquering fear and believing that no harm will come to either of us if I let go of the wheel and put my life in your hands, trusting you to get us safely across those deep waters; then maybe, just maybe, you and I, together, can climb that height and cross that vast, open space.

"You ask: After slavery, war, and disenfranchisement, after hate, terror, resistance, protests, and Civil Rights, after the silence of strangers passing each other with gestures or words spoken and unspoken that cut without intent to hurt, after the rhetoric, finger pointing, and projections, after winter has passed and the spring sun sleeps, and we enter our houses, close our doors, love our children, put them to bed, and turn out the lights, how do we awake to our better, brighter days?

"How do Black and white Americans live as one family? When will Black lives always matter to white people and visa versa? How do we close the racial divide that has existed for four hundred years and divided the sweet soul of this country between two continents and two races of people who now live as one nation under God? How do we solve the problems that sap Americans of life and a sense of worth and dignity? How do we fulfill the promises of democracy for all Americans, regardless of race?

"As complex and perplexing as it seems, the solution is very simple. Each race has answers to those questions, but do we truly listen to one another? By listen, I mean remember but care and forgive. By care and forgiveness, I mean love. By love, I mean imagine *you and I* entering a darkened, unfamiliar room together, with each carrying an unlit lantern. Would we be willing to extend our arms to light, not our own, but one another's lamp? The race problem in this country can only be solved when that happens, when people of all races enter that dark space together to see and feel the realities that each race experiences, even if, in darkness, what we see and feel falls short of truth. Each race must be willing to act out those perceptions in the best interest of the other, knowing that absolute truth is never absolute.

"All races standing together, in one dark, unfamiliar room and lighting each other's lantern is the highest of heights. It requires white people and people of color to step beyond their own front doors far and long enough to see each other's houses, despite the distance and differences between them, and embrace darkness and unfamiliarity without fear or presumption. It requires us to look into our own and each other's hearts to find common goodness, not fearing, forgetting, or shunning the past, but embracing it, while imagining a brighter future. It requires us to climb together, hand in hand, and patiently tread the stony road together, to learn, pray, laugh, and cry together, and be willing to cross the wilderness, valleys, deep canyons, and desert sands together.

"With lamps lit and glowing brightly in the strangeness of darkness, after all we've destroyed and built, after all we've suffered and endured as a divided and united country, we can enter that dark, unfamiliar room. We can leap beyond time, history, and circumstance, but no one but us will carry the light. No one but us will guide, push, or pull us over that vast, open space. No one but us will love enough to get us there.

"Say and do unto me as I say and will do unto you: *I do not have the power to make you love me, but I have the heart to love you, and I will.*"

LETTER TO MY GRANDCHILDREN

My Dearest Children,

Some people write their obituary before they die, telling the world where they lived, how they were educated, what work they did, and how they made the world a better place. I wouldn't think of doing that and I hope that whoever writes my obituary will leave those details unwritten and unspoken. I would hope, instead, that what is written and said about my life is what rests in the hearts and minds of the living about the spirit they came to know me as.

I have lived an imperfect life, filled with missteps, mistakes, and misgivings. I've hurt loving people and turned my back on those who needed love. What good I did pales in comparison to the good I didn't do, times when I didn't give or didn't speak words that could have made a difference in whether another individual was comfortable or at peace or happy. In short, most of me was broken and incomplete, despite how the living might judge my value and contribution to humankind. I received a thousand-fold more than what I gave.

Like all humans, I suffered. I experienced pain. But the storms of life were relatively good to me. The winds, no matter how turbulent and twisting on dark, unseeing nights, were soft, calm, and gentle when compared to the suffering of those much less fortunate than me. I am grateful for grace, for all who struggled, suffered, and died so that I lived more freely and equally as an American citizen. I am especially grateful for those who nurtured, taught, and mentored me, and who prayed for my well-being and protection.

The sum total of any life is too filled with variables to add up, but I am certain that beyond the small parcel of ground that I was given to till, what I have thought and done has had little if any consequence. I have been more like a perennial flower with a name, a season to be planted and bloom, and a time to die. I can only hope that my life was simple and truthful enough to impart some lessons to you of what can make your lives better and beautiful despite the world's pain and ugliness. In the end, I know and have accomplished very little. I am especially blind to the iceberg beneath the surface—the wholeness of me and all the knowledge that came before me, floating in a vast ocean and hidden from my memory and consciousness.

I did not consciously decide to pursue and map a course to seek purpose and what lies undiscovered in me. In a way, the clouded sky and dark, winding paths lured me. The color of my skin caused branches to fall and blocked some roads traveled. My feet were not always firmly planted and there were times when I didn't feel the earth beneath me. I looked before I entered rooms but some doors that I prayed and thought would open did not. Above them were the stars I was meant to gaze. For reasons unknown to me, my destination is being decided for me. Although I am still somewhat adrift without a compass to tell direction, my faith, my sense of unrealized but evolving wholeness, and books that I have read and written along the way make the difference between my being lost and knowing that I am somewhere.

Thirty years ago, I did not know that I would write literature. I was 63 years old when I published my first collection of poetry, but since the very first tablet and pencil I was given to write with there had been guideposts pointing me in that direction. In every sudden rise or twist of the wind, in every solitary walk through the woods or stroll through a still, barren night, in every unanswered prayer and bad decision that sent me spiraling into an abyss where it seemed a sun would never shine, I was being pulled and pushed toward light and a purpose that I had not dreamt or imagined. For that, I am grateful beyond words and measure and will leave this world owing a great debt that I cannot repay.

Admittedly, as blessed as I feel to be an American, I struggle to forgive my country for the ugly past that it wrought. Time and experience have made it difficult for me to separate "my country" from white people in general, because many if not most white people whom I had close contact with at school, work, or in personal relations could not get beyond my black skin and their racial prejudice. They might not have overtly and intentionally shown or spoken prejudice and might not have been aware of my perception of it, but casteism and racism, even in their most subtle forms, have never been something that I simply imagined, felt, or thought. In the absence of obvious discrimination, there was always a look, a body language, or a word spoken or unsaid that triggered my perception of racial intolerance.

In those instances, it didn't matter to white people that I could learn as well as they could or that I was their boss and had the authority to direct, promote, or fire them. It didn't matter that I lived as comfortably and safe as they did, could afford to buy the things they bought, or could travel as freely. At times, I wondered whether it mattered to white people that I was as human as they were. In their minds, they were inherently better and purer simply because they were white and I was black. Something embedded in their history and culture and ingrained in their psyche caused them to believe that they were the upper rung of the ladder and I was beneath them.

I am careful not to view or think of all white people as racists. Nor do I assume that all black people of my generation felt the sting of racism as bitterly as I did. I only speak of the well that I drew water from. Experiences taught me that many white people, who for whatever reason felt or thought that they were intellectually and morally superior to black people, had a good heart, not filled with hatred. I have been extended countless kindnesses by ordinary white people who were total strangers and whose words and actions kindled great faith in the ideals of humanity and racial tolerance. Many turns in my journey that enabled me to learn and to grow professionally and as a writer were influenced and guided by the caring hearts and thoughtfulness of white men and women. But as a whole, my experiences validate my belief that many whose paths I crossed in a personal way thought much less of me solely on the basis of my skin color and either spoke or acted out their biases in some way. I wish I could say that I was being overly sensitive or was merely a victim of time, circumstance, and geography, but the history of my country, the experiences I lived, and the America I know today project a deeper, more pervasive problem that has plagued our nation since 1619, when slaves were first brought to its shores.

My inability to forgive is not entirely attributable to how my country treated your ancestors and me. Experience caused me to be guarded and suspicious of white people and to generally expect their stereotyped view of my blackness. That was the norm, not the exception, and in that respect my instincts nearly always proved to be right. Generally,

I judged them by my perception and feeling about how they judged and responded to me. I always confronted blatant racism directly, but oftentimes my response to ignorance and what I deemed spiritual hollowness was to look past it with cordial friendliness or a stiff, poker face of neighborliness—but never forgetting the encounter.

Whether by their actions or mine, consciously or unconsciously, I can't say that I ever truly loved more than a handful of white people in the Christian sense of brotherly love, which I tried to do with all people regardless of race. In that respect, I failed as much as they did. By love, I mean a total absence of fear, a willingness to lay down my life for another, do for them what I would do for myself, and unconditionally give whatever was needed for their well-being. I got close to only a few white people to really know them and allow them to know me. That was part of the armor that years of experiencing racial prejudice required me to wear. But the absence of love was never bitterness and hate or the desire to hurt anyone; it was merely the comfort zone of civility, where the mind remained cognizant and vigilant, the heart was distant enough to not be vulnerable and bruised, and the soul felt free. Only once did the death of a white person bring me to tears.

A Stranger Loss
(FOR STEPHEN W. CAVANAUGH)

> I seldom think about the river
> that sleeps beside the city,
> but I shun crossing its tallest bridge.
> Today, I climbed it
> in a chrome-polished black limousine,
> thinking about my uneven cuffs
> and clumsily pinned boutonniere,
> wondering why someone stood
> strangely at the top on the ledge.
> I recalled a day that broke
> months ago, when I sat
> looking down on a different city—
> lush hills, steep streets, a scent of fish
> and sea to dream by.
> Suddenly, an email: *Steve Cavanaugh*
> *has pancreatic cancer.*
> *Doctors give him three to six months.*

Steve, in that choked-breath moment,
a distant foghorn
lifted wayward stars
we often searched sitting
like logs splintering in a dying fire
our generation had been given to kindle.
In twenty years of friendship,
I never knew your political party
and didn't hear your recitations
of Chaucer and Seuss.
Through all our God-talk
and bush-burning muse,
I never knew where you worshipped.
Until today, when they covered you
in a bed of irises west of the river,
I had not cried the loss of anyone
of a race other than my own.

I am as much a product of racial hatred as I am of human and civil rights carved through centuries of struggle and resistance to racial tyranny and white supremacy. That was the ground in which I was planted and from which I sprang. I can never escape my African heritage and dark skin and have never been inclined to try to do so. The problem of race in America is complex. Through time, education, experience, and retrospection, I have grown to have my own understanding of it, as limited and shallow as that might be. For me, the most perplexing question is why, after four hundred years, are African Americans still struggling to gain and protect the unalienable rights that our Declaration of Independence decreed as self-evident and uncompromising in the eyes of God? Four hundred years.

Knowing the history of slavery, post-Civil War, Jim Crow, and the fight for Civil Rights in America should have led me to believe that the past fifty years of my life would be less of a struggle. I should not have had to experience racial prejudice as I strived to learn, earn a decent living, and attain what I was humanly capable of achieving. The little that I accomplished, if one could call it that, came at a great price, too great to relish any fruits of it. I now know that for me the "dream" will not be realized. It will be deferred, perhaps for a future generation of Americans. It is a hard pill to swallow, to think that after so much struggle for freedom and equality, after so much bloodshed and sacrifice and such boundless opportunity for achievement, my children live in an American society that is not much less color blind and racially intolerant than the one in which I was born and spent my youth and adult life.

Disenfranchisement is not simply a page written in late-19th century American history. In the South, its ghost still lurks. Political power and all that can be gained by it continues to motivate some men to seek and retain it at the expense of the constitutional rights of black Americans. While the problems and consequences of caste and racial prejudice remain largely the same as they were in the Jim Crow Era of my youth and young adulthood, we live in a different America at a different time. Notwithstanding the bold and courageous cry to make "Black Lives Matter," today's black America has no galvanizing "movement" to tear down the walls of oppression and discrimination that have been built since slaves were first brought to this country. There are no Black Nationalist symbols and rhetoric inspiring and urging a fight for "a more perfect union" and no visible black leaders of a national campaign for the enactment and enforcement of laws that guarantee basic civil rights. That is not to suggest that there should be or that men and women of strong courage and conscience can or should purposefully make themselves martyrs of justice and equality. More often than not, men and women who bend the arc of history with revolutionary ideas and movements are vessels rather than makers of them.

Organized religion, with all its fervor and force, remains a divided, segregated, and powerless institution in the face of racial hatred. The black church is no longer the base for social and political activism and change. Organizational responses and community protests against police brutality and the suppression of black voting rights notwithstanding, the necessary social response to the products and byproducts of racial prejudice in today's society is more individualistic than collective, requiring a realization, understanding, and execution of individuality that is independent of society at-large. Whether contemporary men and women are enlightened, courageous, and caring enough to produce the countless, ordinary, individual acts of tolerance and compassion needed for this moment has yet to be proven.

Despite the tremendous growth of black wealth and the great achievements of black Americans in every walk of life, the mis-education and under-education of many black youth over the last half a century has taken a toll on social awareness and consciousness and on the individual and collective capacity of black Americans to effectively respond to contemporary socio-economic challenges and "the race problem." In many communities and school districts of the South where the doors of school desegregation were slow to open during the early 1960s, economic and educational equity continues to lag too far behind, leaving a trail of social and economic ills that stymie progress and rip apart the fabric of family and community stability. Local news stories are quick to report black-related crime but seldom mention the context of it—poor educational outcomes, joblessness, and high poverty.

In general, black and white middle and high school students are taught little if any history of the struggles of African Americans and of the literature written by slaves and their descendants. Despite the billions of dollars spent on public education, the "re-blackening" of urban schools and the whitening of educators who are failing to effectively teach black children are causing irreparable damage to the educational and economic progress of black people. A narrower, even more short-sighted view is to lay the blame and burden of poverty and poor education on the dysfunctionality of black families. Black mothers and fathers, many argue, are not doing their jobs to nurture, train, and educate their children. Many proponents of that view argue for government subsidized choice that allows poor families to send their children to private schools where teachers are even whiter and less sensitive to the struggles of families who have experienced generations of racism and poverty.

The growing wealth gap in America exacerbates the problem. Many American households are literarily one paycheck from homelessness and starvation, while the overwhelming majority of wealth in America is concentrated in the hands of a small, invisible minority. Ordinary white and black Americans and ethnic minorities are so caught up in the struggles of daily life that they experience a sort of paralysis of action beyond the voting booth. Except in elections and times of crises and natural disasters, they pay little attention to what their governments are doing to make their lives better, let alone get active politically to address pressing socio-economic problems. Polarization and the class-laced sophistication and expense of political campaigns at all levels of government ensure that many poor and middle-class white people who should coalesce in a struggle for equity and fairness vote against their own best interests. Government of, for, and by the people is essentially a government of those who have the means and self-interest to influence and alter its course.

I am ill-equipped to offer solutions to these problems, except to say that the answers to them seem apparent in the nature, scope, and causes of the problems themselves. The task is simply to make the promises of democracy and equality real for all Americans. In many respects, our history of caste and slavery is both an albatross to progress and a front door to our brightest, most humane and united future. We mustn't ignore or shutter our shameful past but embrace and teach it with lessons on humanity, spirituality, and the contributions that all Americans have made to the building of this nation.

There is hope for a society of racial tolerance, I think, in your generation, which blocks out history in the absence of being taught it and which is too busy trying to catch up with a future that is swiftly passing you by. But even the white Americans of your generation bear the guilt and scars of slavery. Frightfully, I find that many youths and young adults of your generation, who have not been taught the history of slavery and its cumulative effects and long-term ramifications, have too narrow and biased a view of government's role in addressing social, economic, and educational inequities. In the absence of the knowledge of history that their country would rather not remember and in their inability to think and act as individuals rather than as a mass society that governs and regulates their means of survival, they, too, are in danger of repeating the mistakes of generations that lived before them, not of slavery or oppression but of thinking that skin color or inherited economic status defines the value and quality of an individual's life. Only time will tell whether your generation and your children can create or shape a society in which all people are truly equal and free.

I often think of what James Baldwin said in the concluding paragraphs of his essay, "Notes of a Native Son." Over the years, Baldwin had grown to hate and despise his unbending, controlling father. On the day of his father's death, Baldwin's eighth sibling was born. On August 3, 1943, the morning after the Harlem riot of 1943, which Baldwin witnessed firsthand, the family drove his father to his gravesite "through a wilderness of smashed plate and glass." That was also the day of Baldwin's nineteenth birthday.

But as Baldwin would later note in his essay, which he wrote twelve years after his father's death, as much as he had hated his father and hated what whites and blacks had made of Harlem in the riot, it was folly. "Hatred, which could destroy so much, never failed to destroy the man who hated." To survive, one must hold on to two ideas which seemed in opposition, the idea of the acceptance of the reality of injustices and the idea "that one must never, in one's own life, accept these injustices as commonplace but must fight them with all one's strength." The fight, Baldwin went on to say, begins in the heart, which must be kept free of hatred and despair. In the words of my mother, "You have to give love to receive love." As short as I have come in fulfilling that truth, I take comfort in knowing that, in time, I have at least grown to understand the realness and power of it.

If I can impart any advice to you about how to deal with or respond to experiences of racism or racial injustice that you will surely encounter at some point in your life, it is to do as Baldwin suggests. Remember that as descendants of slaves, *you* carry the torch to light the cauldron. *You* sail the ship that bounds and carries you. In whatever place, situation, or circumstance in which you find yourself, never accept any wrong done to you because of your blackness simply as the way things are. Never let any injustice make you feel that you are less of an individual or that your goal or dream is unattainable. Fight it with all your strength but with a heart free of hatred.

But remember that you are fighting injustice, not the individuals who inflict it or who passively allow it to exist. They are as broken as all of us are and in need of knowing the wholeness of themselves that is not found in the mirrors they gaze or in what the world sees and thinks of them. Search for that unhidden knowledge of yourself fervently and incessantly. Know that it lies solely within you. The journey will not be lit with night stars and a brightly glaring sun, but the path will be yours, no one else's. Trust the blindness that makes you doubt the turns you take. Trust heart-breaking pain, disappointment, and failure to be the making of you, not the end of you. All that you will discover of yourself will equip you with the means to move or overcome any obstacle or barrier that stands in your way.

Looking back, I believe that I lived a relatively quiet, uneventful life among white students, co-workers, and neighbors, and in the minds of those who read the words I wrote. I could never be invisible to them, but something tells me that I was a black boy and man whom they never quite got to know. In poetry, I discovered a protest voice in me that had been too quiet for too long and demanded to be heard. I unearthed pain that hadn't been spoken. I discovered truth that I had not known, beauty that I had not seen, and fulfillment that I had not felt. To paraphrase Ralph Ellison, I discovered that words can be a weapon—armament for the battle against injustice. Perhaps that would be a fitting end to my journey and the words I leave to carry in your hearts, that when my book was opened, it talked, and a battle cry was sounded. I pray to God that you hear it.

FINAL REFLECTIONS: BEYOND THE VEIL

This is my talking book, a story of a journey in search of who I am becoming, told through memories and reflections of my inner and outward experiences. As best as I could recollect, I gave some accounts of the failures and triumphs of my seventy years, recounting the experiences of places where I lived, studied, and worked and of my interactions with people whose paths I crossed. For better or worse, they influenced how I responded to the branches that fell in the storms of my life. More meaningful are reflections about the parts of me that are unseen—the thoughts, feelings, intuitions, and convictions that shaped my life into the pattern it made of itself.

I recounted experiences of a black boy growing up in poverty in the Jim Crow South and of a man raising a family and striving to be successful in a society in which everything I dreamt of being was in the controlling hands of ordinary people who were descendants of men and women who had either enslaved my ancestors or had embraced the ideal of white supremacy, or people who possessed the wealth, power, and influence to decide whether I would be a shepherd or a sheep led to slaughter. That was the force that my faith, will, and conscious effort were most vulnerable to being destroyed by.

I shared painful moments when I was completely lost and wandered the wilderness, aspiring to reach a mountaintop that I could not see, and was guided only by the good grace of God, the intuitions I followed, and the strangely inexplicable occurrences that blazed the paths I was meant to travel. I am not unique in that respect. Countless individuals have had similar experiences when time, place, and circumstance weaved events and encounters that were synchronistic and foreshadowing. I am also not unique in having been consciously aware of those experiences, but I at least saw their interconnectedness and significance.

I reflected on moments when the sun had never shined more brightly yet my inner self was blind to life's important questions, the most perplexing of which being what would become of the brokenness and incompleteness of me and what purposes I was created to serve. Ironically, it was in the most painful moments when I discovered what those purposes were.

The years 2004 to 2020 were the period of my life when I began to move toward wholeness, knowing that I was still a long way from realizing its fullness. After many falls, turns, and steep climbs, two paths converged in the glade of a forest. After reaching the pinnacle of my work in public service, I discovered a use in which I found much fulfillment and spent the most years of any job I held. As a public education policy advocate for thirteen years, I'd like to think that I did some good for the economically disadvantaged families and children of Louisiana.

Finding a purpose that had been latent since my earliest memory of holding a writing tablet in my hand and that had grown out of an acorn that fell to the ground many years before, I became a university English instructor and a writer, publishing five books of poetry in six years. In August 2019, I was appointed the Poet Laureate of Louisiana, a crowning achievement, as much by a grandfather who raised me as by my hands. Born in 1912, he was Creole, illiterate, barely spoke English, and signed an "X" for his name. Like the stories he told to make me laugh and that I sometimes failed to be attentive to, I had ignored the voices urging me to be a writer, until I finally heeded the words that a reading of Lorraine Hansberry's *A Raisin in the Sun* had spoken to me in a late-night seminal moment forty years before I published my first book.

As wildflowers began to bloom in the spring of 2021, I decided to leave the bare, sunlit opening of the forest, where everything seemed certain and clear, to once again step onto a dark, unfamiliar road, not knowing where it would take me. The journey led to my heightened awareness of the relevance and power of our knowing and telling the true and inclusive story of America, a history that I had been a product of and, in part, a witness to. My writing *For All Those Men* and later accepting the position of executive director at Shadows-on-the-Teche proved to be both a culmination and an affirmation of that growth in consciousness.

In late January of 2025, I resigned from my job at the Shadows to retire from full-time work. I cannot say with certainty that my work at the Shadows will be the final turn in my journey toward self-realization, but I can say with absolute certainty that it is where many decades of seeking and searching for the meaning and purpose of my life had led me. My impact as director of the Shadows was not great and profound, but I had traveled *my* journey, discovered much more of why and who *I* am, and found more personal fulfillment and awareness of self than I could have possibly imagined. Once again, the undiscovered wholeness of me, with the unfathomable depth of personal and collective experiences deeply buried in my mental darkness, had summoned "the other" to come and point a direction that I should go.

I take pride in my professional and literary accomplishments, but what little I accomplished should not be lauded as a heroic achievement of a poor black boy who beat the odds and ended up with fancy job titles and a few material possessions to pass on to his children. In the end, what I achieved pales in comparison to what strong black women and men who came before me gave and sacrificed for me to have the freedom to pursue my aspirations. Because of them, I judge my worth by the extent to which my life enriches the lives of those whose paths I am led to cross for no other reason than to give something required of me with no expectation of something in return. I am not certain that I am measuring up to that standard.

Looking back on the counsel and signposts that I ignored or didn't follow in search of what I thought were the interests and careers I should pursue, I can't help but feel some regret, a sense of time lost, and something not achieved. But I know that "to every time there is a season and a time to every purpose." There was a time for failure and disappointment, a time to heed warnings and advice, and a time to listen only to the still, silent voice within me and go assuredly into dark, unseeing days. Through all of it, a soft, gentle breeze was present—nurturing, protecting, coaxing, pulling, and at times pushing me—daring me to spread my wings and soar. Now, as then, the reasons for that wind lie in the part of me that is unknown.

The only absolute truth that I discovered in my journey is that God exists. As difficult as it is for my mortal, imperfect mind to fully comprehend and explain, I know that the realness of God is irrefutable. Since childhood, I believed that fact and that Jesus Christ, the son of God, suffered, died, and rose from the grave for my salvation and the inheritance of the gift of eternal life. Admittedly, I did not "live" those beliefs during much of my adult life. It is only by the love of Jesus that I lived long enough to repent of sin and, by faith, accept that great gift. In all my weaknesses, failures, and unexpected blessings, and in all that I might become, I have been loved by that unseen amazing grace. The totality of my short life is a testament to that truth.

I am especially grateful to Narva, my wife and best friend for half a century, whose faith and devotion was a constant light in my darkest moments. Her devout worship of Jesus Christ has been the only "church" where I have seen the true healing power of love. Her support of me in my blind leaps of faith and during my unfaithfulness to her was the spirit that sustained us. As on that cold December night when I was in peril, closed my eyes, spun the steering wheel, felt my body spiraling uncontrollably toward death, and saw Daddy pointing, Narva's resolute, unwavering faith was the softest, most gentle breeze to lift and carry me at every turn and fallen branch of the roads I traveled.

The love and sacrifices of my grandparents and parents and the instruction and guidance of my elementary school teachers were my ticket out of poverty but not my ticket out of racism. The books I read broadened my view of the world around and inside me and equipped me with armor to withstand the slings and arrows of racial prejudice, but knowledge could not stop wounds from being inflicted or heal the pain of those experiences.

Memories of racial hatred and prejudice are haunting. Some were no doubt too slight and subtle to leave a strong enough impression to be remembered, but they, too, had effects, if only in an unconscious way. I can offer no model for how one deals with being seen as having less value and virtue or being treated unjustly simply because of the color of their skin, their national origin, gender, body size, or sexual orientation, or the economic status into which they were born. Today, when biases and discrimination are less overt and are coded and disguised in language, political ideals, religion, and mass demonstrations, the greater challenge is *seeing* the face of intolerance, let alone knowing how to effectively respond to it individually or collectively. But I do know, through the trials and struggles of African Americans and through my personal experiences with racism, that the war against injustice will never end, hate will never surrender, and we must always fight to defeat it. Without love, the caste and racial polarization of America will remain an unfortunate consequence of our humanness and continue to rip every thread of humanity we stitch together. Each generation of Americans must bring its own armor and armament to those battles.

Were it not for my introspective search for self-knowledge and the discovery of my uniqueness and value, not as the world saw me but as "I am," I surely would have been more of a victim of mass-mindedness than I turned out to be, tossed by the wind rather than carried by it. I cannot claim complete differentiation between me and the mass society of which I am a part, but I can claim some sense of individuality that enables me to distinguish between the *I* and *Not I* and to embrace reality with the belief that my being a social unit does not totally decide my destiny or how I cope with the daily challenges of life.

My experiences with racial prejudice were very much a contributor to that awareness, turning me inward for strength, understanding, and ways to cope with hostility and injustice. In that respect, racism was as much a maker of me as it was a barrier to my becoming all that I was capable of being. It gave me the determination to persevere and make a good life for myself and my family and fueled my conviction to fight injustice and inequity. But I should not have had to suffer degradation, struggle to beat the odds, and fight for the right to be treated as someone born in America more than three hundred years after the first slaves were stolen from Africa and brought to this country.

As a descendant of slaves, I have had to pay a greater price for the God-given rights of "life, liberty, and the pursuit of happiness," and I might never be fully granted those rights. I offer no apology for my unwillingness to let go of the past, because the past will not let go of me nor my state and country.

If, as Emerson says, "all history is biography," then all history can be told through the individual lives we live. Mine has been only one life but a life shaped by millions who lived long before me. How I live the present and the future in communion with my fellow citizens is to a great degree determined by our collective past, regardless of whether we embrace it, ignore it, or choose to forget it. In life and in death, I am them and they are me.

I, too, am Tar Baby. The American history of my ancestors clings to me as indelibly as the history of enslavers clings to their descendants.

White Americans today are as much a product of our nation's past as I am. We cannot dismiss the generational advantages that slavery, disenfranchisement, and decades of systemic injustice against black people afforded their lives any more or less than we can dismiss the dream-killing effects of those determinants on the lives of African Americans. Our shared past is both a curse and a blessing, enough to smother the hopes and dreams of my descendants as to guarantee the dream fulfillment of the descendants of my white counterparts. Some may choose to forget or ignore the past or attempt to undermine its relevance, but that does not make the past or its effects go away. One can rip pages from a history book but one can never rip history from its pages. America and the problem of race are inextricably bound. As Fannie Lou Hamer put it, "Nobody's free until everybody's free." The sooner white Americans embrace that truth and look beyond the conditions and circumstances they inherit or the molds into which they are cast by birth and ancestry, the sooner we can bridge the divisiveness of race and caste.

After the storm, we cannot fully appreciate the sunlit calm of dawn without any remembrance of the destructive wind and rain of the night before. But America neither slept nor slumbered through the storm. We were wide awake to witness the destruction, death, and suffering of its path. Whether we want to be "woke" or not, the burden is still upon us to deal with the aftermath—to rebuild and "reconstruct" while envisioning a stronger, united, and fair America.

Our nation can never know the true and complete wholeness of itself and realize the fullest potential inherent in its greatness until it, too, embarks on the difficult, soul-searching journey of discovering what and who America is today, a journey that began, not in 1776 but in 1619, when the first free people were stolen from Africa, brought to America, and enslaved solely for the profit of enslavers. Who we are and can become in the context of that history is the question we must answer if we are to achieve our highest aim and purpose as "one nation under God."

Our Declaration of Independence and Constitution bear the fruits of freedom that we cherish so dearly. Our laws reflect the worst and best of us. Our military, systems of governance, and regulated free economy have made us the most powerful and most prosperous nation on the planet. But those pillars have not always worked to the benefit and enrichment of all citizens. In fact, history reveals that those systems have systemically worked to the detriment of the well-being of millions of the descendants of formerly enslaved and marginalized people who, even in freedom, have struggled for over a century and a half to be granted the rights, privileges, and opportunities afforded the majority race.

The belief that Africans and people of African descent are inherently inferior to white people, incapable of reason and creativity, and are therefore fit for nothing except to be enslaved was founded during the so-called period of Enlightenment of the 18th century. Slavery made that lie a truth, hung an albatross around the nation's neck, and spun it into divisiveness, war, and sociopolitical turmoil that we struggle to overcome over one hundred fifty years later. The exhortation that America be true to itself and live up to its creeds, declarations, and religious beliefs is just as old, beginning with abolitionism and reaching its crescendo during the Civil Rights Movement.

Today, over fifty years after Reverend Martin Luther King Jr. was assassinated, we hear the cry for justice in protests against voter suppression and race-based disparities in every measure of the economic and social well-being of African Americans. The rising rate of child poverty, the disproportionately high incarceration rate of black men, the growing number of cases of police brutality against black boys and men, and the January 6, 2021 insurrection against American democracy should be reason enough to reexamine and address the dark shadows of the systems that govern and regulate us. The growing incidences of mass shootings in America that are motivated by hate, albeit attributable to several factors, not the least of which are mental illness and uncontrolled gun ownership, are equally alarming symptoms of a sickness of the soul and psyche of America that remains uncured long after the horrific lashing, lynching, and massacre of African Americans that will forever condemn our national conscience.

The people who are destroying the lives of Americans with unjust incarcerations and policies that create and exacerbate conditions of poverty, and who are slaughtering innocent citizens in mass numbers with military-like firearms are not foreign terrorists; they are Americans themselves. That is not to suggest or imply that our social, political, and economic systems are powerless in the face of such evil, but it clearly is a clarion call to call out and challenge politicians who cloak themselves in American patriotism and oppose legislation to cure these ills while throngs of churchgoing, Bible-believing voters cheer them on.

Racial violence inflicted on Americans by Americans is as old as America. What is relatively new in the war of high principles, indeed in a fight for the soul of the nation, is opposition and resistance to teaching and arguing the generational effects of slavery, disenfranchisement, and racism on contemporary and future American societies, particularly when such teachings and arguments use history to justify affirmative action and other race-preference policies to remedy longstanding, systemic inequality and injustice. Historical fact is the only candle, lantern, or lamp that we can carry into the dreary darkness of that blindness, unrealism, and denial of the truth of the American journey.

In Louisiana, where I live, a state that has the second highest poverty rate in the country and has not elected a black person to statewide office since 1868, the word "liberal" has become a code word for "woke" and Black Lives Matter. After 1873, it took Louisiana 107 years to elect a Republican governor. By then, the Grand Old Party had long been the party of limiting federal power and was beginning to usher in a tsunami wave of "dispassionate" conservatism that would take a direct aim at dismantling federally-supported programs established to uplift economically disadvantaged citizens. Since 1980, the year of President Ronald Reagan's landslide victory over incumbent Democrat President Jimmy Carter, the political pendulum of the governor's office of Louisiana swings frequently. Today, in a state that has 5% more registered Democrats than Republicans, every statewide elected office is held by a Republican, both chambers of the state legislature are majority Republican, both U. S. Senators are Republican, and the only Congressional seats that are not Republican are held by two black men. The last presidential election in which Louisiana voters went Democrat was 1996.

Despite being largely Democrat, Louisianans clearly don't vote "party." I doubt that the average voter of Louisiana gives much thought to how party ideology at the state level affects their daily lives, except when politicians clutter the airwaves and social media with sound bites that subtly pit white people against black people in the guise of conservatism, or until, as was done under former Governor Bobby

Jindal, a Republican, drastic cuts are made to higher education or other vital services. My guess is that Louisiana voters who do vote along party lines seldom if ever discuss politics or political issues with the opposing side. If they did they would discover that they have much more in common than the political principles that divide them.

But when a "liberal" of any color is on the ballot for political office in Louisiana, there is no common ground, even when it means voting against one's own self-interest or voting for candidates who offer no remedies to the longstanding problems of severe poverty, racial inequities in student academic achievement and workforce opportunities, and other ills that threaten the survival, health, and economic well-being of many of the state's children and families. There are many reasons for that behavior, not the least of which are the huge sums of money spent at all levels of electoral politics to spin "liberal" into negative connotations of "race," thus flaming the resistance to bringing the subject of race and the generational impacts of racial injustice into the public discourse.

Erasing the past from our collective memory and social conscience is like gazing darkly into a tarnished glass window that gives no reflection of who we were and are. Notwithstanding the basic goodness and decency in us and the learning, ingenuity, hard work, and perseverance that shape our individualism, there is a more excellent way. To find an answer to the question of what America is and can become after 400 years of slavery we must first make a conscious effort to seek it. As James Baldwin might say, that is foremost the work of the heart. White and non-white Americans will never see and treat themselves as equals until we grow enlightened enough to see the rippling, systemic impacts of the racial cataclysm that tore the nation apart and we commit to addressing those impacts with individual acts of empathy and compassion.

Plowing the ground of "new enlightenment" is not the work of government and career politicians. It is the work of ordinary individuals who greet strangers and their neighbors passing by and who interact with countless others in places where they work, study, shop, socialize, and worship. It is the lonely, unselfish, and unthanked work of individual hearts that treat each other justly and fairly, celebrate each other's triumphs, and feel each other's hardships and challenges through the lens of their collective past. It is the work of visionary business, community, and civic leaders who understand the power and necessity of inclusion and diversity, and the work of religious leaders of all faiths and ethnicities who are spiritually and morally committed to building a loving community of God's people and have the courage to speak out against injustice.

Most adult Americans will never learn or be willing to take the time to learn the full history of this country. The most potentially powerful force for radical enlightenment and the realization of what America is and can become in the context of its racial history is our nation's youth. They offer our best hope for a society not entirely free of ethnic, gender, and religious intolerance but possessing a willingness to work toward reconciliation and fairness—if adults who nurture and teach them will overcome their fears, live up to their Godly beliefs, and not stand in the way of truth-telling.

If there is a will to act justly toward each other, to live the principles of democracy, and to apply the self-evident truths that we proclaim in our Declaration of Independence for "all" Americans, then it is more than possible that our gazing deeply into the darkest moments of the American journey can help to uncover solutions to the complex socioeconomic issues that so often divide us. Our embracing the value of open, honest dialogue about those moments can do much to engender understanding and empathy for the struggles and trials of the disparate and largely separate realities of our multiracial, multicultural society. Ultimately, our reflecting on the individual and collective humanity and inhumanity in us will build a fairer and more equitable society. Only then can we awaken to a new and brighter dawn and realize the greatness that we aspire to be as a nation.

I love my state and country. I count it a great blessing to be of African descent, to have lived enough years to taste the sweet and bitter love of the American journey, and to have been given the freedom to express my thoughts and feelings about those experiences. Like my beloved country, the wholeness of me is still evolving, but I take comfort in knowing, that for whatever good can come of it, the making of us is God's work.

EARLY ESSAYS

On Eliminating Poverty in America
SEPTEMBER 7, 1979

Mankind, so we have learned, has inherited the task of putting to use the resources of this world in a manner that will reap the necessities of life preservation. How we have come to the modern situation of material prosperity bears the marks of ancient conflict and adversity, as effort upon effort brought us nearer to dominion of the planet. In the course of it, some men set out to carve paths that nurtured comfort and security and inspired the confidence of millions. Some, by force, demanded and left no choice but that others should go their way.

The polarities of human nature, the massive, unchecked wave of opposites that divide belief, did indeed make a show of outward events, much to satisfaction, much to regret, yet always tied to whatever future men might possibly conceive or create. This is not a startling realization but one that requires at least a grain of reflection. Take, for example, the ancient tug of war between the haves and have-nots, that inherited tendency of each generation to foster contention of varying degrees about who should be getting what and how much. Because America has been fortunate to have accumulated such an awesome amount of wealth and resourceful value, owing to slavery and the freedom which has been given men to pursue their self-interests, the nation now faces the dual task of preserving its global identity and dominance while answering to its hypocrisies.

Because the elimination of poverty in the midst of American affluence is primarily a legalistic concept, the have-nots make their appeal to the social responsiveness of the so-called majority elected government. Government, as we know and speak of it today, is a very big entity, bigger, perhaps, than what we envision when we speak about it. As a citizen taxpayer, I find it difficult to take sides with many political and socioeconomic issues of our day, even those which appear to be in my interest, because I am uncertain of what unseen forces lurk behind those actions that I would lend support to. I whole-heartedly support the strivings of poor and disadvantaged citizens to achieve economic independence and self-determination. I chose to join the ranks of those who, not having anywhere else to turn and unable to do battle unarmed and ill-equipped, have turned to government to reverse the degrading plight of poverty in America.

But government, I fear, as big as it is and will become, is not prepared to do battle with poverty and achieve lasting results while keeping the nation whole. For as long as countless "individuals" lack the willingness and wisdom to settle directly the conflicts which tug at their humanity and sense of oneness, government is but a puff of smoke, carried on a wave of sentimentalism and choking everything in its path.

Perhaps we are merely yielding to cost efficiency when we witness our neighbor having a hard time, knowing better than anyone what he or she needs and how their condition can be made better. But we choose the scientific way, the way of data processed transfer payments, social scientists, psychologists, administrators, and other government employees, or the more recent trend of consultants and analysts—all filtered through the omnipotent, omnipresent but invisible agencies of government.

I submit the possibility of whether individual and corporate taxpayers could truly begin to think in terms of "self-interest" by taking the entire matter into their own hands, by taking upon themselves the responsibility of lending direct support to the poor and disadvantaged on a "community" as opposed to federal basis, thereby reducing massive outlays of tax dollars to more concrete, manageable proportions. To say the resources for such undertakings don't exist is a fallacy for the smallest and largest cities of America. An underlying assumption of this approach is that people endowed with the capacity to produce wealth would be willing to make the investment of financial and technical resources that would benefit economically depressed communities.

I submit the possibility of whether we as individuals can begin to share the moral responsibility that government has so confusingly transformed into regulations, guidelines, and agencies, if not for the well-being of others, then for the assurance of being in control of our own lives and destinies, holding to the faith that freedom and wealth can co-exist.

Remarkably, positive change is indeed taking place due to the power of bureaucratic policy. But should we not also examine the psychological and humanitarian price we pay for allowing self-worth to be defined by social welfare, ignoring the fact that it was the diligent, self-rising efforts of individuals that created the nation's wealth, and that only the willingness of individuals to propagate wealth for the benefit of the poor offers any promising hope for the elimination of poverty?

Southern Cooperative Development Fund Staff Retreat
GRAND COTEAU, LOUISIANA, DECEMBER 1980

It's been said that life, that miraculous web of experience that we confront and live out as our personal and collective stories are written, can be compared to the sea. Each of our individual experiences is but a tiny drop of water.

"Something quite remarkable," it can be said about the human spirit, "when in spite of its uniqueness, it cannot truthfully deny kinship to a world outside of self."

Not long ago, I sat and listened, watching the waves as they fell upon each other, as they roared and tossed violently against the shore. I wondered about the deepest depth and how different things might be there—what cold darkness, what warm, penetrating light, what overwhelming force. Something unknown is there. But there is more. There is calmness that cannot be judged by the force of surface waters. There is continuity and unity, which certainly cannot be judged by the sporadic, broken pattern of waves we see. There is something eternal, something beyond quest and conquest, something that has been there long before I or any mortal person ever came to be and which, faith tells me, will remain long after I depart.

To a group of people such as us who work to achieve a high purpose, and to black men, women, and children all over the world, I would suggest and pray that we forever cling to a hope that the spirit of our work and achievements can be like the sea, letting the surface water be tossed to and fro by the bustling wind, deceptively allowing others to believe that our force will soon weaken with the changing tide.

Embodied in that hope is the confidence we gain in the knowledge that experience brings us, knowledge about those external forces that come to bear on our changing directions, but most importantly, knowledge about our own depth, worth, and purpose.

There is a current flowing deep beneath the surface. There is a design that in time bends the circumstances to it. Like an old oak tree or a stone that no man has ever touched, there are great, enduring things that simply say "I am."

I would suggest that we cling collectively to that hope, and that our unknown purpose be just as enduring, carving out a quiet good in a world of pain and suffering.

On the 13th Anniversary of the Assassination of Dr. Martin Luther King Jr.

APRIL 4, 1981

In a truly commemorative spirit, the majority of the U. S. Congress and racists factions are proposing legislation that is an insult to the ideals that Reverend Martin Luther King Jr. bravely and tragically committed his life to. Two decades short of the 21st century and the nation seeks to revive an 18th century philosophy whose ghost alone strikes fear in the black community. Economics, politics, religion, madness—call it what you wish. Something very powerful and destructive has taken possession of the hollow men and women who govern this country. We would do well to look at the life of King to seek some insight to truth that time spoke through him.

The sixties decades of the 19th and 20th centuries give vivid account of moments when the black experience evoked turmoil on American soil. In the midst of peaceful, rational, well-meaning plans, widespread dissent and violence was born. A collective-mindedness permeated and a civil rebellion acquired breath of its own. Mental and physical wars were fought. Battles were won and lost. Casualties mounted and a martyr was laid to final rest in the perennial bloom of springtime. The black nation wept.

These events, which occurred in the same decade of two centuries, were an outer manifestation of a singular inner disturbance, the symbolic expression of a stage in the psychic growth of America when the outer face was called to truth and accountability. Indeed, those were times when out of some dark and ancient corner of America's psyche erupted the utterances of freedom, justice, and equality. Reverend Martin Luther King Jr. was an instrument of that utterance.

There is always the danger of America allowing her character to again shift too strongly in the other direction, making faint that special message that King and his dream spoke so eloquently. Such a change can only mean suffering for those whose heritage has prepared them for the task of lifting mankind toward more human and spiritual values.

Today, we stand face-to-face with the great test of whether or not America did awake to the coming and going of King, at test of this nation's readiness to venture further along the journey of becoming what it has so boldly declared itself to be.

Of course, much will depend upon black America. So many contradictions remain unresolved. I truly wonder whether we share a common vision about who we are and whether we see our collective worth from a worldview. Do we face the possibility of losing or permanently weakening the conscious awareness of our spiritually rich heritage? Is it possible that the gulf of materialism has become so vast that we, too, have become hollow and dehumanized? Have we begun to create a seemingly unbridgeable gap between ourselves and the myths that gave so much meaning and hope to our ancestors? Is it possible that we are channeling creative energies too strongly in pursuit of Western values and are not able to carve the path of our own unique journey?

Much more important than being reproof to the attitude and behavior of white America, the civil unrest of the sixties was for black America a psychological assertion, a statement of self-worth, self-identity, and self-determination. Through that struggle, we recognized that the source of our strength lies in our willingness to unite collectively. We should have recognized that deep within the ranks of the poor and oppressed lies the potential to stir the gut and soul of this nation and the world.

We are the creations of a living and just Spirit, not a dollar-inspired god of economic laws and theories. No government or economic system will best serve the interest of a people as peculiar and special as black America. Still, it is the duty and responsibility of black people to ensure that the government and the economy are just. We must always look to the future but be ever mindful of our past, ever conscious of the moment, ever struggling not as ordinary men and women but as a special people, the only people in America who have tasted the bitterness of racial prejudice.

I am reminded of an admonition so often said, that simply knowing right and talking about what is believed to be right does nothing to change what is wrong. Action matched to principle changes things. And in all tasks required of decent, secure survival, a call to discipline, courage, and perseverance oftentimes proves to be the biggest challenge. Virtues are in need of people. And in this country and world house, with ideals contrasting like night and day, courage is in need of young men and women willing to wear it with honor, willing to peaceably challenge any opposing interest.

I am convinced that the gift of life brings with it the will to live, and that there must and will be contention in all things good. All around the world, people of color have historically felt the brunt of this world's strife and contention and of the majority's tendency to exploit everything outside of itself in its attempt to conquer and control. Perhaps the planet has endured for so long and grown so large that ideals prove to be too powerful for one man or woman. King's legacy is that one life can in fact make a difference.

Acknowledgments

Grateful acknowledgement is made to the editors and readers of the journals who published many of the poems that appear in this memoir. I am especially grateful and thankful to everyone who contributed in some way to my journey. My very special thanks to my wife Narva for her support and for contributing to the editing of this book.

ABOUT THE AUTHOR

John Warner Smith was the Poet Laureate of Louisiana from 2019 to 2021 and is the only African American male to serve in the office in its 83-year history. Smith has published five collections of poetry, most recently *Our Shut Eyes* (MadHat Press, 2021). His sixth collection, *From the Flinty Rock: New & Selected Poems*, is forthcoming from MadHat Press in late 2025.

Smith's novella, *For All Those Men: When the KKK Threatened to Take Control of Louisiana*, was published by UL Press in November 2022. His first full-length novel, *Sisters of Gavinville*, was published in December 2024 by Between the Lines (BTL) Publishing. Smith's second novella, *Murders on Red Hill: The Tragedy at Mer Rouge*, will be published by BTL in 2026.

A Cave Canem Fellow, Smith is a 2020 Poet Laureate Fellow of the Academy of American Poets and is winner of the 2019 Linda Hodge Bromberg Literary Award. He earned his MFA at the University of New Orleans.

Smith is retired from full-time work and is an Adjunct Instructor of English at Southern University in Baton Rouge.

www.ingramcontent.com/pod-product-compliance
Lightning Source LLC
Chambersburg PA
CBHW021137130626
46554CB00005B/1546